CW01502332

HISTORY

OF THE

BANK OF ENGLAND.

HISTORY

OF THE

BANK OF ENGLAND,

ITS TIMES AND TRADITIONS.

BY JOHN FRANCIS.

VOL. I.

LONDON:

WILLOUGHBY & CO., AMEN CORNER, PATERNOSTER ROW;
EFFINGHAM WILSON, ROYAL EXCHANGE.

LONDON:

PRINTED BY WILLOUGHBY AND CO., 97, ST. JOHN STREET, SMITHFIELD.

INSCRIBED,

BY PERMISSION,

TO THE RIGHT HONOURABLE SIR ROBERT PEEL.

———————

THESE VOLUMES, ILLUSTRATIVE OF THE ORIGIN AND PRO-
GRESS OF THE BANK OF ENGLAND, FORMING THE FIRST HISTORY
YET ATTEMPTED OF THE GREATEST MONETARY ESTABLISHMENT
IN THE WORLD, ARE, TO THE GREATEST STATESMAN OF THE
DAY, RESPECTFULLY DEDICATED,

BY HIS MOST OBEDIENT

AND VERY DEVOTED SERVANT.

JOHN FRANCIS.

PREFACE.

It is with great diffidence that these volumes are submitted to the public. The writer trusts, however, that as no history has hitherto appeared of an establishment, which, for a century and a half, has held so prominent a position in the public records of England, he may be excused for relating its "strange, eventful" career.

It will be found, from the various authorities which he has put in requisition, that the apprehensions which at one time existed, even among the most enlightened minds, that the intimate connexion between the Bank and the government would be found the precursor of national ruin, have, in a great measure, been quieted by more enlarged experience. The evils anticipated have not arisen; but at more than one momentous crisis the Bank has proved a powerful ally to the state.

The life of William Paterson, the founder of the corporation, one of those men who live before their time, embracing the history of the remarkable Darien expedition—the Mississippi scheme, with its lights and shades, an evidence of the evils arising from the circulation being in the hands of government—the South Sea Bubble, that memorable example of the panics which from time to time have seized this great commercial country—the Mine Adventurers' Com-

pany, pronounced a deception by the House of
Commons, but the origin of the most important
charter hitherto granted the Corporation—the Sacheverell and Gordon riots, with the attack upon the
building—the perplexity of the directors in 1745, and
their extraordinary expedient to meet the evil—the
various runs upon the Bank, with the causes which
produced them—the curious forgeries of Price, which
for a time startled the whole community—the suspension of cash payments, with a historical view of its
causes—the organised deception on the Stock Exchange, almost unrivalled in the history of fraud—
the forgeries of Fauntleroy, when the most trifling
incident which related to the crime or the man
was devoured with avidity, and vast crowds assembled near Carlton-house, anxious to gain, on
the day of the Recorder's report to the sovereign,
the earliest intelligence of the banker's doom—with
the more recent cases of the Continental Conspiracy
and the Will Forgeries, form part only of the contents
of these volumes.

The panic of 1825, its assumed causes and consequences, the varying opinions of the first men of
the day, with particulars of the loans and companies
which ruined half England, have been collected from
past and present authorities, and the writer believes
that in no other work can so complete an amount
of information concerning this fearful crisis be
obtained.

In collecting and arranging the scattered facts relating to his subject, the writer feels that the task might
have fallen into far abler hands; but he ventures to
say, that no exertion has been spared in resorting to
every known source of information, governed in each
instance by an undeviating regard for truth.

CONTENTS OF VOL. I.

Page.

HISTORY

OF THE

BANK OF ENGLAND.

CHAPTER I.

INVENTION OF BILLS OF EXCHANGE—INTEREST FORBIDDEN—
NEAPOLITAN LENDING HOUSES—DEFENCE OF THE HEBREW—
NECESSITY OF HENRY III.—SUCCESS OF THE HEBREW—BANK OF
VENICE—THE LOMBARDS IN ENGLAND—THEIR PERSECUTION—
COMPLAINTS AGAINST THEM—ENGLISH COMPANIES—ADVANCE IN
COMMERCE—ROUTE TO CHINA—ABOLITION OF FOREIGN LOANS.

COMMERCE, the precursor of banking, was in a low
condition at the date of the Norman conquest, when
the English were a pastoral people. The devastating
wars which ensued prevented population from increasing, and commerce from improving. Land also, to a
great degree, remained untilled. The fertilization now
extending over hill and dale was then wanting. The
graceful glebe, the cultivated country, with all the
luxurious evidences of a mature civilization, were
absent. The place of these was supplied by forests,
rich with the hues of their varied occupants, and by
wild extensive tracts of land, which afforded profitable,

and often picturesque pasturage, for large droves of sheep, and horned cattle.

The hides and wool derived from these were the staple articles of merchandize, forming the principle revenue of the proprietor ; and Flanders, even then a manufacturing country of comparative importance, was their chief recipient. As continental languages were almost unknown in London, the business was conducted by foreigners ; but the trade of a whole year only amounted to one or two hundred thousand pounds ; and, for the first two centuries after the conquest, rarely, if ever, exceeded two hundred and fifty thousand. During this period, then, it is obvious that no other bank, save the stronghold of the castle, or the treasury of the convent, was required.

In the proportion, however, that population increased, that fresh branches of commerce were formed, and that the powers of the country began to develope themselves, a new want was likely to arise. It was, in all probability, during such a period that the deficiency of money first made the Jew remarked for the great business capacity which distinguishes him up to the present time, and which even then enabled him to make advances on security. The members of this race, who have always taken the initiative in money getting, had the misfortune, in an age comparatively rude, to attract the cupidity of their masters.

" When a whole people," says the elder D'Israeli, in his " Genius of Judaism," " devote themselves to one great pursuit, one single art, they open sources of invention, they reach to a noble perfection. Unhappily for the present professors, that great pursuit, that single art, was the commerce of money; and to render fortunes invisible, their genius produced the wonderful invention of Bills of Exchange; an object, like the art of printing, become too familiar to be admired; the miracle has ceased, and its utility only remains; yet both are sources of civilization, and connect together, as in one commonwealth, the whole universe. Their successful pursuits worked their own fatality. The Hebrews became the reservoirs of the wealth of the strange lands where they were found. For the steel-clad baron they were sponges to suck in as much water as they could hold, that his protecting hand, as he listed, might squeeze them to their last drop; for the luxurious abbots and the rosy canons, who heaped up their improvident bonds on the Hebrew affecting the poverty he was to relieve, the Jews became the creditors of a whole province."

By a decree of Edward the Confessor, the taking of interest was first prohibited. For a long period the prejudices of priest and people had struggled with the growing wants of trade. To receive interest for money lent, was to incur the invidious name of usurer. With this had each successive phase of commerce wrestled. By this had each growing effort of business been injured. With this, also, had even the lending houses of Italy to contend, when, with a spirit worthy the

Christianity he professed, the Neapolitan of the six-
teenth century attempted to deliver the poor and the
needy from the grasp of the extortioner.* The
religionist, who took too limited a view of the Scripture
he professed to expound, argued that, by the decree
of the Israelitish Legislator, it was a direct violation of
the will of Heaven to receive interest for money
borrowed. This fallacy is most conclusively answered
by Mr. Gilbart, in his " History of Banking." " It
was the object of the Jewish legislator to make the
Jews a purely agricultural people. The promotion of
agriculture was, as Montesquieu would say, the *spirit*
of his laws. Hence he prohibited the taking of interest
for the loan of money. By this means he interdicted
commerce. His design was to prevent the Israelites
associating with the surrounding nations, and learning
their idolatrous practices. But even Moses permitted
the Jews to take interest for money lent to strangers :

* "The lending house at Naples was first established in 1539, or 1540.
Two rich citizens, Aurelio Paparo, and Leonardo or Nardo di Palma, redeemed all the pledges which were at that time in the hands of the Jews,
and offered to deliver them to the owners without interest provided they
would return the money which had been advanced on them. More
opulent persons soon followed their example ; many bequeathed large sums
for this benevolent purpose ; and Toledo, the viceroy, who drove the Jews
from the kingdom, supported it by every method possible. This lending
house, which has indeed undergone many valuations, is the largest in
Europe ; and it contains such an immense number of different articles,
many of them exceedingly valuable, that it may be considered as a reposi-
tory of the most important part of the moveables of the whole nation.
About the year 1635, another establishment of the like kind was formed,
under the title of *banco de' poveri*. At first this bank advanced money
without interest, only to relieve confined debtors ; afterwards, as its capital

a circumstance which proves that the prohibition was
a political, and not a moral precept."

During the period to which we have alluded, the
Hebrews may almost be regarded as the compulsory
bankers of the luxurious monarch, and the iron chief;
for not only were this patient people at the absolute
disposal of the regal oppressor; the war-like baron
also looked down from his stronghold upon the suffer-
ing Jew, as a source of revenue to be measured only
by his own wants, or the capacity of his victim.

"The prejudices of the age," says Hume, "had
made the lending of money on interest pass by the
name of usury : yet the necessity of the practice had
still continued it, and the greater part of that kind of
dealing fell every where into the hands of the Jews,
who being already infamous on account of their religion,
had no honour to lose, and were apt to exercise a
profession odious in itself by every kind of rigour, and
sometimes by rapine and extortion."

We are prone to judge the actions of a preceding
age, by the precepts which guide our own. " Rapine
and extortion" unhappily marked the path of the Christian in his dealings with the Hebrew. History teems
with relations to which " rigour " would be far too
mild a term to apply. John had no charter, save that
of the strong hand, to extract the teeth from the Jew

increased, it lent upon pledges, but not above the sum of five ducats without interest. For larger sums the usual interest was demanded."—*Beck-
mann's History of Inventions*, vol. 2.

who refused to be unrighteously robbed. Henry III. had no right save that of might to wring from this people their hard earned money, in a series of cruel exactions which lasted for half a century. The bold but barbarous baron, licentious alike in all his dealings, asked only his own evil passions for permission to outrage his fellow man.

The Hebrew, acting after the knowledge vouchsafed to him, willing to grasp the only power he was allowed to exercise, happy also in being able to retaliate on the hated race that wronged him, sought and seized on every opportunity which enabled him to gratify at once his love of vengeance and of money.

In a note to Rapin's History, Tindal says, " The King of England was wont to draw a considerable revenue from the Jews residing in this realm : namely, by *tallage* (or assessment,) *and fines relating to law proceedings, by amerciaments for misdemeanours, and by fines, ransoms, compositions, which they were forced to pay for having the king's benevolence ; for protection, for licence to trade, for discharges, for imprisonment, and the like.* He would tallage the whole community or body at pleasure, and make them answer the tallage for one another. In short the king seemed to be absolute lord of their estates and effects, of their persons, their wives, and children."

In this brief passage there is a goodly list of excuses for the exercise of might over right. A goodly list of apologies, with which the Christian attempted to justify his conscience, while he satiated his lust after money.

But "the peculiar people" were neither allowed to leave the land in which they were pursued with so much malignity, or to rest in peace while they remained there. Henry III., their persecutor and their pest, betrayed his evil passions, when memoralized by this people for permission to quit England, in the exclamation : "Is it to be marvelled at that I covet money! It is a horrible thing to imagine the debts wherein I am bound. By the head of God, they amount to two hundred thousand marks, and if I should say three hundred, I should not exceed the truth. I am deceived on every side; I am a maimed and abridged king, yea, now but half a king. *There is a necessity for me to have money, gotten from what place soever, and by what means soever, and from whom soever.*"

History is replete with the oppression of the Hebrew people, written in characters of blood. They were indeed the great source of revenue. They were made use of on all ordinary and extraordinary occasions. "Their command of cash, combined with their acute and business habits, enabled them," says a modern writer, " almost to monopolize the business of traders and money-dealers, and of course their profits were very great. This was their compensation for the state of subjection in which they were held, and that which induced them to remain in the kingdom, notwithstanding all the exactions of the crown.　It was an engine, nevertheless, which there was some art and management required in working.　On the one hand, these Jews were not to be treated with so much severity as to make them wish to quit the country.　They were to be tempted to remain in it.　For this purpose, the process, in which they acted so important a part, while it largely benefited the king, was to be allowed to be also somewhat profitable to themselves.　The pressure of the royal grasp was not to be carried so far as to wring from them the whole amount of their extortionate gains.　Above all, they were to be protected by the law in those rights, without the enforcement of which they could not have satisfied the rapacity of their oppressor.　But, on the other hand, the hatred with which they were naturally regarded by the people was also to be maintained and cherished ; for without this it would have been impossible for the sovereign power to have continued to treat them in the arbitrary and tyrannical manner we have described.　It was, no doubt, found to be somewhat difficult to effect these two objects at the same time, namely, to grant to the Jews the perfect protection of the law against every one else, except the king, and yet to keep the popular feeling against them in so inflamed a state, that it was always ready to approve whatever cruelty and oppression that single and licensed power might exercise upon them."

Another reason, besides " the possession of all the

ready money," of their remarkable success in trade, was the quiet energy with which they pursued their calling. Undisturbed by love of country, for they were an outcast people; unstimulated by the love of war, for they were a peaceful race; uncalled upon by Norman baron, or Saxon chief, to assist him, save with cash and credit, for other help from them was worthless; they devoted themselves with undivided mind to a pursuit, which, while it excited the inexorable passions of their masters, made the Hebrews the possessors of that wealth, which was alike their consolation and their curse.

It appears, then, from the slight sketch given of this remarkable body, that the writer is justified in terming them the compulsory bankers of the period. Their earliest known persecution occurred in 1189, during the reign of Richard Cœur de Lion, about the period that the first European bank, the bank of Venice, was established. While the rude barbarism of the north resorted to the policy shortly to be described, Venice, with all the grandeur of an advanced commercial knowledge, established, upon a scale so just that it has since served as a model for its successors, the earliest bank in Europe.

Towards the end of the thirteenth century, the country ceased to receive support from the Hebrew. Edward I., unable to resist a grant from parliament, and stimulated by the prospect of an immediate booty, consented to the expulsion of this people from

England. With what circumstances of degradation and cruelty it was conducted, let the chronicles of the time repeat; but from this period to their re-admission, during the government of the great and politic Cromwell, in the seventeenth century, they ceased to interfere with the monetary or commercial transactions of the English community.

It is, we think, difficult to account, excepting by the bigotry of the age, for the intense hatred borne to this insulted race. It would perhaps be still more difficult to find a reason for the great folly which prompted their expulsion, at the expense of a revenue so easily obtained,* were it not possible that some light may be thrown on, and some excuse made for, this great political error, by the fact, that, in the same century, the Lombards, by which general term the early Italian merchants of Genoa, Florence, and Venice were known, came over and established themselves in the street which still bears their name. With them came many of the arts and the skill of trade; with them came the only knowledge of banking, then possessed; with them came into more common use, " the wonderful invention " of bills of exchange, by the agency of which they remitted money to their own country. Success followed exertion; a firm footing

---

* "During a space of only about seven years, from the 17th of December, in the fiftieth year of Henry III., till the Tuesday in Shrovetide, in the second year of Edward I., the crown is stated to have extorted from the Jews (amounting in all to probably not more than five hundred families,) the immense sum of £420,000 15s. 4d."—*Popular Tumults.*

was obtained by the skilful Lombard; he was the first who, uniting to the art of the goldsmith the science of the banker, took the initiative in that business, which has since been the agency of so much good, and which has been found to increase with the trade and commerce of the country. The success of the Lombard was not unmarked by the third Edward. With the false policy of a barbarous age, this monarch sought to supply the necessities of the crown by treating the Lombard as his predecessors had treated the Israelite. The reign of Edward was marked by a lavish expenditure of blood and money. The hardy Scot felt his prowess at Halidon Hill. The village of Crecy witnessed the triumph which is yet talked of at our English firesides, and from which the first prince of royal blood derives his motto at the present day. Poictiers, in the capture of the French monarch, was the completion of the great series of conquests, which, while it shed a nearly unparalleled glory over British arms, made the conqueror feel most keenly the want of that money which had hitherto been principally supplied by extortions from the Jew.

Monarchs rarely allow the absence of a reason to stand between them and their desire. If the industry of the Lombards had produced wealth, wealth produced persecution.

To apply the words which the elder D'Israeli wrote upon another topic: " It was their calamity to excel in the arts their neighbours practised. A society which becomes too powerful by their wealth has ever been marked out for the spoil of the government or the people; there are so many passions in human nature which are allied against a flourishing body. First hated, and then calumniated, they become the victims of state; and justice veils her eyes during the popular suppression or destruction. Such was the fate of the order of the Templars, of the English monastic institutions, of the Jesuits throughout Europe. The historical problem is of no difficult solution. Whenever a heavy price is proclaimed to discover offenders, however innocent, offenders will be found; and for the informers there can be no higher price than a share in the confiscation."

Under the pretext that the Lombards were extortioners, Edward III. seized their property and estates. "Perhaps," remarks Maitland, very shrewdly, "the necessity for furnishing him with money for his lavish expenditure might have urged him to this step."

The enmity of the monarch stimulated fresh complaints from his people. Those to whom we are indebted, are seldom regarded favourably by us; and probably the debtor was more to blame than the creditor. The defective laws of the period enabled the former occasionally to evade his just debts; this naturally produced a treble vengeance from the money-lender in the form of increased interest, if the occasion offered, and in imprisonment, if he failed to meet the demand of the Lombard on the appointed day; if not, the wronger is always harsh in his judgment of the man he has wronged.

Persecution produced its accustomed fruits. The Lombards increased in wealth, power, and position. They had gained so much importance by the fifteenth century, that we find them advancing a large sum for the service of the state on the security of the customs. "They dealt," says Robertson, "largely as bankers. They carried on this, as well as other branches of their commerce, with somewhat of that rapacious spirit which is natural to monopolists, who are not restrained by the concurrence of rivals." "Accordingly, we find it was usual to demand twenty per cent. for the use of money, in the thirteenth century." "They enjoyed great privileges, and carried on extensive commerce, particularly as bankers."

It was from such bodies as these, and the "Steel-yard merchants," our masters in the art of commerce, that the kings of England, on any sudden exigency, sought and obtained their principal supplies, on what now appears an exorbitant interest.

The important body of Steel-yard merchants was cherished with great and peculiar privileges. If great privileges were granted, however, great services were often claimed in return. "The Steel-yard Company," remarks Mr. Gilbart, "was a kind of bank to our kings, whenever they wanted money on any sudden emergency ; but the company was sure, in the end, to be well paid for such assistance."

The merchants of the Staple, (so called from their Stapelhoff, or general house of trade for the German nation,) the Mercers, whose existence as a body may be traced to the twelfth century; the Merchant Adventurers, who boldly steered their vessels to unknown shores in search of commerce ; the Traders of Flanders, then in the pride and pomp of wealth derived from successful industry, had all successively ministered to the service of the state.   Nor had the citizens failed in supplying similar assistance.   When Edward III. resolved upon an expedition to France, the wards advanced, according to their several ability, twenty thousand marks, which the parliament voted, in order that the warlike adventures of the monarch might be successfully pursued.

The reign of Henry VII. was distinguished by a great advance in commerce.   This politic sovereign endeavoured to raise and cherish the Commons as an important barrier against the power of the baron.   The independence of the latter was troublesome to peace ; but as the serf grew with the favour of the monarch, and the increase of commerce and agriculture, (the latter of which Henry particularly affected, as the "vigour and nerves of the English state,") so was the baron compelled to retire within his natural and proper boundary.

The great discovery of the greatest man of his, or perhaps any age, occurred this century.   The new world was made known to the old by Christopher Colon, commonly called Columbus ; and though the mind revolts at the cruelties which followed the adventures of the Genoese, yet it is incumbent on us to own the impulse received by commerce throughout that which was termed the civilized world. The movement could not fail to be felt in England; and John Cabot, a Venetian, set sail with his three sons, under a license granted by Henry VII., for the discovery of unknown lands.

In the year 1505, the twentieth of this monarch's reign, the first charter was granted for establishing the " Fellowship of Merchant Adventurers." During this century also the Newfoundland and other fisheries, the Turkey trade, and a trade to Russia, were established, and in its last year was incorporated the East India Company. It was also within the same period that Sir Hugh Willoughby, with three vessels, set sail to discover a near route to China. By the sudden approach of winter, he was compelled to seek refuge within an obscure harbour in Russian Lapland, where, with the crew of two of his vessels, he was frozen to death; and when the Laplanders, in pursuance of their annual custom, sought the sea-coast in summer, for the sake of its fishery, they found the remains of the unhappy adventurer, who, meditating a great discovery, had met with an obscure death. It is a touching picture to contemplate him as he was found, sitting with his diary and papers before him as in life, and to think how little his aspiring, but noble ambition, meditated so melancholy a fate.

The expedition was not without its benefit, as one vessel escaped. Richard Chancellor, its commander, landed near Archangel, and inclined the Czar, Ivan Bazilowitz, then engaged in the Livonian war, to grant considerable commercial privileges to the English.

Such was the state of commerce, when, after the lapse of half a century, a great man arose. The mild, but childish Edward, the persecuting Mary, and the politic Elizabeth, found it equally to their interest to employ the enlarged mind and great talents of Thomas Gresham.

The reign of Elizabeth was marked no less by an advance in poetry and philosophy than by a rapid increase in the science of money. It almost seemed as if nature, hitherto checked in her developement by internal convulsions and unhealthy strife, used extraordinary efforts to repair the evils produced by civil war. Amid the names which adorn the period, that of Gresham takes a noble position. To this great citizen we owe the abolition of loans from foreign states. By his agency the financial difficulties of the reign were ably met. The peremptory necessity which compelled the government to borrow, produced a difficulty on the part of the lender, in exact proportion to the exigency of the borrower. The value arose with the necessity; twelve and even fourteen per cent. was paid for the accommodation. "After negotiating several loans," says the historian of the Royal Exchange, " Gresham felt that, instead of sending such large sums abroad, it would be a desirable thing to secure them for the capitalist at home. With the eye of a statesman, he saw that it would be more convenient for the borrower." By his counsel, Elizabeth was induced, when a loan was necessary, " not to use strangers, but her own subjects, that it might be seen what a prince of power she was."

Her first applications to the citizens were not met with sufficient alacrity to please the imperious queen. She who could imprison a favourite for life, or send a rival to the block, was checked by her plebeian, but wealthy subjects. The pride of the eighth Henry had descended with his crown to his daughter, and she caused it to be intimated to the unwilling merchants that, to borrow their money "was a matter of great grace and favour." On another occasion, the haughty Tudor incarcerated a resolute citizen, who was too modest to place himself under so great an obligation. It is scarcely possible to bestow too much praise on the princely merchant who originated the idea which saved the kingdom from foreign loans, which gave the large interest paid by the state to the English trader, and which, at the same time, offered to the crown a security never possessed through the agency of means so legitimate. It was owing to his active exertions that the principle was carried out, and the objections of the citizens conquered. The accommodation was found to be in some measure reciprocal; at a late period the merchants trading to Turkey acted as bankers to the nation, by borrowing a considerable amount of bullion, previously lying idle in the Tower.

That the character of Gresham has not been overrated is proved by the scheme he devised at Antwerp, for operating on the exchanges, so as to render them favourable to England. He promised Edward VI., during the reign of whom this occurred, that if he might pursue his own views, he would remove all his sovereign's difficulties in two years. The following is his plan, relieved from its antiquated spelling.

"My request shall be to his majesty and you, to appoint me out, weekly, twelve or thirteen hundred pounds, to be secretly received at one man's hands, so that it may be kept secret, and that I may thereunto trust, and that I may make my reckoning thereof assuredly. I shall so use the matter here in the town of Antwerp, that every day I will be sure to take up two or three hundred pounds sterling by exchange. And thus doing it shall not be perceived, nor yet shall be occasion to make the exchange fall. For that it shall be taken up in my name. And so by these means, in working by deliberation and time, the merchants' turn also shall be served. As also this should bring all merchants out of suspicion, who do nothing towards payment of the king's debts, and will not stick to say, that ere the payment of the king's debt be made, it will bring down the exchange to 13s. 4d., which I trust never to see that day. So that by this you may perceive if that I do but take up every day but £200 sterling it will amount in one year to £72,000, and the king's majesty oweth here at this present £108,000, with the interest money that was prolonged before this time. So that, by these means, in two years, things will be compassed accordingly, and my purpose set forth."

" How correct," says Mr. Burgon, in his Life and Times of Sir Thomas Gresham, "he was in the results he anticipated, from these and similar measures, appeared in the sequel by the success which attended them. He found means in a short space to raise the exchange from sixteen shillings Flemish for the pound sterling to twenty-two shillings, at which rate he discharged all the king's debts, and by this means money was rendered plentiful and trade prosperous, while the credit of the crown became established on a firmer basis abroad than it had ever been before."

CHAPTER II.

THE robberies successively exercised upon the Jew and the Lombard, in the dark ages of the Plantagenets, were successfully imitated at a later and more polite period by the Stuarts; but the very blow which appeared likely to crush the infant spirit of banking proved its support. The new features, which in the seventeenth century, were developed in its history, arose from a repetition of one of those tyrannical acts which, in their own opinion, too often form "the right divine of kings." An evil spirit—the spirit of contention—was abroad. The people were beginning to arouse themselves from the apathy with which they had hitherto borne the successive despotic acts of their sovereigns. "Genius and capacity of all kinds," according to Hume, "began to exert themselves, and to be distin-

guished by the public." The danger environing Charles
from an opposition which ranked among its members the "sagacity of Pym, and the ardour of St. John,
the daring impetuosity of Hollis, the chivalric valour
of Hampden, the brilliant eccentricity of Vane, and
the profound subtlety, yet magnificent ambition of
the future master of them all—Cromwell"—rendered
money necessary to the monarch. The treasure arising from the accumulated gains of the merchants had
been deposited by them in the Mint, then within the
Tower, with a perfect conviction of its safety. If the
short-sighted policy of the earlier kings of England
had extorted money from the Jew and the Lombard,
at least they borrowed from their English subjects ; it
remained for the polished Charles to sully his fair fame
by robbing them.

Yet let him not be judged too harshly. Right and
wrong assume new aspects under varying circumstances. The monarch trembled on his throne. His
prerogatives were denied. His favourite minister was
impeached. The claims of his children were endan-
gered. A discontented people were opposed to a per-
fidious court. An irritated parliament were thwarting
a proud aristocracy. The supplies were stopped, and
levies were made in vain. To compass these dangers
money was required ; to gain it by ordinary means
was impracticable. Ere judgment be passed, let these
things be remembered. Rank, family, life, were in
the balance, and the monarch yielded. The money

placed by the merchants in the Mint, amounting to two hundred thousand pounds, was seized ; the sanctuary of a people's commercial faith was violated to supply the royal necessities.

Another palliation to the mind of Charles might perhaps be in the consideration that the money belonged to the merchants ; that the merchants were mostly citizens ; and that the citizens were strenuous supporters of the opposition. Some idea of their feelings toward the monarch may be gathered from the following picture, by the first essayist of the day. " The people of this great city had long been thoroughly devoted to the national cause. Their houses, their purses, their pikes, were at the command of the representatives of the nation. London was in arms all night. The next day the shops were closed ; the streets were filled with immense crowds ; the multitude pressed round the king's coach, and insulted him with opprobrious cries."

The knowledge that the seizure of the merchants money might cripple their power, that in its possession he would gain an important addition to his own strength, and that it was only to be regarded as an equitable punishment for their defalcation, must be accepted as some extenuation of this great wrong. A sufficient amount of evil, which no sophistry can palliate, and no excuse mitigate, rests upon that "grey, discrowned head," without adding another heavy accusation to the many justly brought against him,

" whose popularity with the present generation," says Macaulay, " is owing to his Vandyke dress, his handsome face, and his peaked beard."

The office of royal exchanger must not be omitted. Up to the reign of Henry VII., this prerogative of the monarch continued to be exercised. English coins were not allowed to be exported, and the right of exchanging them for other money, belonged to the crown. The royal exchanger was alone entitled to give the native for foreign coin, or for bullion.

During the reign of Henry VIII., the circulation became so debased as to be difficult of exchange by any one, and the office fell into disuse; the Goldsmiths took advantage of this, and deserting to a great extent their accustomed calling, began to deal in the debased money, exchanging for it, plate and foreign coin. This was continued until the reign of Charles I., a monarch to whom a prerogative, or a monopoly, was almost as dear as his crown. In 1627 he re-established it by royal proclamation, but this interference with the trade of the Goldsmith was received with so little satisfaction, that the king authorized the publication of a pamphlet, vindicating his rights, asserting that " the prerogative had always been a flower of the crown;" " that the Goldsmiths had left off their proper trade, and turned exchangers of plate and foreign coins, for our English coins, although they had no right."

All the important bodies of the City, who could

quickly perceive the evil arising from a monopoly in which they were not allowed to participate, petitioned against the revival of the office; but petitioning was in vain. The duties of " changer, exchanger, and outchanger," were given to one, who twice betrayed his royal master in return, to the handsomest peer, and the basest apostate of a period remarkable for its apostacy. Henry Rich, first Earl of Holland, was installed in possession of the privilege. With the troubles of Charles, the office was abolished; it has not been since established, having yielded to institutions, which have grown out of the circumstances and character of the times.

The return of the Hebrew to that country, from which he had been ignominiously driven, is usually attributed to Cromwell. After the first Charles had paid the melancholy penalty for his dissimulation, a negociation is stated to have taken place with parliament. The demand of the Israelites was, that the laws against them should be repealed, and, provided the Bodleian library were made over to them, with an additional permission to possess St. Paul's Cathedral, as a synagogue, they would pay £500,000. However outrageous this proposal seems, if a letter in the Thurloe state papers may be trusted, it was absolutely discussed, and several debates occurred upon it. The larger sum of £800,000 was demanded; the Hebrews refused to increase their offer, and the negociation was broken off.

The promotion of Cromwell to the Protectorate, once more excited the hopes of the exiled Israelites. The favour this great man evinced towards religious toleration, the grandeur of disposition which led him to the support of principles, requiring two centuries even partially to develope, was not overlooked. In 1654, the French ambassador in Holland, writing to the French minister in England, says, "A Jew of Amsterdam informed me for certain, that the three generals of the fleet have presented a petition to his highness the Protector, to obtain that their nation may be received in England to draw the commerce thither." The mind of Cromwell was undoubtedly aware of all the advantages to be gained by the return of this commercial people. Permission was granted to Rabbi Menasseh Ben Israel to reside in London. In all probability, this permission was made, with the view of testing the feelings of the people. While in England he presented a petition to Cromwell, praying for the Jew, a free exercise of his religion, a permission to exercise the faith of his fathers, and a license to erect synagogues for public worship : at the same time he appealed to the trading propensities of the nation, by a declaration to the Commonwealth, exhibiting the advantages which would accrue to commerce, from the return of his nation. A council was appointed, and in the fashion of the time, disputations were held. Those who were supposed to be most interested were summoned to the debate. Law, trade, and divinity had their representatives. The first was favourable; the second undecided; but the third opposed the return of this people with all the rancour of an ignorant intolerance. The text-quoting fashion of the period, the spirit which led men to dispute in conventicles, and wrest words from their right meanings, the narrowness which only regarded the Hebrew as the outcast, while it forgot that he had been the favoured of God, were all brought into full exercise. For four days were texts which had been uttered in a more genial spirit, narrowed and perverted to party feeling; and for four days must Cromwell's enlarged mind, have been eminently annoyed by the prophetic denunciations of the divinity of the land. At last it appears that something of the determined spirit which had displayed itself on other fields, cut the debate short, Cromwell telling them in very plain language, that they had made the question more intricate than ever; that though he wished no more reasoning, he yet begged an interest in their prayers.

No definite step appears to have resulted from this conference; and the general feeling of hostility which prevailed against the return of the Hebrews, was increased by the discovery of a somewhat similar proposition from their Asiatic brethren. The avowed design of a mission from some of their rabbis, was the establishment of a company to trade to the Levant. But the real object of their visit appears to have been an examination of the pedigree of the Protector, in hopes of tracing a Jewish origin, and of proving him to be the Messiah, after whom the hearts of the people yearned. Whether Cromwell encouraged this idea or not appears quite uncertain, but they obtained permission to repair to Cambridge and examine the library. They then went to Huntingdon, the birth-place of the Protector, to investigate his descent. Some rumours of this design soon propagated; and Cromwell, aware of the ridicule and sarcasm to which he would be rendered liable, ordered them to return to London, from which place they soon departed. After this time, however, the Hebrews obtained admission into England; and in 1689 they must have increased considerably, as, in a petition from some merchants, complaining that the Jews were not subject to the Alien duty, it was stated that £10,000 were lost yearly, from the export Alien duty not being levied.

The next resource of the merchants, after the violent seizure of their treasure by "the royal martyr," was to keep their cash in their own houses. To do this they were obliged to trust their servants and apprentices. As the civil war advanced, however, the love of fighting often overcame the love of honesty; and they, with the money entrusted to them, disappeared.

From the evil arose the remedy. The Goldsmiths, up to this period, were employed, with some exceptions, in the ordinary way of their vocation. They were a rich body; and it was natural that the richest should be most trusted. Those servants, therefore, who yet remained in charge of their master's money, lent it, at 4d. per cent. per diem, to the Goldsmith, who saw a new branch of business opening, and caught the first glimpse of modern banking. The troubles of the time, which prevented country gentlemen from keeping their rents in their own mansions, made them glad to remit it to persons of responsibility. The Goldsmith was equally glad to pay a small interest, with the prospect of lending it at an increased profit. The necessitous merchant applied for loans at a high usance. The rich deposited their cash, for security, without interest. The widow and the orphan received four per cent.; and, with the money thus obtained, the Goldsmith was able to increase his business by the somewhat new branch of discounting bills.

They thus became money borrowers and receivers of rents. "They lent money to the king on the security of the taxes. The receipts they issued for the money lodged at their houses, circulated from hand to hand, and were known by the name of Goldsmiths' Notes. These may be considered the first kind of bank notes issued in England."

A business, at once profitable and safe, increased with the increase of commerce; and, under the prosperous sway of the Protector, must have been found a great convenience. The Goldsmiths gradually arose in reputation with the extension of their transactions. They took the lead in monetary business; and as they allowed interest on cash, however short the period of the loan, it must have been found an important assistance to all those who required a secure depositary for their gains.

The modern principles of banking may thus be traced to the increased importance of business; to the additional facilities required by the latter; and to the disturbed spirit of the time, which gave to it an impulse it might otherwise have wanted. Maitland remarks that, even in his day, there were several eminent bankers who united to the department of banking the keeping of goldsmiths' shops, although they were more frequently separate. Great part of the wealth of Sir Thomas Gresham was found at his death to be comprised in gold chains; while, in 1593, a German writes, that he visited England, and saw in Lombard Street " all sorts of gold and silver vessels exposed to sale, as well as ancient and modern coins, in such quantities, as must surprise a man the first time he sees and considers them."

The celebrity of the first banking house belongs, by common consent, to Mr. Francis Child. This gentleman, who was the father of his profession, and possessed of large property, began business shortly after the restoration. He was originally apprentice to William Wheeler, goldsmith and banker, whose shop was on the site of the present banking house. The foundation of his importance arose from the good old fashion of marrying his master's daughter, and through this, he succeeded to the estate and business. The latter he subsequently confined entirely to the banking department.

The principles on which he founded it, and the remarkable clauses in his will, by which he regulated its future conduct, are well known. It has maintained to the present day, amid all the chances and changes of banking, the same position, and the same respectability, which he bequeathed it.

By the year 1667, the banking business, which had increased in some proportion with commerce, had attained considerable importance.

Wealthy bodies must always hold an important position in the state, and, under a needy government, an influential one. The luxury of the court of the second Charles, combined with his careless disposition, compelled him to have recourse to the Goldsmith. The Goldsmith made him pay interest and premium to an enormous extent. Thus a great portion of the supplies voted by the Houses of Parliament came into the possession of this increasing body. The benefit which should have been derived from the parliamentary grants, was largely absorbed by the necessity which unfortunately existed of obtaining the money immediately. And how could such necessities fail to exist, when the dissipation of Charles produced those scenes of extravagance which were a disgrace to the King, and a dishonour to the people! The pages of Pepys, and the private records of the reign lately

published, tend to prove that the pensioner of Louis
Quatorze must have been utterly and completely at
the mercy of the usurer.

In a curious pamphlet, published in 1676, it may
be seen that the Goldsmith took great advantage of
the necessities of Charles. The monarch who lives
beyond his revenue must pay the same penalty as the
subject who outruns his income. He found himself
at the mercy of the rich Goldsmith, who made the
royal debtor pay ten, twenty, and thirty per cent. for
accommodation, while he allowed only six per cent.
for the money which went to alleviate the difficulties
of the "merry monarch." A business so profitable,
induced the Goldsmith "more and more to become
lender to the King, to anticipate all the revenue, to
take every grant of Parliament into pawn as soon as
it was given; also to outvie each other in buying and
taking to pawn bills, orders, and tallies, so that, in
effect, all the revenue passed through their hands."

The extravagant luxury of the court, however,
together with the utter want of principle of Charles,
produced a nearly fatal result upon this important
interest. The imbecility with which the contest with
Holland had been carried on, had involved the nation
in debt and dishonour.

"The Government of Charles," says Mr. Babington
Macaulay, "had suffered a succession of humiliating
disasters. The extravagance of the court had dissipated all the means which Parliament had supplied for

the purpose of carrying on offensive hostilities. It was determined to wage only defensive war; and even for defensive war the vast resources of England were found insufficient. The Dutch insulted the British coast, sailed up the Thames, took Sheerness, and carried their ravages to Chatham. The blaze of the ships burning in the river was seen at London; it was rumoured that a foreign army had landed at Gravesend; and military men seriously proposed to abandon the Tower. To such a depth of infamy had a bad administration reduced that proud and victorious community, which a few years before had dictated its pleasure to Mazarine, to the States General, and to the Vatican."

The people, accustomed to the secure reign of Cromwell, were in utter consternation. The monied portion of the community were seized with a panic. The country was in danger. London itself might be invaded. What security was there then for the money advanced to the crown? The people flocked to their debtors; they demanded their deposits; and London witnessed the FIRST RUN UPON THE BANKERS.

The fears of the people proved fallacious, as the Goldsmiths met all demands made upon them; confidence was restored by a proclamation from the King, stating that the demands on the Exchequer should be met as usual; and the run ceased.

From this period up to 1672, the Goldsmiths continued their money-making trade. The difficulties of

Charles had increased ; he wanted money without the aid of Parliament. He was ambitious of absolute power; and his reign had been a succession of abortive attempts to obtain it.

The infamous cabal ministry were in office; nothing was too bad for them to attempt. If there were some palliations for Charles I., when he seized the money deposited in the Mint, what can be urged for Charles II. ? His throne was secure ; his person popular ; money was freely advanced to him on the security of his revenues. No necessity of the monarch justified the act we have to record. Charles I., under the pressure of unexampled necessity, had made a forced loan, Charles II., to gratify his immoderate passions, ordered the Exchequer to be closed, and no payments made ; were this not vouched for by contemporary history, we should hesitate, as we now blush, to recite it.

The relation of Hume is worthy repeating. "The King had declared that the staff of Treasurer was ready for any one that could find an expedient for supplying the present necessities. Shaftesbury dropped a hint to Clifford, which the latter immediately seized and carried to the King, who granted him the promised reward, together with a peerage. This expedient was the shutting up of the Exchequer, and the retaining of all the payments which should be made into it.

" It had been usual for the bankers to carry their money to the Exchequer, and to advance it on security

of the funds, by which they were afterwards reim-
bursed when the money was levied on the public ; the
bankers by this traffic got eight, sometimes ten per
cent. for sums which either had been consigned to
them without interest, or which they had borrowed at
six per cent. ; profits which they dearly paid for by
this egregious breach of public faith. The measure
was so suddenly taken, that none had warning of
the danger ; a general confusion prevailed in the city,
followed by the ruin of many ; the bankers stopped
payment : the merchants could answer no bills ; distrust took place everywhere ; and men full of dismal
apprehensions asked each other, what must be the
scope of those mysterious counsels, whence the Parliament and all men of honour were excluded ; and
which commenced by the forfeiture of public credit, and
an open violation of the most solemn engagements."

The Goldsmiths were ruined, and their clients
ruined with them. Both had fallen by an act which
stamped the monarch and his minions with infamy.
But a general burst of honest indignation arose. The
large sum of one million three hundred thousand
pounds affected, directly or collaterally, the remotest
provinces of the kingdom. The bankers were besieged ;
but they, innocent of this great transgression, could
yield no redress. A thousand families were deprived
of bread. The widow and the orphan suffered with
the merchant and the trader. The universal feeling
which spread throughout the length and breadth of

the land, had it been resolved into words, would have uttered, with one loud voice, in the solemn warning of the psalmist, " Put not your trust in Princes." The press was resorted to, and language, stronger than the Stuarts liked or usually permitted, was boldly circulated among the people. Several pamphlets, and one octavo volume, were published, and it is a proof of the general feeling of the nation, that one writer ventured to say, " A step of this kind could proceed from nothing less than a resolution of the court to borrow no more hereafter, but to take."

The outcry assumed so much importance, that Charles was compelled to yield, and we learn that six per cent., out of the hereditary excise, was paid for this sum during the remainder of his reign. It is a curious circumstance that, only two years after this, the King was able to borrow money at eight per cent., being nominally the same rate of interest charged before that event. The principal was never repaid. It was, however, made part of the national debt by William ; this act was confirmed by Anne; and the Stock ultimately became part of the celebrated South Sea fund.

We abridge from " Knight's Pictorial History of England," a remarkably clear and succinct account of the progress of the debt.

" Interest had been originally paid upon this sum at six per cent. up to the last year of Charles's reign. From which time no provision was made for it till 1701, the last of William's reign, when interest was granted on the whole from 1705, at three per cent., and the principal made redeemable on payment of half its amount. The entire amount to which the unfortunate bankers and merchants were plundered by this arrangement exceeded three millions. The £664,263 thus ultimately awarded in satisfaction of equitable claims to six times the amount was called the Bankers' Debt, and still remains undischarged with other public debts, of which it may be regarded the foundation."

CHAPTER III.

THE important position assumed by England towards the middle of the seventeenth century, renders the absence of a national bank somewhat surprising. Under the sagacious government of Cromwell, the nation had increased in commercial and political greatness : and although several projects were issued for banks, one of which was to have branches in every important town throughout the country, yet a necessity for their formation not being absolutely felt, the proposals were dismissed. During the Protectorate, however, Parliament, taking into consideration the rate of interest, which was higher in England than abroad, and that trade was thereby rendered comparatively disadvantageous to the English merchant, reduced the legal rate from eight to six per cent., and this measure, although it had been carried by the Parliament of Cromwell, almost every act of which proved odious in the eyes of the Stuarts, was nevertheless confirmed by the legislature of Charles II. In 1546 the payment of interest had been rendered legal, and fixed at ten per cent. In 1624 the rate had been reduced to eight per cent. ; and with the advance of commercial prosperity it has been found advisable to lower it still further.

There were many reasons for the establishment of a national bank. It was necessary for the sake of a secure paper currency. It was required for the support of the national credit. It was desirable as a method of reducing the rate of interest paid by the state ; a rate so high, that, according to Anderson, men were induced to take their money out of trade, for the sake of securing it ; an operation " big with mischief." The truth is that the times required it. The theorist may prove to demonstration the perfection of his theory ; the speculator may show the certainty of its success ; but unless it be a necessity, called for by the onward progress of society, it must eventually fall to the ground.

That the want of such an establishment was felt is certain. But as such firms as Childs,—the books of whom go back to the year 1620, and refer to prior documents—Hoares, dating from 1680, and Snows, from 1685—were able to assist the public demand, although at the exorbitant interest of the period, it does not occasion so much surprise, that the attempt made to meet the increasing requirements of trade, proved insufficient. In 1678, however, sixteen years previous to the foundation of the Bank of England, "proposals for a large model of a bank" were published : and in 1683, a "National Bank of Credit" was brought forward. In a rare pamphlet, entitled "Bank Credit; or the usefulness and security of the Bank of Credit examined, in a dialogue between a Country Gentleman, and a London Merchant," this idea is warmly defended. It was, however, simply to have been one of credit ; nor was it proposed to form a bank of deposit; although by the following remark of the "Country Gentleman," it is evident that such an establishment, on a secure scale, was desirable. He says,

"Could they not without damage to themselves have secured the running cash of the nobility, gentry, merchants, and traders of this city and kingdom, from all hazard, which would have been a great benefit to all concerned, who know not where to deposit their cash securely."

To this, which time has proved to be a reasonable suggestion, the following reply is made by the "London Merchant."

"They are unwilling to meddle with money, because the scarcity of it, would, perhaps, by ignorant or malicious men, be imputed to them. Possibly for the sake of ease and convenience, they may be induced to receive and secure the running cash of such as shall desire it, yet dealing in money is not the business they purpose."

One of the objects was, " that tradesmen, when they have a considerable quantity of goods or wares made, may, by the help of this bank, deposit their goods, by raising a credit on their own dead stock, employ their servants, and increase their trade, till they get a good market instead of selling them at a loss."

In other words this bank was to act as a great capitalist for the merchant, and enable the speculative man to inflict on the country the evils of over-trading. However desirable such an establishment may be as a resource on an emergency, it is far from being so ordinarily ; as it would invariably tend to increase the mischief, arising from undue speculation.

The directors proposed also, to encourage any " ingenious invention" tending to the promotion of linen, woollen, silk, lace or other useful manufactures.

The danger of forgery, a fearful question, and involving many interests, is met by a reply of which time has unhappily proved the fallacy. " I am well assured," calmly and confidently replies the London merchant, " that the bills are so contrived, that it is morally impossible that they should be counterfeited." The pages of the Newgate Calendar afford a melancholy, but conclusive reply to this assertion.

After much trouble this bank of credit was

established at Devonshire House, in Bishopsgate Street. Its object, as we have related, being principally to advance money to tradesmen and manufacturers, on the security of goods. Three fourths of the value was lent on these, and bills for their amount given to the depositor.

In order to render these bills current, an appointed number of persons in each trade, was formed into a society to regulate commercial concerns. Any individual possessed of such bills, might therefore obtain from this company goods or merchandize, with as much ease as if they offered current coin.

The bank of credit does not appear to have flourished. The machinery was too complicated, and the risk of depreciation in the value of manufactures too great. It was next to impossible for such a company to exist after the Bank of England came with its low discounts, and free accommodations.

The wild spirit of speculation, that spirit which at various periods has created fearful crises in the commercial world, commenced in 1694. The fever which from time to time has flushed the mind of the monied man, and given a fierce excitement to the almost penniless adventurer, was then and in the following year in full operation. The great South-sea scheme in 1720,—which it will be our melancholy duty to refer to—is ordinarily considered the earliest display of this reckless spirit. But a quarter of a century before, equal ingenuity, and equal villany, were exercised.

Obscure men, whose sole capital was their enormous impudence, invented similar schemes, promised similar advantages, and used similar arts to entice the capitalist, which were employed with so much success at a later period. The want of a great banking association was sure to be made a pretext. Two "Land Banks" and a " London Bank" to be managed by the magistrates, with several other proposals were therefore put promisingly forward. One of these was for another " Bank of Credit;" and a pamphlet published in 1694 under the title of " England's Glory," will give some idea of its nature.

" If a person desires money to be returned at Coventry or York he pays it at the office in London, and receives a bill of credit after their form written upon marble paper, indenturewise or on other paper, as may be contrived to prevent counterfeiting." It was also proposed that government should share the profits; but neither of the projects were carried out.

The people neglected their calling. The legitimate desire of money grew into a fierce and fatal spirit of avarice. The arts so common at a later day, were had recourse to. Project begat project. Copper was to be turned into brass. Fortunes were to be realized by lotteries. The sea was to yield the treasures it had engulphed. Pearl fisheries were to pay impossible per centages. " Lottery on lottery," says a writer of the day, " engine on engine, multiplied wonderfully. If any person got considerably by a happy and useful invention, others followed in spite of the patent, and published printed proposals, filling the daily newspapers therewith, thus going on to jostle one another, and abuse the credulity of the people."

Anderson, the historian of English Commerce, says, " the projectors of these made a great noise in town, for drawing on people to join with them, making use of various tricks and stratagems. At first they pretend a mighty vein of gold, silver, or copper, to have been discovered in a piece of ground of their knowledge, then they agree with the lord or patentee, for a small yearly rent, or a part reserved to him, to grant them a lease for twenty-one years, to dig that ground, which they immediately fall to ; and give out it is a very rich mine. Next they settle a company, and divide it usually into four hundred shares : and pretend to carry on the work for the benefit of all the proprietors, who at the beginning purchase shares at a low rate, say ten or twenty shillings. Then all on sudden they run up the share to £3. £5. £10. and £15. : when those originally and principally concerned, sell out their interest, and by this· and other under-hand dealings, tricking and sharping on one another, the whole falls to the ground, and is abandoned by every body." Thus it would seem, that they who lived in the " good old times," were not deficient in craft, cunning and duplicity.

Amid the many delusive and impracticable schemes, were two important projects which have conferred great benefits on the English people. The first of these was the New River Company, the conception of Sir Hugh Middleton; the second was the corporation of the Bank of England. Nature, and the great nations of antiquity, suggested the former; the force and pressure of the times demanded the latter. It is from such demands that our chief institutions arise. By precept we may be taught their propriety ; by example we may see their advantages. But until the necessity is personally felt they are sure to be neglected ; and men wonder at their want of prescience and upbraid their shortsightedness, when with a sudden and some-times startling success, they arise through the energy of another.

William Paterson, one of those men whose capacity is measured by failure or success, was the originator of the new Bank ; and it is perhaps unfortunate for his fame, that no biography exists of this remarkable person. As the projector of the present bank of Scotland, as the very soul of the celebrated Darien Company, and as the founder of the Bank of England, he deserves notice. A speculative as well as an adventurous man, he proved his belief in the practicability of the Darien scheme by accompanying that unfortunate expedition ; and the formation of the Bank of England was the object of his desires and the subject of his thoughts for a long time previous to its establishment.

William Paterson was born in Traillflatt in the

county of Dumfries in 1658. Having been educated
for the church, he indulged a naturally adventurous
disposition, by visiting the West Indian Islands under
pretext of converting the Indians. His real occupation is stated however to have been very different, as
he mingled with, and perhaps formed part of those
daring buccaneers, the exploits of whom form so
romantic a chapter in the byeways of history. During
this period Paterson made himself thoroughly acquainted with the capabilities of the Isthmus of Darien,
better known as the Isthmus of Panama. "This place,
which is between Mexico and Peru," says a modern
writer, "is within six weeks' sail of most parts of
Europe, the East Indies, and a part of China. It is in
the heart of the West India Islands, and not far from
North America. It is one of the best situations for
a colony from a trading and manufacturing country on
the face of the earth." The same opinion was entertained by Paterson, who must have been thoroughly
acquainted with the position and natural advantages of
the place ; and from his youth contemplated its
colonization. "The expense of navigation to China,
Japan, the Spice islands, and the far greatest part of
the East Indies will be lessened more than half, and
the consumption of European commodities and manufactures, will soon be more than doubled. Trade will
increase trade, money will beget money, and this
trading world shall need no more to want work for
their hands, but will rather want hands for their work."

While roving about the beautiful islands of the western Indies Paterson loved to listen to the buccaneers, who after a stormy and eventful career delighted in relating the glories of their early achievements ; and with memories which still lingered on their past lives, recounted with transport the ease with which they had passed from one sea to another, driving before them the plunder they had acquired.   From them he heard of precious metals in the bowels of the earth, of fine tracts of land little known to Europeans, and of rivers sparkling over sands of gold.   The romance which fired the imagination of the youth, was productive in the maturity of his manhood, of the unfortunate Darien expedition ;   as before leaving he satisfied himself that there was one portion of this fine country, which still belonged to the Indians,—the original proprietors of the soil,—from whom it had never been alienated.   The situation was between Portobello and Carthagena, and although under a tropical sun, the air was temperate.   The soil also was rich and productive, yielding almost spontaneously the refreshing fruits of a warm and luxuriant climate.

A desire to participate in advantages similar to those enjoyed by the East India Company, was prevalent among many commercial nations, about the end of the seventeenth century.   This feeling being noticed by Paterson, he first mentioned his project to the English people, by whom it was coldly received.   He then proposed it, through the agency of a rich Walloon banker, to several European states, but without success. On his return to London he formed a friendship with Mr. Fletcher of Saltoun, a man who " hated England, because he loved Scotland to excess." Struck with the proposal, the advantages of which he was anxious to secure for his country, Fletcher took Paterson to Edinburgh, and introduced him to the minister for Scotland, who with the secretaries of state, warmly countenanced the project. The prospect of participating in the profits of the East India Company stirred all the accumulative propensities of human nature. Every thought of a nation remarkable for an absence of undue speculation, was embarked in a scheme which promised universal riches. " The phrensy," says Sir John Dalrymple, "of the Scotch nation to sign the solemn league and covenant, never exceeded the rapidity with which they ran to subscribe to the Darien Company. The nobility, the gentry, the merchants, the people, the royal burghs, without the exception of one, and most of the other public bodies subscribed. Young women threw their little fortunes into the stock ; widows sold their jointures to get the command of money for the same purpose." Four hundred thousand pounds—half the cash in Scotland—was subscribed. To this, England added three hundred thousand, and Hamburg and Holland, two hundred thousand more.

An agreement had been entered into by which Paterson was to be paid two per cent. on the stock,

and three per cent. on the profits, but in the greatness
of this success, he tendered a discharge of both claims ;
a testimony to his entire disinterestedness. In doing
so, Paterson contrived to throw a grandeur of expres-
sion over a simple law release. " It was not suspicion
of the justice or gratitude of the company, nor a
consciousness that my services could ever become
useless to them, but the ingratitude of some individuals
which made it common prudence to ask a retribution
for six years time and ten thousand pounds spent in
promoting the establishment of the company. But
now I see it standing on the authority of parliament,
and supported by so many great and good men, I
release all claim to that retribution, happy in the noble
concession made to me, but happier in the return I
now make for it."

The English were startled at the enthusiasm of
their neighbours. The East India Company remonstrated. The parliament impeached some of their
countrymen for joining it. The king grew alarmed, and
said "he had been ill advised in Scotland," changed
his Scotch ministry, and withdrew the promised aid.
The Scottish people, far from being depressed, were
animated by this. They regarded the profit as likely
to be greater ; undertook the vast project themselves ;
and neighbouring nations, with surprise and respect,
saw the poorest country in Europe send forth the
most gallant and numerous colony, which had ever
passed from the old to the new world.

The 26th July, 1698, is a day memorable in the annals of Scotland, when twelve hundred persons, three hundred of whom were men of birth and influence, embarked in five stout vessels from Leith. The entire population of Edinburgh thronged to witness their departure. Tears mingled with smiles, and praises of their courage were blended with prayers for their safety. Many a fond heart looked forward with confident anticipation; and none among that earnest crowd had power to weaken the present joy, with anticipations of future sorrow. Those who had been refused for want of room, hid themselves in the ships, and clung to the ropes and timbers, imploring permission to accompany the expedition. The eyes of that anxious crowd followed the white sails of the vessels as they left the harbour, and few who were interested in their progress, left the pier of Leith, so long as they could trace the course of these bold adventurers.

September witnessed their arrival at the proposed colony. Paterson honourably purchased land of its Indian possessors, sent messages of amity to the Spanish settlers, and to his eternal honour, he who at an earlier period had said, "A people and their industry are the true riches of a nation," proclaimed as the two great principles of his commonwealth, freedom of faith and freedom of trade, to all sects and to all nations. The new settlers built a fort, established a station, and consecrated both with mingled feelings of hope and love. Hope for the place where they had cast their destinies, love for the home which a Scot never forgets. They found the land of unequal surface, varied by swelling hills and fair vallies, abounding with rivers, brooks and springs. Delighted with the beauty of its situation, the golden sands of its rivers, and the treasures assigned by tradition, which Paterson at a later period had witnessed, they worked with all the strong good will of settlers anxious to make a fruitful harvest from the fertile soil, and the earnestness of men willing to earn their bread by the sweat of their brow. And as the followers of " stout Cortes,"

" Silent upon a peak of Darien,"

gazed in " mute surprise" upon the broad Pacific, so upon many a fair summer's eve did the companions of Paterson find themselves on the summit of the loftiest " peak," gazing through the clear air of that fine climate towards the bleak mountains of their northern home. In the watch tower which they had built upon a mountain a mile above the surface of the sea, Dalrymple says they often sate enjoying the beautiful air, and speculating upon their future prospects.

The first letters from the colony were written with enthusiasm. " The wealth, fruitfulness, health and good situation of the country are much above our expectation." " In fruitfulness this country seems not to give place to any in the world." One river was named the Golden River. Another place was called the Golden Island. The seas were filled with turtle. Hunting, fowling and fishing were abundant. Grand

and stately trees, without any underwood, enabled a horseman to ride for miles beneath the pleasant shade so acceptable to the inhabitants of a sultry climate. " Strong in body and hardy in habits," says a writer in " Chambers' Journal," they behaved differently to the effeminate Spaniards in a similar situation. In place of shrinking with disdain from the labour which could alone command success, the Caledonian settlers nerved themselves to their task. Unhappily their stock of provisions ran low, and they were compelled to accept the hospitality of the Indians who hunted and fished to supply their necessities. Summer brought disease ; provisions grew scarcer ; the other colonists were forbidden to trade with them. With a deficient supply of food, their numbers daily diminishing, beneath the wasting sun of a tropical climate, the bold Scots began to shrink from the dangers they had dared. But worse and more perilous evils were in reserve. The fort was attacked by the Spaniards from another portion of the isthmus, who were said to be covertly instigated by the English monarch. Their numbers were thinned by disease, the remnant were weakened by famine, and the unhappy settlers, commanded by Captain Campbell, after gallantly supporting the credit of the national name, had no resource but to surrender. The terms were favourable. The honours of war, and safety for personal property were guaranteed them. This, added perhaps to the strong home feelings which a Scottish exile ever cherishes, decided their homeward course; and William Paterson, the first to leave his native soil at Leith and the last to quit Darien, saw with an anguish almost inexpressible the failure of his cherished scheme. His conduct was worthy his character. A letter of the period says, " The colonists give Paterson due praise, for he had been diligent and true to the end. He looks more like a skeleton than a man." The following is a touching picture drawn by his own pen. " When the rest were preparing to go away, I was left alone on shore in a weak condition. None visited me, except Captain Drummond, who with me still lamented the thoughts of our leaving the place, and prayed God that we might hear from our country before we left the coast." The utmost precaution could not have guarded against the miseries which assailed them. So weak were they when they left this inhospitable spot, that they were unable to weigh the anchor of the leaky vessel destined to convey them home. Thirty only of those who left the pier of Leith with such bounding yet honourable ambition, again set foot on their native soil. The projector, though seized with temporary derangement during the voyage, was one of them. With him the greatness of the failure was in proportion to the vast grandeur with which his imagination had invested the scheme. Not a family in Scotland escaped. In cash or kindred all suffered. It was a national calamity which fell alike on peer and peasant. That it was not the mere dream of a speculative enthusiast, is certain from the interest taken in discouraging it. That it was eminently practical, is almost proved from a people, so cautious as the Scotch, adventuring so freely. The mere fact that Paterson embarked in it, if not a direct evidence in its favour, is at least a direct proof of his faith in its practicability. It appears indeed to have been a remarkably grand scheme; grand in its conception; grand in its attempted execution; and was worthy the mind of that man with whom the idea of the Bank of England originated.

The accounts of Paterson's after life are various. One historian reports that he assisted in forming the union; that he was recommended by the Scottish Parliament to Queen Anne; and that he received an appointment in connection with the South Sea scheme; while another says, "Paterson survived many years in Scotland; pitied, respected, but neglected." It is equally doubtful whether any reparation was made, as Anderson states that for his great merit and public services the House of Commons voted him £18,241 10s. as a compensation; but Sir John Dalrymple writes "After the union he claimed reparation for his losses from the equivalent money given by the English to the Darien Company, but got nothing, because," he adds bitterly, "a grant to him from a public fund, would have been only an act of humanity, and not a political job." Thus ended the attempt of the founder of the Bank of England to colonize Darien, an expedition so important, and at the same time so disastrous, that it lives in the memory of the Scottish peasant, and forms a part of his familiar superstitions to the present day. Robert Chambers says, the peasantry of Torwoodlee in Roxburghshire yet believe that on a night—afterwards ascertained to be that of the death of the Laird's son at Darien—all the bells in Torwoodlee house rang violently and simultaneously, without the appearance of mortal agency.

CHAPTER IV.

OPPOSITION TO THE BANK—SCARCITY OF SUPPLIES—DISTRESS OF
THE ARMY — VARYING OPINIONS — ESTABLISHMENT OF THE
BANK—ANALYSIS OF THE ACT.—BANK AT GROCERS' HALL—
BENEFICIAL EFFECTS—TRIAL OF THE BANK—WILL OF THE
BANK—DEATH OF THE FIRST DEPUTY GOVERNOR—JEALOUSY
OF THE GOLDSMITHS.

FROM that political change which has been so justly
termed the " great revolution," to the establishment
of the Bank of England, the new government were in
constant difficulties ; and the ministerial mode of procuring money was degrading to a great people.   The
duties in support of the war waged for liberty and
protestantism, were required before they were levied.
The city corporation was usually applied to for an
advance ; interest which varied probably according to
the necessity of the borrower rather than to the real
value of money, was paid for the accommodation.
The officers of the city went round in their turn to the
separate wards, and re-borrowed in smaller amounts
the money they had advanced to the State.   Interest
and premiums were thus often paid to the extent of

twenty-five and even thirty per cent., according to the exigency of the case, and the trader found his pocket filled at the expense of the public.   Mr. Paterson gives a graphic description.   " The erection of this famous bank not only relieved the ministerial managers from their frequent processions into the city, for borrowing of money on the best and nearest public securities, at ten or twelve per cent. per annum, but likewise gave life and currency to double or treble the value of its capital in other branches of public credit, and so, under God, became the principal means of the success of the campaign in 1695 : as particularly in reducing the important fortress of Namur, the first material step towards the peace concluded in 1697."

To remedy this evil the Bank of England was pro-jected, and after much labour, William Paterson, aided by Mr. Michael Godfrey, procured from government a consideration of the proposal.   The King was abroad when the scheme was laid before the council, but the Queen occupied his place.   Here considerable opposi-tion occurred.   Paterson found it more difficult to procure consent than he anticipated, and all those who feared an invasion of their interests united to stop its progress.   The Goldsmith foresaw the destruction of his monopoly, and he opposed it from self interest. The Tory foresaw an easier mode of gaining money for the government he abhorred ; with a firmer hold on the people for the monarch he despised, and his antagonism bore all the energy of political partisanship.

The usurer foresaw the destruction of his oppressive extortion, and he resisted it with the vigour of his craft. The rich man foresaw his profits diminished on government contracts, and he vehemently and virtuously opposed it on public principles. Loud therefore were the outcries, and great the exertions of all parties, when the bill was first introduced in the House of Commons. But outcries are vain, and exertions futile in opposition to a dominant and powerful party. A majority had been secured for the measure ; and they who opposed its progress covered their defeat with vehement denunciations and vague prophecies. The prophets are in their graves, and their predictions only survive in the history of that establishment the downfall of which they proclaimed. " The scheme of a national bank," says Smollett, " had been recommended to the ministry for the credit and security of the government, and the increase of trade and circulation. William Paterson was author of that which was carried into execution. When it was properly digested in the cabinet, and a majority in Parliament secured, it was introduced into the House of Commons. The supporters said it would rescue the nation out of the hands of extortioners ; lower interest; raise the value of land ; revive public credit ; extend circulation ; improve commerce ; facilitate the annual supplies ; and connect the people more closely with government. The project was violently opposed by a strong party, who affirmed that it would become a monopoly, and engross the whole money of the kingdom; that it might be employed to the worst purposes of arbitrary power; that it would weaken commerce by tempting people to withdraw their money from trade; that brokers and jobbers would prey on their fellow creatures; encourage fraud and gaming; and corrupt the morals of the nation."

Previous governments had raised money with comparative ease because they were legitimate. That of William was felt to be precarious. It was feared by the money-lender that a similar convulsion to the one which had borne him so easily on the throne of a great nation, might waft him back to the shores of that Holland he so dearly loved. Thus the very circumstances which made supplies necessary also made them scarce. In addition to these things his person was unpopular. His phlegmatic Dutch habits compared unpleasingly with those of the graceful Stuarts, whose evil qualities were forgotten in the remembrance of their showy characteristics. Neither his Dutch followers or his Dutch manners were regarded with favour; and had it not been for his eminent kingly capacity, these things would have proved as dangerous to the throne as they tended to make the Sovereign unpopular. In a pamphlet published a few years after the establishment of the new corporation, is the following vivid picture of this Monarch's government. "In spite of the most glorious Prince, and most vigilant General the world had ever seen, yet the enemy gained upon us every year; the funds were run down, the credit jobbed away in Change Alley, the King and his troops devoured by mechanics, and sold to usury, tallies lay bundled up like Bath faggots in the hands of brokers, and stock-jobbers; the Parliament gave taxes, levied funds, but the loans were at the mercy of those men (the jobbers); and they showed their mercy indeed, by devouring the King and the army, the Parliament and indeed the whole nation: bringing their great Prince sometimes to that exigence through inexpressible extortions that were put upon him, that he has even gone into the fields without his equipage, nay even without his army; the regiments have been uncloathed when the King has been in the field, and the willing brave English spirits, eager to honour their country, and follow such a King, have marched even to battle without either stockings or shoes, while his servants have been every day working in Exchange Alley to get his men money of the stock jobbers, even after all the horrible demands of discount have been allowed; and at last, scarce 50 per cent. of the money granted by Parliament has come into the hands of the Exchequer, and that late, too late for service, and by driblets, till the King has been tired with the delay." This is a strange picture; beating even Mr. Paterson's account of the "processions in the city," to gain money, and adds another convincing proof of the necessity which then existed for some establishment, capable of advancing money at a reasonable rate, on the security of parliamentary grants.

The scheme proposed by William Paterson was too important not to meet with many enemies, and it appears from a pamphlet by Mr. Godfrey, the first Deputy Governor, that " Some pretended to dislike the bank only for fear it should disappoint their Majesties of the supplies proposed to be raised." That "all the several companies of oppressors are strangely alarmed, and exclaim at the bank, and seemed to have joined in a confederacy against it." That " extortion, usury and oppression, were never so attacked as they are likely to be by the bank." That "others pretend the bank will join with the Prince to make him absolute. That the concern have too good a bargain and that it would be prejudicial to trade." In Bishop Burnet's " History of his Own Times," we read an evidence of Mr. Godfrey's truth. "It was visible that all the enemies of government set themselves against it with such a vehemence of zeal, that this alone convinced all people that they saw the strength that our affairs would receive from it. I had heard the Dutch often reckon the great advantage they had had from their banks, and they concluded that as long as England remained jealous of her government, a bank could never be settled among us, nor gain credit among us to support itself, and upon that they judged that the superiority in trade must still be on their side.

The advantages that the King and all concerned in

tallies had from the bank were soon so sensibily felt that all people saw into the secret reasons that made the enemies of the constitution set themselves with so much earnestness against it." Another writer says: "Some prophetic politicians intimated their apprehensions, that an institution of this kind would soon become a mere creature of government; that care would be taken to give it none but government operations; that on any sudden emergency, or even general panic, the bank might be unable to answer the demands of its creditors; and that the failure of a national bank must be attended with national ruin—that such an institution under the influence of the executive government, would throw more real power into its hands, and add more facility to the projects of arbitrary and despotic ministers, not to say Monarchs, than the erection of a citadel : that the shutting up of the Exchequer in the last reign but one, after the Bankers had been induced to deposit the money there, was alone sufficient to manifest the danger of trusting any mighty mass of wealth within the reach of power : and that from the time this new wheel was added to the machine of government, all its motions would be mysterious and unintelligible; and a very little cunning might serve to destroy what all the wisdom and virtue of the nation could never restore."

All these varied interests were vainly exerted to prevent the bill from receiving the royal sanction, and the Bank of England, founded on the same principles which guided the Banks of Venice and Genoa, was incorporated by Royal Charter dated the 27th July 1694. From Mr. Gilbart's "History and Principles of Banking" we present the following brief analysis of this important Act. " The Act of Parliament by which the Bank was established, is entitled " An Act for granting to their Majesties, several duties upon tonnage of ships and vessels, and upon beer, ale and other liquors, for securing certain recompences and advantages in the said Act mentioned, to such persons as shall voluntarily advance the sum of fifteen hundred thousand pounds, towards carrying on the war with France." After a variety of enactments relative to the duties upon tonnage of ships and vessels, and upon beer, ale, and other liquors, the Act authorizes the raising of £1,200,000 by voluntary subscription, the subscribers to be formed into a Corporation and be styled " The Governor and Company of the Bank of England." The sum of £300,000 was also to be raised by subscription, and the contributors to receive instead annuities for one, two, or three lives. Towards the £1,200,000 no one person was to subscribe more than £10,000 before the first day of July, next ensuing, nor at any time more than £20,000. The Corporation were to lend their whole capital to government, for which they were to receive interest at the rate of eight per cent. per annum, and £4000 per annum for management; being £100,000 per annum on the whole. The Corporation were not allowed to borrow or owe more than the amount of their capital, and if they did so the individual members became liable to the creditors in proportion to the amount of their stock. The Corporation were not to trade in any " goods, wares, or merchandize whatever, but they were allowed to deal in bills of Exchange, gold or silver bullion, and to sell any goods, wares, or merchandize upon which they had advanced money, and which had not been redeemed within three months after the time 'agreed upon." The whole of the subscription was filled in a few days ; twenty-five per cent. paid down ; and as we have seen, a charter was issued on the 27th of July, 1694, of which the following are the most important points.

" That the management and government of the corporation be committed to the governor, deputy-governor, and twenty-four directors, who shall be elected between the 25th day of March, and the 25th day of April each year, from among the members of the company, duly qualified.

" That no dividend shall at any time be made by the said governor and company save only out of the interest, profit, or produce arising out of the said capital stock or fund, or by such dealing as is allowed by act of parliament.

" They must be natural born subjects of England, or naturalized subjects ; they shall have in their own name and for their own use, severally, viz., the governor at least £4000, the deputy governor £3000, and each director £2000, of the capital stock of the said corporation.

" That thirteen or more of the said governors or directors (of which the governor or deputy governor shall be always one), shall constitute a court of directors for the management of the affairs of the company, and for the appointment of all agents and servants which may be necessary, paying them such salaries as they may consider reasonable.

" Every elector must have, in his own name and for his own use, £500, or more, capital stock, and can only give one vote ; he must if required by any member present, take the oath of stock, or the declaration of stock if it be one of those people called Quakers.

" Four general courts to be held in every year in the months of September, December, April, and July. A general court may be summoned at any time, upon the requisition of nine proprietors duly qualified as electors.

" The majority of electors in general courts have the power to make and constitute by laws and ordinances for the government of the corporation, provided that such by laws and ordinances be not repugnant to the laws of the kingdom, and be confirmed and approved according to the statutes in such case made and provided."

When the payment was completed, it was handed into the Exchequer, and the Bank procured from other quarters the funds which it required. It employed the same means which the bankers had done at the Exchange, with this difference, that the latter traded with personal property, while the Bank traded with the deposits of their customers. It was from the circulation of a capital so formed that the bank derived their profit. It is evident, however, from the pamphlet of the first Deputy Governor, that at this period they allowed interest to their depositors ; and another writer, D'Avenant, makes it a subject of complaint. " It would be for the general good of trade if the bank were restrained from allowing interest for running cash ; for the ease of having 3 and 4 per cent. without trouble, must be a continual bar to industry."

In Grocers' Hall, since razed for the erection of a more stately structure, the Bank of England commenced operations. Here, in one room, with almost primitive simplicity, were gathered all who performed the duties of the establishment. " I looked into the great hall where the Bank is kept," says the graceful essayist of the day, " and was not a little pleased to see the directors, secretaries, and clerks, with all the other members of that wealthy Corporation, ranged in their several stations according to the parts they hold in that just and regular economy." The secretaries and clerks altogether numbered but fifty-four, while their united salaries did not exceed £4350. But the picture is a pleasant one, and though so much unlike present usages, it is a doubtful question whether our forefathers did not derive more benefit from intimate association with and kindly feeling towards their inferiors, than their descendants receive from the broad line of demarcation adopted at the present day.

The effect of the new Corporation was almost immediately experienced. On the 8th August in the year of its establishment, the rate of discount on foreign bills was six per cent, and although this was the highest legal interest, yet much higher rates had been previously demanded. The name of William Paterson was not long upon the list of directors. The Bank was established in 1694, and for that year only was its founder among those who managed its proceedings. A century and a half has passed ; the facts which led to his departure from the honourable post of director are difficult to collect ; but it is not at all improbable that the character of Paterson was too speculative for those with whom he was joined in companionship. Sir John Dalrymple remarks, " The persons to whom he applied made use of his ideas, took the honour to themselves, were civil to him awhile, and neglected him afterwards." Another writer says, " The friendless Scot was intrigued out of his post, and out of the honours he had earned." These assertions must be received with caution ; accusations against a great body are easily made ; and as it is rarely consistent with the dignity of the latter to reply, they are received as truths either because people are too idle to examine, or because there is no opportunity of investigating them.

Success provoked competition. A bank was proposed by Dr. Hugh Chamberlain to advance money on the security of landed property ; and though the Bank of England had no occasion to fear rivalry, they petitioned against it, and were heard by their counsel. A pamphleteer of the day says, "Estates to a very great value were subscribed in a short space, a deed settled, a company formed, and all things disposed to put this wonderful project into execution." All that the projectors required was money ; and as that was not ready at the appointed period, "the romantic Land Bank" failed. The pamphlet of Mr. Michael Godfrey offers some particulars of the Bank of England which may account for this failure. We learn "that the directors had no fixed remuneration, but submitted themselves to what the general court chose to allow them ; that such a reputation had been given to tallies, they were currently taken by private persons at fifteen and twenty per cent. less discount than they were previous to the establishment of the Bank ; that it was the only fund ever settled in England which had lowered the interest of money ; that though the nation had been engaged in an expensive war, though thirty millions had been expended in it, and several millions captured by the enemy, yet there was a fall in interest, since the Bank had exerted itself;

and previous to it, interest had been constantly rising, and must have come to a strange exorbitancy, without the bank ; that in the short space of thirty years, between two and three millions had been lost to the people by the Goldsmiths breaking." With such a list of benefits conferred by one bank, the monied men, who believed the other to be impracticable, were wise enough to refuse their support. A paper war was carried on between the supporters of the rival companies, and the following extract will prove that, however great the sarcasm, it was at least surpassed by the ill-nature of the writer. It is entitled "The trial and condemnation of the Land Bank at Exeter Change for Murdering the Bank of England at Grocers' Hall." A will, by no means complimentary to the directors of the latter, is supposed to be produced at the trial. " Know all our creditors by these presents, that we, the Governor and Company of the Bank of England, being weak in body, through the wounds received from the Land Bank at Exeter Change, to whom we lay our death, but of as good sense as ever we were, finding ourselves impaired in our credit and reputation, and despairing of recovery, do make our last Will and Testament. 1st. We bequeath our soul to the devil, in order to serve the publick out of our creditors' money , and as to the qualities of our mind, we dispose them as follows, namely, all our skill in foreign exchanges, and our probity and candour in making up the accounts of the loss thereof, we give to all and every of our directors except four or five, jointly and severally, to hold to them, and to their successors, as heir looms, and indelible monuments of their skill and probity for ever. All our obstinacy and blunders, we give unto our present Governor, upon trust, that he shall employ one equal third part thereof, as one of the Lords of the Admiralty, and the other part thereof as Governor of the Bank of England. All our oaths, impudence, &c. we give unto our present Deputy Governor, and our dear Sir Henry Furnese to hold in joint partnership during their lives; and the survivor to have the whole. All our shuffling tricks we give to our dear Sir William Gore. All our cynicalness and self conceit we give to our directors, Sir John Ward, and Sir Gilbert Heathcote, equally to be divided betwixt them, share and share alike, as tenants in common. All our blindness and fear we give unto our dear Obadiah Sedgwick— and we also give him £5 in money to buy him a new cloth coat, a new half beaver hat, a second-hand periwig, and an old black sword to solicit with in the lobby, and also to buy him a pair of spectacles to write letters to Lords with. As to the residue of our temporal estate, (besides the said £5,) we dispose thereof as followeth. Imprimis we devise to our own members, (when they shall have paid in their whole £100 per cent.) our fund of £100,000 per annum charged and chargeable nevertheless with the sum

of £1,200,000 for which it stands mortgaged, by
Bank bills, in full satisfaction of all their great expectations from the probity and skill of our directors,
advising them to accept a redemption thereof by Parliament whenever they can have it. Item, all our
ready monies, before any of our debts are paid, we
give to our executors, hereinafter named, in trust, that
they shall, from time to time, until 1st August 1696,
lend the same into the Exchequer upon condition to
defeat the establishment of the Land Bank ; and from
and after the said 1st August, then to lend out
the same into the said Exchequer upon security of
premises to establish our executors the next session,
instead of the Land Bank, and for such other premiums as our said executors can give to themselves,
for doing thereof. And we do direct our said executors to continue the stock and pensions already
allowed to our past friends,—they know where. And
after all our ready moneys so disposed, we leave the
residue of our effects for payment of bills and notes,
at such days and hours, and in such manner and
proportion, and with such preferences as our said
executors shall think fit. And we do hereby constitute our directors executors of this our will, giving
each of them power out of our cash to discount their
own tallies, bills, and notes, at par : and the bills and
notes of other of our creditors at the highest discount
they can get for the same. And our body we com-
mit to be burned, with all privacy, lest our creditors

arrest our corpse. In witness whereof we have here-
unto set our Common Seal, 4th May, 1696."

"The epitaph succeeded only in being coarse and
dull, and the two," says Malcolm, in his "History of
London," "may serve to excite astonishment that an
institution, which has baffled every art foreign and
domestic aimed at its ruin, should have attained such
a pinnacle of splendour in little more than 100 years.

"Here lies the body of the Bank of England, who
was born in the year 1694, died May 5, 1696, in the
third year of its age. They had issue legitimate by
their Common Seal, 1,200,000 called Bank Bills, and
by their cashier two million sons of ——— called
Speed's notes."

The small extent of the affairs of the Company at
the commencement of its existence, compared with
their present magnitude, appears from an account
delivered to the House of Commons on 4th December,
1696, by which the balance in favour of the Bank
amounted to £125,315 2s. By an act to regulate
their proceedings, the Bank were authorised from 25th
March 1698 to pay their dividends half yearly, instead
of quarterly, as they had been accustomed to do up
to that period.

Mr. Michael Godfrey, whose pamphlet has been
quoted, and to whose exertions, with those of William
Paterson, may be traced the successful establishment
of the Bank, met with a somewhat singular fate in
1695. Previously to this year, the allied armies had

retreated before the wisdom of Louis, and the bravery
of his soldiers. The funds supplied by the new Corporation changed the scene ; but the transmission of
specie was difficult and full of hazard, and Mr. Godfrey
left his peaceful avocations to visit Namur, then
vigorously besieged by the English monarch. The
Deputy Governor, willing to flatter the King, anxious
to forward his mission, or possibly imagining the
vicinity of the sovereign to be the safest place he
could choose, ventured into the trenches. " As you
are no adventurer in the trade of war, Mr. Godfrey,"
said William, " I think you should not expose yourself
to the hazard of it."

" Not being more exposed than your Majesty,"
was the courtly reply, " should I be excusable if I
showed more concern ?"

" Yes !" returned William, " I am in my duty,
and therefore have a more reasonable claim to preservation."

A cannon-ball at this moment answered the " reasonable claim to preservation," by killing Mr. Godfrey
with several officers near the King, and it requires no
great stretch of imagination to fancy a saturnine smile
passing over the countenance of the Monarch, as he
beheld the fate of the citizen who paid so heavy a
penalty for playing the courtier in the trenches of
Namur.   Tradition states that Mr. Godfrey's remains,
which were buried in the Church-yard of St. Christopher
le Stocks, were disinterred, to make room for the

enlargement of that prosperous establishment in which he once felt so deep an interest, and in the service of which he may be said to have fallen.

The journals of the period prove that the Bank had no pleasant path to pursue. The Goldsmiths were jealous of their great competitor. Their business was diminished; their discounts were lowered; their transactions with government had passed to their opponents. The writer has seen sufficient evidence to convince him of the great difficulties, arising out of foreign feuds and internal division, experienced by the directors of the Bank for the first ten years. Nothing but strong will, unconquerable energy, and a healthy perseverance, could have borne them on to so triumphant an issue. Looking upon the Bank in its present pre-eminent position, it is difficult to imagine it borne down by jealous rivalry, struggling for a precarious existence; its notes at a heavy discount, without specie to meet the demands of its creditors, compelled to advertize for defaulters, and actually obliged to cash the notes payable on demand in quarterly instalments. With a government always borrowing and always exigent, even they who so zealously supported the interest of the Corporation, must sometimes have shrunk from the responsibility, must sometimes have feared for the result. The plans adopted during the first few years, were very different to those in use at present. The great responsibility undertaken by the direction, was then unknown. Courts of proprietors were suddenly called to discuss loans to government. Emergencies which must arise in every establishment, were not met by the directors, but by meetings of the proprietors. Novel positions—and the position of the directors must have been eminently novel — were placed before the assembled courts and discussed by them. Their first and greatest difficulty has now to be related.

CHAPTER V.

THE rash scheme of the land bank had done some
mischief to the young establishment ; the re-coinage
of the silver did more.   This important measure was
supported by Mr. Montague, who acted under the
advice of Sir Isaac Newton ; and although the enemies
of the expedient urged all the reasons their imaginations could suggest, the proposition, after long and
vehement debates, was passed.   The difficulties which
already environed the bank,—partly from a prevalent
feeling of discontent, and partly from the efforts of an
opposition, which saw its cause grow weaker in proportion as the Corporation assisted the government—
were considerably increased by the new measure,
which prevented them from meeting their engage-
ment to pay their notes in cash.   It is probable also,

that their funds were partially locked up in advances
on merchandize; as, on the 6th May 1695, an advertisement appeared in the "London Gazette," that
" the Court of Directors of the Bank of England give
notice they will lend money on plate, lead, tin,
copper, steel, and iron at four per cent. per annum."
The coins had been diminished by clipping and
filing; many of the shillings contained only three-
pence in silver—an enormity attributed to the Goldsmiths, who appear to have been rather sharp traders:
counterfeit coins had also been clipped and filed, that
they might pass the more readily. While the coinage
was proceeding money grew scarce. The bank were
placed in a peculiar position. They had received the
clipped money at its full value; they had taken
guineas at thirty shillings, and when the notes issued
by them in exchange came in, there was not sufficient
specie to meet the daily demand. Had they paid in
full, they must soon have been drained of specie, and
they resorted to the plan of paying cash, at first in
instalments of 10 per cent. once a fortnight, and afterwards 3 per cent once in three months. But that
this was only a temporary pressure arising from extraordinary circumstances and not discredit, was proved
from sealed bills, bearing interest, being received by
their creditors in lieu of specie. Bank notes were
advertised at 20 per cent. discount, but it must be remembered that guineas were at 50 per cent. premium.
The energy with which the Bank directors met these

difficulties, and the vigour with which they were
assisted by the ministry, prevented the evil from
spreading. They made two separate calls on their
shareholders of twenty per cent. each, and issued bills,
bearing interest at the rate of six per cent., which
they gave in exchange for bank notes. That the calls
on their proprietary were not responded to by all, is
proved by the following advertisement on the 6th May
1697, to pay " the last call of twenty per cent. which
should have been paid by 10th November, 1696 : and
also those indebted to the Bank on mortgages, pawns,
notes, bills, or other securities, to pay in the said
twenty per cent., and the principal and interest of
these securities by 1st June next." So late as the
22nd June, 1697, we read in a well known newspaper
of that date, " Bank notes were yesterday at 13 and 14
per cent. discount." The Bank advertised also, " that
for the convenience of trade while silver is re-coining,
such as think fit to keep an account in a book with
the bank, may transfer any sum under £5 from his
own to another man's account." This was a plan
originally adopted by the bank of Amsterdam, and in
all probability copied from it. Exchequer bills were
also issued for £5 and £10 ; and as they were received
in payment of the revenue they passed as ready
money, and were of great service during the crisis.

Exchequer tallies had been at forty, fifty, and sixty
per cent. discount in 1696. The duties granted by
parliament frequently proved less than the amount

advanced on them. This deficiency was soon observed by the monied men. They also noticed the remoteness of the payments on other advances ; that the tallies varied in value, and a new trade arose in government securities. Forty and fifty per cent. was frequently lost if the owner was compelled to part with them, and the monied man availed himself of his capital to become the tally or stock-jobber of that day. With the notes of the national bank at twenty per cent. discount, and public securities thirty per cent. worse, we must suppose the public credit to have been insecure. William III. was far from popular, and frequent conspiracies were formed against his person and his throne. The Jacobites were still a numerous and important body. The Stuart family were yet the desire of many who disliked the present monarch. If it be added that the expences of the war were greater than the parliamentary supplies, no further reason can be required to account for the disrepute into which the credit of the country had fallen. The evil called loudly for a remedy, and the difficulty was boldly met. The government empowered the corporation to add £1,001,171 10s. to their original stock, and public faith was restored by four-fifths of the subscriptions being received in tallies and orders, and one-fifth in bank-notes at their full value, although both were at a heavy discount in the market.

The past services of the Bank were not forgotten. The ministry resolved that it should be enlarged by new subscriptions ; that provision should be made for paying the principal of the tallies subscribed in the Bank ; that eight per cent. should be allowed on all such tallies, to meet which a duty on salt was imposed ; that the charter should be prolonged to August 1710 ; that before the beginning of the new subscriptions the old capital should be made up to each member one hundred per cent. ; and what might exceed that value should be divided among the new members ; that the Bank might circulate additional notes to the amount subscribed, provided they were payable on demand ; and in default they were to be paid by the exchequer out of the first money due to the bank ; that no other bank should be allowed by act of parliament, during the continuance of the Bank of England ; that it should be exempt from all tax or imposition ; that no contract made for any bank stock to be bought or sold should be valid unless registered in the bank books, and transferred within fourteen days. It was also enacted that not above two-thirds of the directors of the preceding year should be re-elected in the succeeding year. These vigorous measures were thoroughly successful. "The nation," says Smollett, "did not know its own strength till it was put to trial." The Corporation, also, were not to owe more than the total amount of all their increased capital. With these arrangements the charter was extended until 1710, nor could it then be taken away until government paid the debt owing by them to the Bank. By this act the forgery of the company's seal, notes, or bills, was made felony without benefit of clergy. Great gains were made; great fortunes even were won by the capitalists of the day. Sir Gilbert Heathcote, one of the Bank directors, gained £60,000 by the liberal scheme; and numerous estates were raised in a shorter time than was ever known.

A pamphleteer of the period states that the Bank offered to lend a million without interest, for 21 years, if government would extend the charter to the same period. The writer good-naturedly adds, " As the Bank discount at four per cent., the directors will have more command to this favour, and beyond others. They therefore, or any of them, being merchants, easily foreseeing the great advantages by monopolizing several commodities, will be able to provide themselves, and thus monopolies may be spread." Time has pronounced this to be an unworthy objection. It may as a principle be confidently asserted, that, up to the present time, no accommodation has been afforded to a director by virtue solely of his office, which would not have been awarded him as a merchant of the city of London. · Another writer, in " a letter concerning the Bank, and the credit of the nation " says, " The directors upon a pressing occasion of the king's, had stretched their credit to a degree that could not consist with any measure of prudence, nor could the directors answer it to their members, had it been for any less occasion than the preservation of the kingdom." The reason given is sufficient excuse for the offence. The "preservation of the kingdom" was the preservation of the Bank of England. But the most triumphant answer which could be given to all these attacks was the remarkable fact that bank stock, given to the proprietors in exchange for tallies at fifty per cent. discount, rose to one hundred and twelve per cent. There is no reply to a fallacy so triumphant as a fact, no rejoinder to a sparkling sophism so unanswerable as a plain truth. Nothing can mark more strongly the triumph of this corporation over its enemies, nothing can more plainly evince that it was founded on safe principles, than that bank stock maintained so great a value. In addition to these things it must be remembered, that money, which ten years before had borne so high a rate of interest, was sufficiently plentiful to realize the prophecies contained in the pamphlet of Mr. Michael Godfrey. "The bank will infallibly lower the interest of money." "And now the bank is established, all who want money and have security, will know where to be supplied, and the terms, and there cannot be such advantages made in the public or private men's necessities for the future." The truth of these remarks is to be found in the fact, that, on 16th of January, 1695, foreign bills, having three months to run, were discounted at six per cent.; and to those who kept accounts at the bank, only three per cent. was charged : that on 19th of May running notes and bills

were discounted at three per cent.; and that money
was advanced on merchandize at four per cent.

So early as 1697, in " Some thoughts of the interest
of England " a proposal was made " that the Bank of
England be branched into every city and market town
in England, and that the several branches be ac-
countable to the general Bank in London for the
profits of their respective branches." Had this plan
been carried into effect, some of those crises which
have borne ruin into many happy homes would have
been averted. The entire circulation would have been
in the hands of an establishment equal in stability to
the government. The " London Gazette " would not
have borne testimony to the ill-fortune or faithlessness
of many firms with which the profits of a life were
placed. The provinces would not have rung with
the desolation which penetrated to the hearth and
heart of the English peasantry. The cottager who
had hoarded his gains, earned by the waste of sinew
and of strength, would not have been crushed by the
intelligence that the banker of his district had failed
in his great trust. The father who left his home with
a light heart would not have returned with news
which he dreaded to communicate. The grandsire and
the infant, the widow and the fatherless; the maiden
and the matron, would have been saved the stony
bread of charity ; nor would society have been startled
by so many disgraceful monetary failures, had the
Bank of England possessed the entire management of

that circulation which, as a responsible body, should have been placed under its control. At a later period Mr. Horner stated in the House of Commons, that the destruction of country bank paper had given rise to a universality of wretchedness only to be equalled by the bursting of the Mississippi bubble. " Thousands upon thousands found themselves sunk, as if by enchantment, and without any fault of their own, in the abyss of poverty." Next to a government, with which, from various reasons, it would be most unwise to place it, the greatest bank of the empire has an indisputable claim to the circulation of the country.

By the various extracts given above, it may be seen that the directors did not repose upon a bed of roses. Constantly invited to aid a needy government, and as constantly abused and upbraided by those inimical to it, they had but one path,—the path of probity and rectitude — to pursue ; and by it they attained a triumphant success. During their early career, the violence with which they were assailed by their opponents stimulated their efforts. It is probable, and the course of nature justifies the supposition, that had they been unopposed, they would have failed in attaining equal importance. Uninterrupted prosperity produces presumption, and presumption is often the precursor of failure. An arrogant confidence in their good fortune, therefore, might have produced the practical conviction that they were fallible to the precise extent they considered themselves infallible.

Opposition, however, induced caution, stimulated their energies, and produced an eminent and honourable success.

The ambitious spirit of France was signally displayed in 1700 to the injury of the credit of the nation. The alarm of all Europe, indeed, was excited by Louis, who, under the pretence of a will in favour of his grandson, seized upon the entire Spanish monarchy. By the possession of the imperial fiefs in Italy, the empire was concerned. By his grasp on the Spanish Netherlands, the Dutch were deprived of their barrier against his ambition. By his hold on Spain, the great Mediterranean commerce rested at his mercy. Terror spread throughout the land ; the public funds were affected ; and the credit of the Bank of England, which has always paid a heavy penalty, in times of national fear, for its connexion with government, was shaken with the general apprehension. The same effect was produced in 1704, and the prices of public securities were again lowered. From an insurrection in Hungary, and the invasion of the German empire by the French, great evils were apprehended, which so much affected the public faith that the Bank directors were once more obliged to issue sealed bills, bearing interest, for a large sum, in order to keep up their credit. The scene, however, soon changed. Blenheim witnessed our superiority ; the proud fortress of Gibraltar yielded before British prowess ; and the public credit of the country arose

with her victories. The sealed bills enabled the bank
to bear up until happier times, when its character was
restored, and its usefulness once more experienced by
the community.

In the year 1707, one of those invasions which were
periodically threatened by the Pretender excited the
accustomed alarm. The expedition was assisted by
Louis XIV., and great splendour was affected in the
appointments. The head of the holy Catholic faith
subscribed towards the expedition. Sumptuous tents,
rich tapestries, and splendid liveries, gave it the
appearance of a triumph for a kingdom won, rather
than a trial to regain an empire lost. Religious
mottoes were wrought upon the standards, which
looked more like the colours of a crusade than those of
a political enterprise. Louis, with a grace that distinguished him, and with a compliment worthy his
finished grace, " trusted he should never see the
royal adventurer again." Alarm spread throughout
the country. It is difficult to say whether, at the
period, the pope, the devil, or the Pretender, was
feared the most. The probability of an invasion by
the Chevalier startled the people, and a demand was
immediately and extensively made for gold by the
excited populace. " The late hurry of an expected
invasion," says a pamphlet entitled "The Anatomy of
Exchange Alley," " sunk the price of stocks fourteen
or fifteen per cent. Who were the men that made a
run upon the Bank of England, and pusht at them

with some particular pique too, if possible to have run them down, and brought them to a stop of payment? Is not this disabling the government, discouraging the King's friends, and a visible encouragement of the King's enemies?" The feelings of the private bankers towards their great rival do not appear to have been very conciliatory. The same writer says, " I humbly refer to a case recent in memory, of two Goldsmiths, (Knights also, and one of them Member of Parliament too) in Fleet Street who pushed at the Bank of England at the time of the Pretender's invasion from France. One of them, it was said, had gathered a quantity of Bank bills to the value of near £100,000; and the other a great sum, though not so many, and it was said, resolved to demand them all at once. Let the gentlemen I point at enquire with what difficulty Sir R. Hoare wiped off the imputation of being a favourer of the rebellion, and how often in vain he protested, he did it with no such view, and how hard the Whigs were to believe him. Sir Francis Child indeed carried it with a higher hand, and afterwards pretended to refuse the bills of the bank, but still declared he did it as a Goldsmith, and as a piece of justice to himself, on some points in which the Bank had as he alledged used him ill." The proposed invasion proved the esteem with which the Bank was regarded by those whose good opinion was worth possessing. It was found that the Protestant succession had supporters as ardent as the adherents to the house of Stuart. When the run took place, many, instead of withdrawing their deposits, carried all their cash to assist the establishment. The Lord Treasurer Godolphin, who, as an astute and able financier, felt that the credit of the country was connected with that of the Bank, informed the directors that the Queen would allow, for six months, an interest of six per cent. on their sealed bills. Nor was this all; the Dukes of Marlborough, Newcastle, and Somerset, with others of the nobility, offered to advance considerable sums of money to the Corporation. A private individual, who had but £500, carried it to the Bank; and on the story being told to the Queen, she sent him £100, with an obligation on the Treasury to repay the whole £500. It is pleasant to read of such chivalrous devotion repaid in so royal a manner. Encouragement such as this gave a firmness to the establishment, and, united with a call of 20 per cent. on the proprietors, enabled the directors to meet their difficulties and preserve their credit.

CHAPTER VI.

PRIOR to 1708, the government had paid off the
principal and interest of the additional debt incurred in
1697; by this the capital of the Bank was reduced to
its original amount, and in the first-named year the
extension of the charter was again proposed till 1732.
The same plans of passive and active resistance which
had hitherto been pursued by the opponents of the
Bank,—an opposition renewed whenever the opportunity has offered—were again resorted to with great
energy. Pamphlets bearing such titles as " Remarks
upon the Bank of England:" " A short view of the
apparent danger and mischief from the Bank of
England :" " Reasons against the continuance of the
Bank of England :" poured from the press with a
vehemence that must have proved dangerous to the

young establishment, had it not been based upon a firmer foundation than the breath of popular opinion. An answer was written by Nathaniel Tench, whose name forms one of the earliest directors. Stow says, "The chief purpose of this defence was to vindicate the corporation and the management thereof. Not so much from the crimes they had already been guilty of in the experiment of eleven or twelve years, as the fear of what they might do hereafter." This pamphlet contained a very able defence of the directors, and an enumeration of their services, of which the following is the conclusion; tending to prove that there were in this, as in most cases, two sides to the question. "It might be with truth concluded that, since their first establishment, they never bought one foot of land, they never monopolized any one commodity; that they had been so far from obstructing trade, that they had very much encouraged and enlarged it. That they had never put any hardships upon the government, as those authors would insinuate; but had at all times served it to the utmost of their power. That they had been so far from raising the interest of money, that they were the great, if not the only cause of lowering it. That they had never concerned themselves in the election of any one member of parliament, nor never advanced a single penny to influence any election. Neither could any man complain, that he did not receive his money on demand that called for it. In short, that, notwithstanding the clamour and noise their adversaries made against them, they had not brought any instance that they had been guilty of any base or unworthy action, in any one fact committed by them since their first establishment. So that all the clamour of their ill-willers had been raised upon a bare suspicion of what their successors might do hereafter." It is satisfactory to read such a succession of services emanating from an establishment not fourteen years of age, penned also by one who could well appreciate the troubles of his brother directors. There was another champion in the field, who published " Reasons for encouraging the Bank of England." " The Bank," remarks the writer, " has been the sole cause of lowering the interest of money, which is the only fund that ever lowered it—and that too in time of war, when usually interest rises—by which the nation, since the Bank was erected, has saved a great sum of money, having been supplied at a much cheaper rate than formerly, which doth excite industry, raise the value of land, and increase trade."

The eminent services of the Bank of England to the political and commercial community, the integrity with which it had ever been conducted, and the aid rendered to government, the importance of which it had assisted to maintain, were now to be acknowledged and rewarded. Its "important banking privileges," as Mr. Fenn in his " English and foreign Funds" truly terms them, were conveyed in return for these. By the act of 1708 their charter was

extended until 1732, and it was therein provided
" That, during the continuance of the said Corporation of the Governor and Company of the Bank of
England, it shall not be lawful for any body politic or
corporate whatsoever created or to be created, other
than the said Governor and Company, or for any other
persons whatever, united or to be united in covenant
or partnership exceeding the number of six persons in
England, to borrow, owe, or take up any sum or sums
of money on their bills or notes payable on demand,
or at a less time than six months from the borrowing
thereof."

A circumstance, which appeared to threaten the
prosperity of the bank, tended to produce the above
favourable clause. The " Company of Mine Adventurers" at the head of which were peers and baronets,
but which nevertheless proved a most melancholy
bubble, arrogated many prerogatives belonging to the
Corporation. They erected themselves into a money
bank, issued cash notes, and circulated sealed bills,
until restrained by the above act. The hopes of the
proprietors had been stimulated by Sir Humphrey
Mackworth, the projector, who carried on his chi-
canery with an ability worthy a better cause. He
imposed upon the proprietors for five years by " false
and sham calculations of their profits,—by purchasing
lead from other persons' mines and declaring it to
be digged from the Company's mines,—and by buying
silver extracted from other men's lead, and getting it

coined in the King's mint as coming from the Company's mines." So dishonourable a course could not be pursued without discovery, and the scheme met with the fate it merited. Like the South Sea Company at a later period, it was pronounced a bubble by the House of Commons, who voted that Sir Humphrey Mackworth was guilty of " scandalous frauds," and brought in a bill to prevent the Secretary and Treasurer from leaving the kingdom. The bill, however, did not pass the House of Lords, for Sir Humphrey was a high Tory, and the Tories were in power. Another object was gained by the government in the above Charter. They were desirous of circulating Exchequer bills on the security of the house duties, and the Bank undertook to cancel £1,500,000 at six per cent. interest until redemption of the principal, in consideration of the privileges granted them : this, with interest, amounted to £1,775,027 17s. 10½d. The measure procured the favour of government, as it tended to relieve the ministers from difficulty. It was the first time that the Bank had undertaken the circulation of Exchequer bills, and they again issued sealed bills at an interest of 2d. per cent. per diem. These transactions rendered a new subscription of £1,001,171 10s., and another of £2,201,171 10s., necessary, which, with a call on the proprietors of fifteen per cent., amounting to £656,204 1s. 9d., increased the total capital to £5,058,547 1s. 9d. Anderson gives some curious particulars. " The

Bank," he says, "continued to permit new subscriptions for the doubling their present stock by selling the additional stock at the rate of £115 for every £100 subscribed. All which was subscribed for between the hours of nine in the morning and one in the afternoon. Nearly one million more could have been subscribed on the same day, so great was the crowd of people coming with their money to the books."

The Bank obliged themselves to advance to government £400,000 without interest, which made their original capital of £1,200,000 at eight per cent. amount to £1,600,000 at six per cent. to commence from 1st August, 1711. Discount being allowed on the said £400,000 till the 1st August 1711 and the fifteen per cent. advance on the sale of their additional stock enabled them to pay this £400,000 to the public.

In 1709 a new danger arose to the Bank of England. The importance of the Corporation, and the great wealth possessed in its treasury, have always rendered it liable to attack in times of political excitement. Large bodies, collected in haste, and agitated with passion, are rarely discriminatory. There are always a number of idle and profligate men to whom the very name of the Bank possesses a charm ; and up to the present day it has been periodically liable to attacks from the mobocracy. In the present case the piety of the people created a religious riot. One Dr.

Henry Sacheverell, an apostate whig, was appointed to preach the annual sermon at St. Paul's, before the Lord Mayor and Court of Aldermen. An apostate is usually violent in proportion to his apostacy, and Dr. Henry Sacheverell was no exception to the rule. The sermon was used as an engine of attack upon some of the members of her Majesty's government. Among others the Lord Treasurer was characterised as *Volpone*. The measureless impudence of the preacher attracted attention, and Sir Gilbert Heathcote, a director of the Bank of England, and a wise man in his generation, for we have seen he made sixty thousand pounds by one transaction—protested against it : nor did the city authorities make the ordinary request to have it published. But as publicity was the worthy doctor's object, and the truth of no importance, he pretended that Garrard, the Lord Mayor, had desired him to print it, and to him he dedicated it with an inflammatory epistle. Impudence is generally successful for a time, and the Doctor attracted attention. He was arrested and impeached, in revenge for the liberties he had taken with government, " I know," says Lord Dartmouth, " neither the Doctor nor the doctrine had been called in question, if the word *Volpone* had been left out of the sermon." The populace, — skilful judges of a sermon,—chose to support the divine, and London became a scene of confusion. To the lower class the prospect of a riot is generally pleasant ; and if they can flatter themselves that it is for the cause of

religion, they are doubly riotous. They now determined to support the worthy Doctor; and a body
guard of London butchers accompanied him to his
trial at Westminster Hall, which the Queen honoured
with her presence. " God bless the church and Dr.
Sacheverell," was echoed from mouth to mouth among
the pious populace. Multitudes followed, pressing
about him, and striving to kiss his hand. Money was
thrown among them, by some of the better classes
who followed in hackney coaches. The anxiety of
the Bank directors during this period of tumult must
have been great, as every day rendered them liable to
attack. The divine, inflated with his popularity,
looked upon himself as half hero, and half martyr. The
people sought the dissenting chapels, collected the
hymn books and bibles, broke up the pews and tore
down the pulpits, and made a great bonfire in Lincoln's Inn Fields. There was one trifling error in
destroying a church for a chapel, owing to its wanting
a steeple; but the populace arc not nice discriminators.
Bishop Burnet only escaped by the bold and determined courage of some of the more respectable inhabitants, and their great ambition was to place a dissenting minister on the top of one of the piles; but in
this they were disappointed. The Queen and Court
were in the utmost consternation. The citizens were in
equal alarm. Intelligence reached the Bank directors
that the rioters were moving towards their locality.
As a pious mob was no more to be trusted than a

political one, the Court assembled to " concert measures proper to be taken, and sent to the principal
Secretary of State for a guard to prevent any attempt
they might make on the Bank." When the message
was received, the Earl of Sunderland made its tenor
known to the Queen, who immediately ordered both
horse and foot out to quell the tumult, leaving her
own person without any protection. " God will be
my guard," was her regal reply, when reminded of her
danger. A detachment under Captain Horsey was
immediately ordered into the city to prevent the meditated attack on the alarmed directors. " Am I to
preach or fight?" was the question of the blunt soldier
on receiving his instructions. There proved to be no
occasion for either. The rioters retreated in alarm.
The Bank was saved from pillage, by the self sacrifice
and devotion of the Queen ; and the affair—which
was a trial of party strength—terminated without
difficulty.

Much inconvenience having been experienced from
directors of the East India Company being also in
the direction of the Bank, it was decreed by a clause
in the 9th act of Queen Anne, that no person should
be governor, deputy governor, or director of the Bank
of England and the East India Company at the same
time.

The Bank first undertook to receive the contributions to a lottery, consisting of 150,000 tickets at
£10 each in 1710. A great rise took place in Bank

Stock. The nation had been depressed by war, which, though victorious, was expensive. The pride of the French had been humbled by the triumphs of the allies, and they were compelled to sue for peace; a prospect so gratifying to the nation, that on the mere probability Bank Stock rose from 110 to 129. The prospect proved illusive. Louis resolved to risk another campaign; and on the negociation being broken off, the stock fell to 107. From " the life and times of Bishop Burnet " a remark may be gleaned which strongly illustrates the opinion entertained by government of the importance of the Bank of England. "The Queen's intention to make a change in her ministers now began to break out. In June she dismissed the Earl of Sunderland from being Secretary of State, and presented the seals to Lord Dartmouth, a Tory. This gave the alarm both at home and abroad, but the Queen, to lessen that, said to her subjects here, *in particular to the Governor of the Bank of England,* that she should make no other changes." These few words mark the importance of the Bank to the state; nor do they show less strikingly the political tendencies of the Corporation, which regarded with suspicion a change of ministry as paving the way to power of the exiled Stuarts. These tendencies are also a sufficient reason for the panics which have seized the English people, when an invasion in favour of this family was expected. It will be seen that, on all such occasions, the Bank has experienced a call for its gold.   In 1713 this effect was produced, when, at her ancient palace of Windsor, the Queen was seized with an alarming illness.   The buoyant hopes of the malcontents arose.   An armament was reported to be ready in the ports of France.   The directors of the Bank were overwhelmed with consternation by a great run made upon them; and the imminence of their position may be conceived from the fact, that one of their body was sent immediately to the Treasurer, to announce the danger which threatened public credit.   Measures were promptly taken for its support; the health of the Queen was soon happily renewed; the armament proved an idle alarm; the Pretender was in Lorraine; and the phantom which threatened the safety of the Bank ceased with the fears which had given rise to it.

The same year was marked by a renewal of the charter until 1742, an extension of the privileges of the Bank for ten years.   Of course the proprietors had to pay for the extension.   The reign of Queen Anne had been gilded by the splendid victories of Marlborough, and the chivalrous achievements of Peterborough; but victories and achievements must be paid for.   An act was therefore passed to raise £1,200,000 for public uses, by circulating a further sum in Exchequer bills, which the managers of the great Corporation,—for the establishment already deserved the title—undertook at three per cent. in consideration of their renewed privileges.   They were also to receive

£8000 yearly until all the Exchequer bills in existence should be paid off. To enable the directors of the Bank to effect this, they were allowed to call in money from the proprietors to form additional stock ; and the Corporation was to continue until the government debt was paid off ; twelve month's notice being given from the 1st of August, 1742.

In the following year the last monarch of the unfortunate house of Stuart was approaching her end, and London became a scene of confusion and intrigue. The succession was uncertain, and it was equally doubtful whether the Queen would name the exiled Chevalier, or whether the House of Hanover would obtain the splendid prize. In 1714 she died ; her death-bed agitated by the wrangling and plotting of political partisans. The fine genius of Bolingbroke and the sagacity of Oxford failed before the bold energy of their opponents. Letters were sent to the Elector of Brunswick ; a squadron was prepared to convey him to England ; the Heralds at Arms were kept in waiting to proclaim the new King ; the malcontents were overawed in Scotland ; and the head of the house of Brunswick ascended the English throne as George I. A period fraught with so much anxiety to the whole kingdom could not fail to affect its great monetary establishment. The uncertainty of the future dynasty produced a run upon it which lasted without intermission for several days, although without any unfavourable result, as its resources were equal to the demand. The price of Bank Stock, however, fell from 126 to 116.

· The accession of the first George must have caused some uneasiness to the friends of the Bank. The policy of the new King was unknown, and it appeared equally uncertain whether he would endeavour to win over the great landed proprietors, and with them all the important Jacobites, or, to use the words of Smollett, "declare himself the head of a faction, which leaned for support on those who were enemies to the church and monarchy, on the Bank and monied interest, raised on usury and maintained by corruption." The race of Brunswick, however, like previous princes, found that a wealthy body which could assist in procuring supplies was worthy the support of the state. A power was given to the latter which it once wanted, and the Bank maintained in return a close connection with government, which gave additional confidence in their credit, additional importance to their establishment, and additional dividends to their proprietary.

· The rebellion of 1715 being checked before any demonstration could be made in England, it produced no effect upon the Bank, and the excitement—kept alive by numerous trials, and exasperated by successive executions — was soon subdued. Tranquillity being thoroughly restored, the ministry and Parliament determined to reduce the legal rate of interest from six to five per cent. To do this the aid of the directors of the Bank was necessary, as well as that of the other powerful monetary bodies, and they agreed to provide cash for those creditors preferring their principal to a reduced interest. Three bills passed, under the names of the South Sea Act, the Bank Act, and the General Fund Act. The former (established in 1711) by some advances to government, procured several advantages. By the Bank Act, the Governor and Company accepted an annuity of £88,751 7s. 10½d or the principal of £1,775,027 17s. 10½d in lieu of the present annuity of £106,501 13s. 5d.; they likewise cancelled as many Exchequer bills as amounted to £2,000,000 at five per cent., redeemable after one year's notice, and agreed to circulate the remaining Exchequer bills at three per cent. and one penny per day: it was enacted that the former allowances should be continued to Christmas, and then the Bank should have for circulating the £2,561,025 remaining Exchequer bills, the last named interest. By the same act the Bank was required to advance at five per cent. part or all of £2,500,000 towards discharging the national debt. The legal rate of interest was thus easily reduced; and it is worthy of remark that all the fundholders accepted the terms proposed.

In 1718, subscriptions for government loans were first received at the establishment; and this practice being beneficial for various reasons, is still continued.

CHAPTER VII.

THE MISSISSIPPI COMPANY — FINANCIAL DIFFICULTIES — ROYAL
BANK—PRIVILEGES OF THE COMPANY OF THE WEST—INFATUA-
TION OF ALL CLASSES—INCREASE OF LUXURY—COUNT VAN
HORN — MURDER OF A STOCK-BROKER—ENORMOUS PROFITS—
DEMAND FOR SPECIE—PANIC COMMENCES—THE BANK BESIEGED
—UNPOPULARITY OF LAW—DESTRUCTION OF THE COMPANY.

A HISTORY of the Bank of England and its times,
would scarcely be complete without a report of that
monetary convulsion which shook France to the
centre, and preceded the bubble of the South Sea
scheme. The unfortunate interference of the Regent
of France with the Mississippi Company, is too
remarkable an evidence of the evils which may rise
from the circulation of a country being under the
entire control of the state, not to demand a place in
the present work.

John Law, the son of a Scotch goldsmith, was born
in Edinburgh. From an early age his attention was
directed to the somewhat abstruse studies of public
and private credit, the state of trade and manufactures,
the theory of taxation, and other matters connected

with political economy. His early life was marked by irregularities, and after a career noticeable for its dissipation, he proposed a scheme to the Scottish people, for the circulation of notes on the security of land. The project was rejected, and in a few years Law found himself in Paris about the period of the death of Louis XIV. To a nation like France, Law was a dangerous visitor. The country groaned beneath its debt. The luxurious court of Louis had burthened the people with taxes, which yet fell short of the necessity. The nation was on the verge of bankruptcy. The circulation of the country was injured. Industry was checked and trade destroyed. The financial difficulties of the Regent were great. During the last years of Louis the expenditure of the nation had reached 260,000,000 livres. Paper money was issued on the credit of the state, but it sunk to an enormous discount. To supply cash, offices were created and then sold. A controllership for piling wood, and an inspectorship of wigs, may offer some idea of the extreme difficulty which could compel a great government to resort to means so ludicrous. At this moment Law came forward and proposed a paper circulation on the security of landed property, and the royal revenues. The project was declined; and Law, not a man to be easily discouraged, procured letters patent to establish a Bank, which proved so fortunate, that while the notes of the state were at a heavy discount, those of Law's bank were at fifteen

per cent. premium. The Regent D'Orleans grew
jealous of this success. By an arbitrary decree, in
1718, he abolished it, and established a Royal Bank,
of which he made John Law director-general. The
notes rose to one per cent. premium, and the Duc
D'Orleans became impressed with the idea that he
had only to issue notes according to his necessities.
From this period Law's cherished project began to
be developed. The scheme that rang throughout
Europe as the Mississippi scheme, was near its
accomplishment.

The proposition which he made to the Regent was
to vest the privileges and possessions of all the foreign
trading Companies, the great farms, the Mint, the
King's revenues, and the management of the Bank,
in one Company, which having all the trade and royal
revenues, might multiply the notes of the Bank to any
extent, doubling, or even trebling at will, the circulating medium, and by the vastness of their funds,
carry foreign trade and colonial improvements to a
height hitherto unattainable. This monopoly, alike
unparalleled and impracticable, met the approbation
of the Regent; and letters patent were granted to a
commercial company, under the title of the "Company of the West." The whole province of Louisiana,
watered by the noble river Mississippi, was granted to
the association, and 200,000 shares were issued of
500 livres each, and *billets d'etat*, then at 60 to 70 per
cent discount, were received at their full value in

payment. So liberal a scheme, together with the prospect held out by Law of 120 per cent. per annum, procured a favourable opinion not only from the speculative, but from the thinking. The shares were filled up, and the Company became creditors to the state to the extent of a hundred million of livres, the interest of which was settled at four per cent.

Law, who enjoyed the Regent's favour, was made director-general of the new association, which assumed the title of the Company of the Indies, from the exclusive privileges of the East India Company being added to its already extensive prerogatives. Fifty thousand new shares were issued at 550 livres each, and they immediately rose to 1000. Ever volatile and inconsiderate, the French people received Law's promises as gospel. The new shares were applied for with avidity. The dirty street Quincampoix, in which Law resided, was impassable. People of the highest rank clustered about his dwelling to learn their destiny, and delicate women braved all weathers with the hope of enriching themselves. 300,000 applications were made for 50,000 shares; and the destiny of an empire, remarkable for its national *hauteur*, seemed in the hands of John Law, the son of a Scottish jeweller. Advantage was taken of this eagerness. 300,000 new shares were issued at 5000 livres each, and the Regent availed himself of the popular excitement to pay off the national debt. The whole of the foreign trade was placed in the possession of the Com-

pany, and the public ran with increased eagerness at
each creation of stock. Prelates, Marshals, and Peers
of that old aristocracy which once boasted a Bayard,
cringed to the lackies, and swarmed in the ante-
chamber of a Scottish adventurer. A rumour of his
indisposition sent the stock down nearly 200 per cent.,
and the announcement of his recovery sent it up in
the same proportion. The frenzy became general.
A rage for shares infatuated every rank. The price
reached 10,000 livres in September, 1819, and the air
echoed with Mississippi and Quincampoix. There
appeared but one aim and one pursuit. From six in
the morning until eight in the evening the street was
filled with fervent worshippers of mammon. The dissolute courtiers of the yet more dissolute Regent shared
in the spoil. The princes of the blood were not too
proud to participate. They mingled with the eager
crowd, they added their voices to the Babel-like confusion, and when they won the money of the *canaille*,
thought they did them too much honour in accepting
it. The ante-chamber of Law was crowded by women
of rank and beauty—the mistress of Law was flattered
by ladies as irreproachable as the court of the Regent
would allow them to be—and interviews with Law
were sought with so much assiduity, that one lady
caused her carriage to be upset to attract his attention ; and another stopped before his hotel, and
ordered her servants to raise the cry of " Fire."
The people emulated one another in luxury. Equi-

pages more remarkable for splendour than taste rolled about the streets. Footmen got up behind their own carriages, so accustomed were they to that position. One of those who had done so recollected himself in time to cover his mistake by saying he wished to see if room could be made for two or three more lackeys whom he had resolved to hire. The son of a baker, wishing a service of plate, sent the contents of a jeweller's shop to his wife, with directions to arrange the articles properly for supper. The opera was crowded 'with cooks, ladies' maids, and *grisettes*, dressed in the superbest style of fashion, who had fallen from a garret into a carriage.

The Rue Quincampoix became too confined for the mighty fever which infested the metropolis; and the Place Vendome, chosen in its stead, soon presented the appearance of a fair. But Law was again compelled to move, owing to the complaint of the Chancellor, who could not hear the pleading of the Advocates. The projector then purchased the Hotel de Soissons, and in its beautiful gardens established his temple. "In the midst, among the trees," says Dr. Mackay, "about five hundred small tents and pavilions were erected. Their various colours, their gay ribands and banners, the busy crowds which passed in and out, the hum of voices, the noise, the music, the strange mixture of business and pleasure, combined to give the place the air of enchantment."

The various anecdotes of contemporary literature

attest the mania. The private letters of the period confirm it. A few hours often witnessed an alteration in the price of ten, twenty, and thirty per cent. A servant who was sent by his master to sell two hundred and fifty shares, found the value had risen sufficiently to enable him to make £20,000 sterling by the difference, with which he departed. The nobility sought alliance with many of the vulgar rich ; and that feeling, so nearly allied to contempt, with which they too often regard the poor, though refined man, faded away before an eager desire to associate with and profit by the rich, but coarse speculator. Law's coachman made a fortune ; and when his master requested him to supply a substitute, brought two, saying, whichever the projector refused he would take for himself. Luxury reigned pre-eminent. The arts were encouraged. Beautiful paintings were imported. The graceful bust, the sculptured marble, the pictured tapestry, were no more the exclusive property of the peer. The aristocracy were no longer the sole pos-sessors of the elegancies which refine the mind. "Money lightly gained, was lightly spent," says Chambers ; "palaces rose on all sides with the rapidity of enchantment ; fortunes were lavished on furniture, equipages, dress, and jewels; and entertainments were habitually given, which seemed to have had their pro-totypes in the fairy tales." Paris was filled with foreigners, tempted by the reports which circulated far and wide. Nearly half a million were located there at one time. In vain did Marshal Villars, with more zeal than discretion, harangue the people in the open street upon their " disgusting avarice." They indulged themselves with a laugh, as they hurried towards the mart of mammon, to purchase shares in this unrivalled bubble. That the passion for paper was carried to a great length may be collected from the phraseology of the day. To the question, " Have you any gold?" " Nothing to do with it," was the regular answer. The herald's college was disregarded. The armorial bearings of a peer were placed on the carriage of a *parvenu.* Folly came in the train of wealth ; and the gaiety of the people was great. But the provinces grew envious of the profits of the capital. Land was sold for any price it would bring; and the proprietors hastened to Paris with the proceeds to make or mar their fortune. Bishops consecrated by partaking of the follies, and the clergy forgot the precepts which they enjoined in the practice they pursued. " At that epoch of scandal and opprobrium," says M. de Tocqueville, " there was no folly or vice in which the high society did not take the lead. The degradation of men's minds was equal to the corruption of their manners." Assassinations and robberies were common. The Count Antoine Van Horn, brother to a reigning prince, related to half the noble families of France, and connected with the Regent Orleans, was an evidence of the crime produced by this epoch. The description given of Van

Horn is striking: "his face was as pale and as beauti-
fully chiselled as that of an antique statue ; and a
pair of singularly wild and brilliant eyes, shed over the
whole what might have seemed preternatural light."
A contemporary states that the ladies of the period,
with whom Van Horn was a greater favourite than
with their husbands or brothers, declared that it was
" almost impossible to support his ardent gaze." The
man thus remarkable for beauty became yet more
remarkable for crime.   The gay city of Paris was
suddenly startled by a rumour that a Hebrew stock-
broker had been robbed of property worth one
hundred thousand crowns, and afterwards murdered ;
not in some lonely and unfrequented place, but in the
broad day, in a crowded house, and in the very heart
of the city.   The rumour spread ; the excitement
increased ; a name, more known than respected, was
whispered, and Count Antoine Van Horn, the scion
of one of the haughtiest houses in Europe, was openly
accused of the murder.   The unfortunate broker had
been allured to a cabaret ; cries were heard from the
interior of the room ; the waiter locked the door ; and
the aristocratic Count was taken almost redhanded.
The trial of Van Horn commenced on the following
day, and "the relatives of the accused," says Chambers,
" now adopted a plan which throws a curious light
upon the feelings and manners of the time.   On the
day of trial, they assembled at the place of justice in a
body of fifty-seven, both male and female, and lined

the long corridor which led to the court room. As
the judges passed through this proud array, they were
saluted in a mournful and supplicatory manner by the
highest and noblest of Europe, and passed into the
hall of trial with their minds strongly impressed, even
if their hearts were not melted, by the imposing scene."

The evidence was clear, and the punishment of being
broken alive on the wheel was awarded to the criminal.
Disappointed in their efforts in one way, the nobility
connected with the house of Van Horn attempted
another mode of saving the assassin. A petition,
praying for mercy on the ground of insanity, signed by
Cardinals, Archbishops, Dukes, and Marquisses, was
presented to the Regent. Many were not sufficiently
noble to sign the paper, and the honour of claiming
blood-relationship with a murderer was keenly contested. The Regent was, however, inexorable; and
when, as a last resource, it was represented that, in
the armorial bearings of his mother, there was the
escutcheon of Van Horn, he only signified his will by
saying, "Very well, gentlemen, I will then share the
disgrace with you." Another writer says his reply
was in the words of Corneille:

"Le crime fait la honte, et non pas l'echafaud."

The prince remained firm, and the murderer perished
on the wheel, after refusing to take a cup of poison,
handed to him by one of his relatives.

In the mean time, the mania continued. The
profits acquired by Law were enormous. Fourteen

estates, the titles of which were attached, were purchased by him. The Marquisate of Rosny, a title
originally belonging to the illustrious Sully, he who
honoured Henri Quatre by being his minister and
friend, was amongst the number. The people of the
Scottish capital were proud of calling him fellow-
citizen, and conveyed the freedom of the good town
in a golden snuff-box. The only obstacle to the projector's advancement to the highest offices of the
State, was his religion ; and Law, who probably would
have turned Hindoo as easily, changed his profession
of faith from Protestant to Catholic, to secure the
·Controller-Generalship of the Finances. Scientific
Academies honoured him by electing him a member,
says a modern writer, and " the flattering incense of
poetry was offered up at the same shrine with the
homage of an infatuated people." In one week, Law
paid the Count D'Evreux for the Compte of Tancar-
ville, 80,000 livres ; offered to the Prince of Carignan
1,100,000 for the Hotel de Soissons ; 500,000 to the
Marchioness Beuvron for her estate of Lillebonne, and
1,700,000 livres to the Marquis of Sully for his
Marquisate of Rosny.

The credit of the Bank was at its height in November, 1719, when six shares were sold for ten thousand
livres, and the directors lent any amount of money at
two per cent. The first blow was struck by the Prince
de Conti, who sent an enormous quantity of paper to
change into metal. Three waggons were required to

remove it, and Law drew the attention of the Regent to the mischief such conduct must occasion; two thirds of the specie, by a despotic decree, were ordered to be refunded. But there were others who saw the coming storm, and acted more judiciously. One house famous for their funded operations, sent notes quietly, and by degrees, and when they had amassed a sufficient quantity of treasure, placed it in a cart, covered it with straw, and carried it off in triumph; others purchased extensive jewellery, and sent it to England or Belgium, whither they soon followed. These symptoms increased. There was a constant drain of bullion from the Bank. The speculators began to think of realizing their immense profits. It was computed that five hundred millions of livres, in specie, were sent out of the country. "Knowing no means," says Mr. Gaspey, in his Pictorial History of France, "by which he could arrest the great and alarming decline in price, which speedily commenced, Law prevailed on the Regent to issue an ordinance, proscribing the use of gold and silver as money, and forbidding private individuals to keep in their houses more than five hundred livres, in specie. This odious measure caused, in the course of a single month, forty millions to be deposited in the coffers of the Bank. But it was not by such means that damaged credit could be restored. The distrust of the paper constantly increased; every one sought more anxiously from day to day, to convert his notes into cash; and in consequence of this an order was issued, dated May 21st, 1720, which reduced their value one-half, and suspended their payment by authority. Then rose the cry of rage, wild and menacing, against the author of the system, and against those who had taken him under their patronage. They had, however, allowed the payment of notes of ten livres. The men of the market-halls, sailors, and others, bought these at low prices, and pressed towards the doors of the Bank, making a passage for themselves by blows. None but such persons could venture to approach."

On 17th July, three men were killed in the crowd. Sinister voices were heard to exclaim, "if there are any who are weary of life, let them follow us." Notes like the following were sent from house to house, " Sir, or Madam. Notice is hereby given, that it is intended to make another St. Bartholomew on Saturday or Sunday. Do not go out yourself, nor suffer your servants to do so. God preserve you from fire. Make your neighbours acquainted with this.—May 25th, 1720." In the month of September, for a single mark of gold, 1800 livres, in bank notes, were given, which, ten months before, were valued at 160,000 livres in specie; and all the ecclesiastics and hospitals of France were prohibited from depositing their money in any security, excepting Mississippi stock. Still it continued to decline. Various means were tried to prevent this; the sole property in one island was given to the company; and pamphlets were published to demonstrate to the proprietors that the stock had no right to fall. On 21st May, the fatal decree, just alluded to, came out. Under pretence of having lowered the value of the coin, it was declared necessary to reduce the nominal value of the notes and India stock, the former to half, and the latter from nine thousand livres a share to five thousand. Bank notes instantly lost their currency; and, to prevent tumults, the guards were placed everywhere The Parliament remonstrated, and another decree revoked the former. On 29th May, 1720, Law resigned his office of Controller-General of Finance, and it was thought necessary to allow him a detachment of Swiss soldiers, to save him from being torn to pieces by the populace.

Every three or four days some new decree was issued. A sufficient number to fill two quarto volumes were circulated, and are now collected. The people were filled with indescribable terror, and began to send their valuables abroad, and a decree came out to prevent them. Merchants began to refuse the notes at any price, and a decree was immediately promulgated forbidding any one to reject them. This made the possessors run with them to the Bank, and then another decree decided "That, owing to the tumult at the Bank, on account of paying the notes, the Regent thought fit to suspend the payment of them till further orders." "There was not cash in the Bank," says Anderson, " to pay the fiftieth part of them." Persons were forbidden from meeting, or assembling together, under any pretence ; and the military were placed in various situations to disperse them.

A consternation, soon converted into rage, seized all ranks. Disorder and confusion reigned everywhere. Inflammatory libels were posted up, and seditious papers distributed. The life of the Regent was threatened. Great allowances must be made, however, as upwards of ninety millions of notes were in circulation when the bank stopped, and all classes and all conditions were in a state of bankruptcy. The depreciation of this paper was so great, that a man might have starved with a hundred millions in his pocket. Law was compelled to seek interviews with the Regent by night, as he had on one occasion narrowly escaped with life from the enraged multitude. Fifteen people were pressed to death at the doors of the Bank, in their eagerness to obtain specie, and eight or nine thousand of the indignant sufferers proceeded with three of the bodies to the gardens of the Palais Royal, where they destroyed the coach of Law, and demanded his punishment. The Chamber of Deputies was sitting, and the report spread of the destruction of the carriage. Such was the vindictive feeling, that one account says, " the members rose simultaneously, and expressed their joy by a loud shout; while one man, more zealous in his hatred than the rest, exclaimed, " And Law himself, is he torn to pieces?" Another report says, the President, over-

powered with joy, was seized with the spirit of rhyme,
if not of poetry, exclaiming,

"Messieurs! Messieurs! bonne nouvelle!
"Le carosse de Lass est reduit en Canelle!"

The death blow to all hopes that the Company would
redeem its credit came in November, 1720. Their privileges were taken from them, and they were reduced
to a mere private Company. Law left the kingdom
escorted by some horse-guards, after declining the
assistance proffered by the Regent. It is a remarkable proof of this man's faith in the success of his
plan, that whatever money he had made during the
infatuation, he invested in the soil of France; and that,
when he left the country, the only property he carried
with him was a diamond, worth about £5000.
Various other methods of abating the evil were
adopted. Commissioners and tribunals were instituted.
Six hundred millions of notes were turned into stock,
and many large sums created into terminable and life
annuities. All the malversations which had been
committed with impunity during the excitement were
rigidly enquired into. Many dishonest deeds were
brought to light. Some peculators were fined, and
others imprisoned. An abbé and a master of requests
were condemned to decapitation. By these and other
means, together with the consolation which time ever
brings, the good people of Paris recovered their gaiety.

After a short residence on the continent, Law came
to England, where he dwelt during the existence

of that bubble, which must have forcibly reminded him of his own career, and which followed in the train of the Mississippi scheme. It seemed as if they who had escaped from Paris had brought the epidemic with them ; and that the sober London citizens were seized with the same mania which but a few months before had turned all the heads in Paris. Many who, away from that furious phrenzy, had laughed with national heartiness at the Parisians, found themselves, at a later period, weeping and wailing at their madness in following the example.

It is difficult to calculate to what extent the English bubble may have resulted from the French project. It is certain that the Mississippi Company arose in some degree from the Darien undertaking. Mr. Law confessed that the facility with which he saw the love of enterprise communicate itself throughout all classes of Scottish society, convinced him of the ease with which a similar effect, on a grander scale, might be produced ; and this knowledge increased, if it did not cause, the great delusion of which he was the officiating high priest. As the Mississippi project was encouraged in some degree by the Darien scheme, so may the fever of the South Sea bubble have been caught from the contagion, and magnified by the proximity of the Company of the West. For this reason a slight sketch has been given of that enormous fraud, which preceded the project about to be related.

CHAPTER VIII.

THE history of the year 1720 is the history of the
South Sea delusion. Anderson says, "it is a year
remarkable beyond any other which can be pitched
upon for extraordinary and romantic projects." It is
a history of wild excitement, and of wilder despair.
It extended to all ages and to all classes; it created
hopes which it never realized; it changed magnificent
dreams into dark realities. We have seen in our own
time how a fierce lust after money has overcome the
calm calculation of the financier, the cool deduction
of the mathematician, and the equability of the
christian; how the caution of the capitalist has
yielded to the phrenzy of desire; how the merchant,
whose name stood highest in the annals of commerce,
and whose credit was only limited by his conscience,

has placed both name and credit in the hands of the
unscrupulous adventurer. We have seen the names
of men whom their country delighted to honour,
stand side by side with those whose reputation was
more than dark or doubtful. We have seen the man
who, in his regular business, would cautiously weigh
and coldly scan every circumstance that might affect
the gain of fifty pounds, throw the honourable profits
of a life into a scheme which promised fifty per cent.
Such are the fevers and inflammations of commercial
life at present; and they were the same a century ago.
"Were it not in its consequences so full of the
materials that make tragedy," remarks a writer of the
present day, "the South Sea bubble might have been
represented on the stage as an admirable farce, satirizing more broadly than comedy would have thought
befitting her dignity, or the common sense of probability, the eternal passion for wealth." Although the
propriety of public competition is as unquestionable
in governments as in individuals, yet the doubt may
fairly arise how far it is to be encouraged to the
prejudice of a valuable assistant, or to what extent the
bidder, who offers extravagant advantages, is to be
supported. We pause before we enter the shop of
the man who marks his goods below the cost price ;
we respect the trader who keeps the even tenor of his
way without professing to sell at enormous sacrifices ;
how much longer then should a state hesitate to
accept proposals which are not only extravagant,

but utterly impracticable. Upon these grounds the ministers of 1720 are chargeable with the ruin and the wretchedness shortly to be related. Smollett writes :

" The King having recommended to the Commons the consideration of proper means for lessening the national debt, was a prelude to the famous South Sea Act. The scheme was projected by Sir John Blunt, who had been bred a scrivener, and was possessed of all the cunning, plausibility, and boldness requisite for such an undertaking : he communicated his plan to Mr. Aislabie, the Chancellor of the Exchequer, as well as one of the Secretaries of State ; he answered all their objections, and the project was adopted ; they foresaw their own private advantage in the execution of the design, which was imparted in the name of the South Sea Company, of which Blunt was a director, who influenced all their proceedings." The pretence for the scheme was to discharge the national debt, by reducing all the funds into one.

Upon the 22nd of January, 1720, the House of Commons resolved itself into a Committee to take the subject into consideration : and a subsequent proposition, made by the South Sea Company, to unite the whole of the debts of the state—amounting to £30,981,712—at five per cent. until 1727, and after that period at four per cent.,—for which they were to pay three millions and a half—met with great approbation from the members of the government.

But the Bank of England had many friends in the House of Commons. The great services rendered by this Corporation were brought forward; a strong representation was made of the injustice of thrusting so important a body aside for those who had done nothing to assist the state; and a postponement of the question for five days was obtained. This time was not lost upon the Bank authorities, who offered five millions for the same privileges, being an advance of one million and a half on the proposition of the South Sea Company. The government found that the delay was highly favourable; no sooner was the offer of the Bank known, than the directors of the South Sea Company called a meeting; and at a general court they were instructed to obtain the preference at any cost; their offer of three millions and a half was increased to upwards of seven and a half millions. But the members of the first monetary establishment in the kingdom were not to be outdone; and seized with the same emulation which animated the South Sea Company, they proposed more advantageously in several respects, and offered to give £1700 Bank stock for every hundred pounds irredeemable long annuities. "Let any one," says Anderson, "consider how this was possible." Fortunately for the Bank of England, but unfortunately for the country, the offer of the South Sea Company met with most favour. The former ceased its bidding; the latter remained in possession of its

dangerous bargain. At one time there appears to
have been some idea of dividing the advantage between the Bank and the South Sea Company, but
Sir John Blunt is stated to have exclaimed, "No,
Sir! we will never divide the child."

The very rumour, in 1719, that the South Sea
Company were ambitious of incorporating with their
own all the funds of the Bank, East India Company,
and Exchequer, raised the price of their stock to 126 ;
and no sooner was the preference given to them over
their competitors known, than a signal phrenzy marked
alike the city and the suburb. Large premiums were
paid for the refusal of stock at high prices, and on the
2nd of June, 1720, it rose to 890. Some of the
directors were created baronets for "their great
services;" and in a short time it reached 1,000.
Artifice and exaggeration were resorted to, to maintain
this unnatural elevation. Fifty per cent. was confidently
predicted ; inestimable markets and valuable acquisi-
tions in the South Seas were promised ; and mines of
hidden treasure mysteriously alluded to by the agents
of the scheme. The public mind was dazzled ; all
the available resources of the kingdom were embarked
in wild speculations and rash undertakings. Change
Alley was crowded with peers of the realm, who
forgot their pride ; country gentlemen, who forsook
their homes ; clergymen, who disregarded the dignity
of their calling ; and ladies, who forgot their natural
timidity, in the hopes of making money. The

monarch was said to have profited by it. His ill-
favoured German mistresses made great fortunes and
sent them over to Hanover ; and the only exceptions
among the ministry and nobility of the day were
asserted to be the Dukes of Argyll and Roxburgh,
and Lord Stanhope.   On the 5th August may
be read in a contemporary journal, "Our South
Sea equipages increase every day ; the city ladies
buy South Sea jewels ; hire South Sea maids ;
take new country South Sea houses ;   the gentlemen set up South Sea coaches, and buy South
Sea estates ; they neither examine the situation, the
nature or quality of the soil, or price of the purchase,
only the annual rent and the title : for the rest, they
take all by the lump, and pay forty or fifty years, purchase."

That the King favoured this unhappy scheme, may
be gathered from the correspondence of the day.   On
the 18th April, 1820, the Duchess of Ormond wrote
to Swift, "You remember, and so do I, when the
South Sea was said to be my Lord Oxford's brat, and
must be starved at nurse.   Now the King has adopted
it and calls it his beloved child : though perhaps you
may say, if he loves it no better than his son, it may
not be saying much ; but he loves it as well as he
does the Duchess of Kendal, and that is saying a good
deal.   I wish it may thrive, for some of my friends are
deep in it : *I wish you were so too !*"   What a proof
is the latter sentence of the prevailing madness.

Prior writes, " I am tired of politics, and lost in the
South Sea.   The roaring of the waves, and the madness of the people, were justly put together.   It is all
wilder than St. Anthony's dream ; and the bagatelle
is more solid than any thing that has been endeavoured
here this year."

And all these anticipations were indulged in of a
scheme, which, according to Smollett, promised no
commercial advantages of importance, and was buoyed
up by nothing but the folly and rapacity of individuals.
He says, " During the infatuation produced, luxury,
vice, and profligacy increased to a shocking degree of
extravagance.   The adventurers, intoxicated by their
imaginary wealth, pampered themselves with the
rarest dainties, and the most expensive wines that
could be imported : they purchased the most sumptuous furniture, equipage, and apparel, though without
taste or discernment : they indulged their criminal
passions to the most scandalous excess : their dis-
course was the language of pride, insolence, and the
most ridiculous ostentation.   They affected to scoff
at religion and morality, and even to set heaven at
defiance."

In the periodicals of the time the course of the
fraud may almost be traced.   At first gay and satirical,
we read,

> " In London stands a famous pile
> And near that pile an alley,
> Where merry crowds for riches toil,
> And wisdom stoops to folly ;

Here sad and joyful, high and low,
  Court fortune for her graces;
And as she smiles, or frowns, they show,
  Their gestures and grimaces.
Here stars and garters too, appear,
  Among our lords the rabble;
To buy and sell, to see and hear,
  The jews and gentiles squabble;
Our greatest ladies hither come
  And ply in chariots daily;
Or pawn their jewels for a sum
  To venture in the alley;
Longheads may thrive by sober rules,
  Because they think and drink not.
But headlongs are our thriving fools,
  Who only drink and think not.
What need have we of Indian wealth,
  Or commerce with our neighbours,
Our constitution is in health,
  And riches crown our labours."

Where credulity is plentiful, promises are equally so : where men desire money they appear to credit any falsehood, however monstrous, provided only it be plausible ; " the wish is father to the thought," and while they imagine they are cheating they often become the cheated. Exchange alley was thronged with the duper and the duped, and Cornhill was impassable for fools and knaves. Ballads were sung about the streets, and the caricaturist was busy in his legitimate calling of satirizing the folly and the vices of the people. But who cares for caricatures when money is to be made? The spirit which levels rank, and destroys distinctions, which ruins virtue and engenders vice, that fierce thirst which " grows by what it feeds on," continued to spread. The South Sea company was a legitimate trade to some of the speculations which arose.

Schemes were proposed which would have been extravagant in 1825, and which stamped the minds of those who entertained them with what may be truly termed a commercial lunacy. One was for the " discovery of perpetual motion." Another for subscribing two millions and a half to " *a promising design hereafter to be promulgated.*" A third was a " Company for carrying on an undertaking of great advantage, but nobody to know what it is ; every subscriber who deposits £2 per share, to be entitled to £100 per annum." Even this insolent attempt on the credulity of the nation succeeded ; and when the arch-rogue opened his shop, the house was beset with applicants. In five hours £2000 were deposited in the hands of the projector, and from that day he ceased to be heard of in England. Projects like these enlisted the lowest with the highest. On some sixpence, and on others one shilling, per cent. was paid ; and as no capital was required, the comparative beggar might indulge in the same adventurous gambling, and enjoy the same bright castles in the air, which marked the dreams of the rich and the great. Some came so low as to ask only one shilling deposit on every thousand pounds. Persons of quality, of both sexes, were engaged in these. Avarice triumphed over dignity ; gentlemen met their brokers at taverns ; ladies at their milliner's shops.

The English historian says, "All distinctions of party, religion, sex, character, and circumstance, were swallowed up in this universal concern, or in some such pecuniary project. Exchange Alley was filled with a strange concourse of statesmen and clergymen, churchmen and dissenters, Whigs and Tories, physicians, lawyers, tradesmen, and even multitudes of females. All other 'professions and employments were utterly rejected; the people's attention wholly engrossed by this and other chimerical schemes, which were known by the denomination of bubbles."

Among the schemes advertised in derision of the propensity of the day, was one " for making Butter from Beech trees;" another for "an engine to remove the South Sea House to Moorfields ; " a third " for teaching wise men to cast nativities." The clerks of the South Sea Company found it a prosperous period. As the lapse of a day might make 100 per cent difference, a £20 note was frequently given to expedite the transaction. These perquisites were so great, that they wore lace dresses, and answered when remonstrated with, that " if they did not put gold upon their clothes, they could not make away with half their earnings."

The following is selected from among the many epigrams of the period, to prove that a few yet retained their senses.

> " A wise man laughed to see an ass
> Eat thistles and neglect good grass;

> But had the sage beheld the folly,
> Of late transacted in Change Alley,
> He might have seen worse asses there,
> Give solid gold for empty air !"

But while the speculator "put money in his purse," he little heeded the admonitions of the satirist. It is evident, from the following, that there were some who shrewdly guessed the advantages which the directors proposed taking to themselves.

> " As fishes on each other prey,
> The great ones swallowing up the small,
> So fares it in the Southern Sea,
> But whale-directors eat up all.
>
> " Oh ! would these patriots be so kind,
> Here in the deep to wash their hands ;
> Then, like Pactolus, we should find
> The sea indeed had golden sands.
>
> " The nation too, too late will find,
> Computing all their cost and trouble,
> Directors promises but wind,
> South Sea, at best, a mighty bubble."

New companies started up every day under the countenance of the prime nobility. The prince of Wales was constituted governor of the Welsh Copper Company, (by which he made sixty thousand pounds, and then withdrew his name ;) the Duke of Bridgewater formed an association for building houses in London and Westminster ; and the Duke of Chandos appeared at the head of the York Buildings Company.

Another ingenious fraud consisted of the " Globe permits," square bits of playing card, on which were impressed in wax the Globe tavern, and inscribed on them " sail cloth permits." These cards were merely permissions to subscribe to some future Sail Cloth Company, and were currently sold at sixty guineas each. The confusion and crowd were so great that the same shares were sometimes sold at the same moment £10 higher in one part of the Alley than another.

It is impossible to peruse the contemporary papers without surprise. The absurdity seems too glaring to excite anything but ridicule. "The London Journal" of 11th June, says, " The hurry of our stock-jobbing bubblers has been so great this week, that it has exceeded all that was ever known. There has been nothing but running about from one coffee-house to another, and from one tavern to another, *to subscribe without examining what the proposals were.* The general cry has been, ' *For G—'s sake let us but subscribe to something, we don't care what it is.*' So that, in short, many have taken them at their words, and entered them adventurers in some of the grossest cheats, and improbable undertakings, that ever the world heard of ; and yet, by all these, the projectors have got money, and have had their subscriptions full as soon as desired."

Mr. Mackay, in his " History of Popular Delusions," says, " Besides these bubbles, many others sprung up daily, in spite of the condemnation of the government, and the ridicule of the still sane portion

of the public. The print-shops teemed with caricatures, and the newspapers with epigrams and satires,
upon the prevalent folly. An ingenious card-maker
published a pack of South Sea playing cards, which
are now extremely rare, each card containing, besides
the usual figures, of a very small size, in one corner,
a caricature of a bubble company, with appropriate
verses beneath. One of the most famous bubbles
was 'Puckle's Machine Company,' for discharging
round and square cannon balls and bullets, and
making a total revolution in the art of war. Its
pretensions to public favour were thus summed up in
the eight of spades,

'A rare invention to destroy the crowd
Of fools at home, instead of fools abroad.
Fear not, my friends, this terrible machine,
They're only wounded who have shares therein.'

The nine of hearts was a caricature of the English
Copper and Brass Company, with the following
epigram,

'The headlong fool that wants to be a swopper
Of gold and silver coin for English copper,
May, in Change Alley, prove himself an ass,
And give rich metal for adulterate brass.'

The eight of Diamonds celebrated the Company for
the colonization of Acadia, with this doggrel. The
reader cannot fail to admire the ease and elegance of
the rhyme.

'He that is rich and wants to fool away
A good round sum in North America,
Let him subscribe himself a headlong sharer,
And asses' ears shall honour him or bearer.'

And in a similar style every card of the pack exposed some knavish scheme, and ridiculed the persons who were its dupes. It was computed that the total amount of the sums proposed for carrying on these projects was upwards of three hundred millions sterling, a sum so immense, that it exceeded the value of all the lands in England at twenty years' purchase."

It would be curious, were it practicable, to know the feelings of the directors of the Bank of England during this important period. It seems almost impossible for them to have escaped the universal fever. A golden prize appeared in the possession, and human nature must have repined at the success of their opponents. During a time so full of excitement it was almost impossible to argue calmly; and they probably looked upon the gigantic success of the rival company as calculated to injure their own Corporation, if not utterly to destroy it. But whatever their ideas were, the revulsion which followed must have more than compensated for them by their entire security, when the remainder of London was one great commercial wreck. Out of this universal phrenzy arose two great corporate bodies. The Royal Exchange and London Assurance Companies owe their origin to this speculative period. The civil list was in arrears; and the heads of the above Companies offered £600,000 on condition of obtaining charters. There is rarely great evil without accompanying good; and these bodies, which have tended to so much individual advantage, the benefits of which have been moral as well as pecuniary, which have provided for so many sorrows and dried so many tears, as much by their own transactions as by the great impulse afforded to the principle of Life Assurances—have in some respects atoned for the despair which followed the "delusion and the drunkenness" described. The evil was confined to a few years; the good will be spread over centuries. While the excitement was at its height, the Royal Exchange and London Assurance shares were respectively forced up to £250 and £175. East India Stock, under the same influence, rose to 445, and Bank Stock to 260 per cent.

But the South Sea company grew jealous of their rivals, and commenced legal proceedings against some of the companies. This brought the whole affair to an issue, and a general panic seized the conductors of the bubbles. The "York buildings" fell at once 100 per cent.; and in two days this company, with some others which were specially named, had no buyers at any price whatever. The more bare-faced bubbles immediately shrunk to their natural nothingness. The various offices were shut up; the contractors disappeared; and Change-alley was a comparative wilderness. When the law proceedings began, South Sea stock was 850 per cent., and from that time it rapidly declined, until, on the 29th September, the following month, it fell to 175.

The Directors grew alarmed. In vain they promised

that the Christmas dividend should be at the rate of 60 per cent. and that 50 per cent. should be guaranteed for the following twelve years. The public refused to believe, and men ran to and fro, alarm and terror in their countenances, their imaginations filled with dismal pictures of calamity. The fear was in proportion to the hope ; and no one knew where the evil would cease. Thousands of families were reduced to beggary. Many were not able to withstand the shock, but died brokenhearted. Others withdrew to remote parts of the world, and perished in exile. The very name of a South Sea director was an abomination, nor could one of them appear in the streets without danger of being insulted.

In the London Journal we read, "There appeared the utmost consternation in Change alley, the day the act for suppressing them took place, which, because of the terror and confusion it struck among those brethren in iniquity, they called the day of judgment. Many of those who have been most assiduous in drawing other poor wretches into their ruin, have, besides their wealth, acquired an infamy they can never wipe off; they being followed with the reproaches, threats, and bitterest curses of the poor people they have deluded to their destruction." The Weekly Packet says of the schemers, "they have been used to such dishonest ways of living, and hardly will take up with any course of life that is not so; insomuch that it is feared many of them will go out marauding; then *stand clear the Bristol mail.*"

Public credit sustained a tremendous shock. Many Bankers and Goldsmiths who had lent money on the security of the stock, were compelled to stop payment through its depreciation; and the Sword-blade association, hitherto the chief cashiers of the company, followed their example. There was but one hope left to the nation. The directors of the Bank of England, always applied to in distress, and not always remembered in prosperity, were persuaded, at the instance of Sir Robert Walpole, to come forward during the early part of the panic. A general court was held, at which the Governor and Directors were empowered, without a dissentient voice, to agree with the South Sea Company to circulate their bonds, in hopes of sustaining the credit of the country. A memorandum was hastily drawn up, to be the foundation of a future agreement, by which the bank undertook to circulate £3,500,000 at 400 per cent. The mania which affected all England must have seized partially on the proprietary, or so high a rate would never have been allowed. Fortunately the memorandum had not been legally ratified. The first effect of this arrangement was to support the price of the stock. Books were opened at the Bank to receive subscriptions, and large sums were brought in. The bankruptcy of some large companies, however, produced a run upon the Bank, and the directors renounced the agreement. The losing party commenced legal proceedings, but a hundred reasons prevented a continuance. The fear of publicity; the knowledge of their own nefarious transactions; the conviction that they had been and were acting dishonestly; the influence of those parties in power who had profited by the rascality of the transaction; the certainty that everything would be brought to light, and that they could not, to use an expressive but homely phrase, "go into court with clean hands," wrought upon the directors of the South Sea Company; and legal proceedings were quickly abandoned.

The managers of the Bank of England retained the even tenor of their course. They had wrought no evil, they feared no reverses. They had not entered the market to raise or depress the stock; and, without alarm, they saw it daily fall in value. The South Sea Company had commenced into a distinct and positive rivalry with them. They had sought to obtain from Government those advantages which had been paid for at a high rate by their competitors; and which could only be procured by their injury. If therefore a certain degree of satisfaction pervaded the minds of the Bank directors at the downfall of their rivals, it reflects a higher degree of credit on them, that, setting aside the littleness of jealousy, they came promptly forward to render all the assistance in their power. When they found the terms, hastily named, were more in accordance with the inordinate ambition of the South Sea Directors, than with the intrinsic worth of the stock, it was a duty which they owed to themselves, to their proprietary, and to the nation, to abandon the connexion at once, rather than add to the misery of the people, by being engulphed in the whirlpool. "The overbearing insolence of ignorant men," says Dr. Mackay, "who had arisen to sudden wealth by successful gambling, made men of true gentility of mind and manners blush that gold should have power to raise the unworthy in the scale of society. The haughtiness of some of these "cyphering cits," as they were termed by Sir Richard Steele, was remembered against them in the day of their adversity. In the Parliamentary inquiry, many of the directors suffered more for their insolence than their peculation. One of them, who, in the full blown pride of an ignorant rich man, had said that he would feed his horse upon gold, was reduced almost to bread and water for himself; every haughty look, every overbearing speech, was set down, and repaid them a hundred fold in humiliation." One of the members made a motion concerning this man, whose name was Grigsby, to the following effect: "that, since that upstart had been so prodigally vain as to bid his coachman feed his horses with gold, no doubt he could feed on it himself; and therefore, he moved that he might be allowed as much gold as he could eat, and the rest of his estate go towards the relief of the sufferers."

During this period the King had been in Germany; but the confusion of the nation compelled him to return, and on the 11th of November he arrived in England. Many expedients were started, when the Bank, fearful of compromising their own safety, withdrew from the field. Amongst others, an engraftment of nine millions of the South Sea Stock into Bank and nine into East India Stock. Warm and varied debates occurred at the Courts; and the proposition, though at last agreed to, and confirmed by act of Parliament, was afterwards abandoned. In the mean time the most infamous transactions were discovered; and Parliamentary language was not much regarded in the debates. A few of the speeches indulged in by the senators strike somewhat curiously on the modern ear.

The Bishop of Rochester said, " the scheme was like a pestilence." The Duke of Wharton added, that " he would give up his dearest friend if engaged in the project." Lord Stanhope thought " every farthing of the criminals' property ought to be confiscated ;" and Lord Molesworth, with a fine philanthropic spirit, remarked that " the directors ought to be tied in a sack, and thrown into the Thames." Mr. Shippen, the Jacobite member, said, " he was glad to see a British House of Commons resuming its pristine vigour; and that there were other men, in high station, who were not less guilty than the directors." Mr. Craggs, Secretary of State, against whom this inuendo was directed, arose, and offered to demonstrate his innocence by fighting any man in or out of the house. Lord Molesworth "wondered at his boldness; but though he was past sixty, there were plenty of young men who would not be afraid to look Mr. Craggs in the face." Vociferous cries of order arose; Mr. Craggs was compelled to apologise; and a secret Committee appointed to enquire into the transactions of the South Sea Company.

It was found impossible to please the losers, who absolutely besieged the House of Commons. On one occasion the tumult was so great that the members could not proceed with the ordinary business. The riot act was read; and one from the crowd called out, with the bitter boldness of a ruined man, "You pick our pockets, and then imprison us for complaining." The governors, directors, and officers of the Company were brought before the bar of the House of Commons. The treasurer, who was deeply implicated, absconded; and fear being entertained that the directors might follow his example, a proclamation was issued that none of them should leave the kingdom.

General Ross, with more energy than elegance, informed the house a train of the deepest villainy that hell ever invented to ruin a nation, had been discovered. Bribery had been effected in procuring the act to be passed; and all officers of this Company holding government situations were immediately removed from them. It had, indeed, been a delusion from beginning to end. A fictitious stock, amounting to £574,000, had been created and distributed among Secretaries of State, Chancellors of the Exchequer, Duchesses, Earls, and Countesses. The conduct of Mr. Aislabie, Chancellor of the Exchequer, was more infamous than that of any other, as he had advised the Company to increase their second subscription half a million, without any other authority than their own, and appears to have benefited to the amount of £800,000. His punishment rapidly and deservedly followed his crime. He was ignominously expelled the house, sent to the Tower, restrained for a year from leaving the kingdom, and ordered to make a correct account of his estate for the benefit of the sufferers. Dwellings were illuminated in testimony of delight at the sentence; a mob assembled on Tower Hill to witness his degradation; bonfires were kindled in all parts of the city, and London wore the appearance of a great festivity. The hand of Providence was on the betrayers of their country. Several members of the lower house, directors of the Company, were expelled. Mr. Secretary Craggs and his father died while proceedings were pending, the latter leaving a million and a half for those he had assisted to ruin. The legislature restrained the persons of the directors, and marked their characters with ignominy. An impartial tribunal was scarcely to be expected. Those who had lost money were revengeful. Those who had gained endeavoured to hide it under the appearance of zeal. The devices of party, the application in the name of friendship, the appeal under the plea of kindred, were all used to shield the guilty, and in some instances were successful in procuring a small majority. The more violent recommended hanging; and one of the members most pathetically lamented that "after all there was nobody's blood shed!"

The great historian of the "Decline and fall of the Roman Empire" complains, "Instead of the calm solemnity of a judicial enquiry, the fortune and honour of thirty-three Englishmen were made the topics of hasty conversation, the sport of a lawless majority; and the basest member of the committee, by a malicious word or silent vote, might indulge his general spleen or personal animosity. Injury was aggravated by insult, and insult was embittered by pleasantry. Allowances of £20 or one shilling were facetiously moved. A vague report that a director had formerly been concerned in another project, by which some unknown persons had lost their money, was admitted as a proof of his actual guilt. One man was ruined because he was grown so proud, that one day, at the Treasury, he had refused a civil answer to persons much above him. All were condemned, absent and unheard, in arbitrary fines and forfeitures, which swept away the greatest part of their substance."

The pens which had been employed in prophesying
mischief, were not backward in affecting commisera-
tion for the sufferers. The following is another, and
the last specimen of the literature of the South
Sea bubble.

> " Behold a poor dejected wretch,
>   Who kept a South Sea coach of late,
> But now is glad to humbly catch
>   A penny at the prison gate.

> " 'Tis strange one set of knaves should sour,
>   A nation famed for wealth and wit ;
> But stranger still that men in power,
>   Should give a sanction to the cheat.

> " Fools lost when the directors won ;
>   But now the poor directors lose,
> And where the South Sea Stock will run,
>   Old Nick, the first projector, knows."

The most difficult process was yet to come ; it was
easier to punish the delinquents than to relieve the
sufferers. Through the abilities of Mr. Robert
Walpole, however, this was adjusted. It was partially done by giving to the public seven millions of
the money which belonged to the Company in their
corporate capacity, being the profits arising from the
delusion. Of their Capital Stock a sufficient sum to
pay the claimants £33 6s. 8d. per cent., amounting
to £8,900,000 was taken ; and this was necessarily
a great relief. Of a debt of eleven millions sterling,
advanced by the Company to the public on stock,
the latter were relieved on paying ten per cent. on it.
Thus the Company would have received £1,100,000

instead of eleven millions, had all consented to the agreement, but many debtors refused to make any payment whatever.

Who can read these things and not mourn? They are not asked to deplore rapid reverses, they are not called upon to grieve for the rich man, made suddenly poor, for luxury turned to want, or the insolent man made humble; but they are called upon to grieve for our common humanity. For that melancholy madness which crushed all good feeling, which made the poor man insane from the hope of riches, and the rich man mad from the hope of extravagant wealth; which trampled alike upon human ties and natural desires, and embarked all England in a scheme destructive of moral feeling and national strength.

Thus ended this delusion, alike memorable and melancholy. There are no fine deeds standing prominently forward to redeem it; there are no noble acts which, while we deplore the cause, make us admire the effect; there is no unselfish sacrifice tending to make us proud of human nature. The prospect is one wide waste of degradation; there is nothing to sanctify, there is nothing to redeem it.

The course of this history may lead to new instances of intense thirst for gold. Speculative epochs may again occur; the events of the past may reappear in the future. Legitimate business may again be deserted for unlawful callings, and the history of that which is gone cease to be received as a warning.

Yet will the great delusion of this period stand alone in its infamy, its disgrace, and its misery; and though we dare not venture to hope that the spirit, which shook the country to its centre, has passed away— for nations, like individuals, are liable to their fevers and their crimes,—yet, let it be hoped that, if witnessed again in England, a prince of the blood may not sanction it; an officer of state profit by it; members of the senate be bribed with it; peers of the realm be disgraced through it; or a Chancellor of the Exchequer be denounced, degraded, and dishonoured in its discovery.

The following copy of an agreement, entered into with the Duke of Rutland, will serve to shew the form of compact:—" I promise to pay to the Duke of Rutland £10,000, upon his transferring to me or my order 1,000 capital South Sea stock, sometime on or before the shutting of the Company's books for the next Christmas dividend."

More than two millions were confiscated. The following deductions are rather in proportion to the delinquency of the speculators than to the magnitude of their estates.

PERSONS.	ESTATES.			ALLOWANCES.
Sir John Fellows, Sub. Gov. . .	£243,096	0	6 . .	£10,000
Charles Joye, Esq., Dep. Gov. . .	40,105	2	0 . .	5,000
Mr. Astell, ...	27,750	19	8¾ . . .	5,000
Sir John Blunt	183,349	10	8¾ . .	1,000
Sir Lawrence Blackwell	83,529	17	11 . . .	10,000
Sir Robert Chaplin	45,875	14	5 . .	10,000

PERSONS.	ESTATES.			ALLOWANCES.
Sir William Chapman	£39,161	6	8½.	£10,000
Mr. Chester	140,372	15	6	10,000
Mr. Child	52,437	19	1	10,000
Mr. Eyles	34,329	16	7	20,000
Mr. Gibbon	106,543	5	6	10,000
Mr. Hawes	40,031	0	2¾	31
Sir Theodore Janssen	243,244	3	11	50,000
Sir John Lambert	72,508	1	5	5,000
Mr. Read	117,297	16	0	10,000
Mr. Surman, Dep. Cash.	121,321	10	0	5,000

CHAPTER IX.

In 1722, the South Sea Company were allowed to
sell £200,000 government annuities; and the Bank
of England took the whole at twenty years' purchase,
at a price equal to par. To meet the payment,
amounting to four millions, their corporate capital
was increased £3,400,000, by £3,389,830 10s. being
subscribed for at 118 per cent. By this transaction
the Bank made a profit of £610,169 10s., and the
capital amounted to £8,959,995 14s. 8d. This year
may be regarded as somewhat memorable. In all
commercial bodies, a reserve fund, in proportion to
the importance of the partnership, is desirable. Unexpected liabilities and losses must frequently take
place, and periods of difficulty, demanding extensive
capital, must occasionally arise. The dividends of the

Corporation had hitherto varied considerably, as extra losses could only be met by decreasing the interest. If such claims occurred in the earlier part of the half-year, it is probable that they were only to be met by disposing of valuable securities at a serious sacrifice. That some such cause was in operation is evident, from the Bank, for the first time in its history, maintaining a reserve fund, which, under the name of REST, has increased with the business of the house, and has frequently proved of invaluable service. In the earlier history of the Bank a want of money must have been sometimes experienced, as the subscribed capital was lent to government in payment of the charter. The importance given by the latter, the growing requirements of trade, the interest allowed on deposits, together with private influence, produced clients to the young establishment. In exchange for deposits, notes were issued to the public, which readily circulated. The deposits, cash, and credit, together with the notes, formed indeed the chief fund upon which the Corporation traded; but as the profits made in the first few years were nearly, if not altogether, consumed by the expenses, the dividends continued until 1698, at the rate paid by government of eight per cent. The preliminary expenses in obtaining a charter, the outlay prior to the establishment, the incomes of the officers, together with the rent and bad debts, must have greatly diminished the early banking profits. It was during this period that its notes were at a discount; that the most strenuous efforts were made to destroy it; and that its opponents were most zealous in their attempts to crush that Bank which they hated as much as they feared. When the business augmented, an increased, though uncertain dividend was paid, which necessarily varied with the profits, as there was no fund to meet extraordinary claims, and the goldsmiths and bankers, jealous of the importance of their competitor, were not to be relied on for assistance. It is always desireable to have a steady dividend, as many of the shareholders rely on it for their support. The variations of the interest, therefore, were probably inconveniently felt. It is, indeed, a question how much the credit of a corporation is benefited by an uncertain dividend; and an addition to an uniform rate may always be appended as a bonus. A large reserved capital prevented the interest from fluctuating; and while it added stability to the Bank, was of great importance to the direction, by giving them confidence in their resources, and enabling them to triumph over those perils which must ever surround a new establishment, and which are often only dangerous in proportion to the smallness of its capital.

It is true that calls might have been made on the proprietary whenever an urgency occurred; but this would not have been in character with the great respectability already acquired by the Bank of England. For such reasons a reserve fund was desirable; and for these, with other and more powerful causes, THE REST, that great capital which has often been attacked and more often envied, was commenced in the year 1722.

It has been already seen that conspiracies against the state have usually produced an effect upon the Bank. The confidence reposed in it vanishes rapidly under the appearance of difficulty; and the more implicit the previous trust the greater the alarm when the balance of the public mind is disturbed. Men act when they should reason; and the hazard of the Bank is in proportion to the mystery which confuses the people rather than to the danger which environs the state. An obscure conspiracy which ended, as it was perhaps founded, in nothing, was communicated by the Duke of Orleans to King George I., and was stated to be formed against the person and throne of the latter. A proclamation of the exiled Pretender was gravely produced, which as gravely proposed a peaceable cession of the throne, by the English monarch, who in return, was to be made King of his native states. Every effort, both foreign and domestic, was reported to have been made. The people were to be intrigued with; government was to be subverted; money was said to be provided; officers engaged from abroad; arms and ammunition procured; and the city of London was to be marked with bloodshed and confusion. The Royal Exchange was to witness the proclamation of the Pretender; the Exchequer was to be seized; and the Bank of England to be plundered. At this period the Jacobites were a numerous, and even a powerful party ; and a plot conveyed from so important a personage as the Regent of France, struck alarm throughout the nation ; and once more the Bank paid the penalty of its greatness, by the public running to demand its cash. The stock fell in value. South Sea funds sympathised, and decreased in price. Vigorous measures were had recourse to, to meet an evil so sudden and alarming. A camp was formed in Hyde Park. Troops were ordered from Ireland. The States of Holland prepared to embark their guarantee troops. The Bishop of Rochester and Bishop Atterbury, with some of the nobility, were seized. The proclamation of the Pretender was burned at the Royal Exchange, and the House of Commons passed a bill in support of the means adopted. These proceedings overawed the malcontents; the run upon the Bank soon ceased ; and the city was restored to its propriety.

In 1725, the Bank consented to reduce the interest on two millions, advanced in 1716, from five to four per cent.; and in 1728, Government again resorted to the Bank of England to assist in meeting a vote of four millions, to pay the expenses of the preceding year. In times of war the ministry have always applied to this establishment to support them during those periods of danger and distrust, which must ever arise in a long contest with a powerful enemy. But that danger had ceased, and the nation had enjoyed a period

of profound quiet ; notwithstanding this, the directors
were again applied to for assistance in the above year ;
and the application was met by an advance of
£1,750,000, (on the security of the coal and culm
duties,) at four per cent. per annum. They were
enabled to advance this large sum without a further
call on their proprietary, in consequence of one million
having been repaid them, in 1727, of the previous
debt.   In the following year they advanced a further
sum of £1,250,000 at four per cent. on security of
the lottery, and were repaid £775,027 17s. 10½d. for
redemption of the remainder of the capital, due to
them for cancelling exchequer bills in 1709 ; and also
£500,000 towards redeeming the capital of two
millions, due for exchequer bills delivered up in 1717.

The notes issued at this period were made out in
the various names of the public ; and as part only was
printed, it was the duty of the clerk to enter that
portion which was not engraved. No note was circulated for less than £20 ; and though the demand was
limited, this mode must have added materially to the
business of the officers. If we may judge also from
the dividends, the directors did not shrink from their
share of work, as each warrant was signed by two of
their body. The number of fund-holders was considerable, and the labour, therefore, was not of a
trifling character.

Prior to the year 1732, the Court of directors had
carried on their business within the hall of the

Grocer's Company.   They had commenced their
career unostentatiously, and they had met with their
reward.   With fifty-four assistants, whose names and
salaries are recorded in the appendix, they had gone
on prospering, until the business demanded a building
exclusively devoted to its interests.   The time had
now arrived when an enlarged edifice was not only
advisable but necessary; and on 20th January, 1732,
it was unanimously resolved to erect a hall and office
in Threadneedle Street; and the site chosen for the
new edifice was that of the house and garden of Sir John
Houblon, first governor of the Bank.   The structure
was contracted for by Dunn and Townshend, eminent
builders of the day, after designs by Mr. George
Sampson.

On Thursday, the 3rd of August, at one o'clock in
the afternoon, the new building was commenced; a
stone, on which the names of the directors were
placed, being made the foundation for one of the
pillars.   Twenty guineas were presented to the workmen for distribution; and on the 5th of June, 1734,
business was commenced in that edifice, the present
importance of which is unparalleled in the history of
monetary establishments.   Notwithstanding the sagacity of those who governed its concerns, it may
reasonably be questioned whether they imagined the
time would ever arrive when its buildings would occupy
acres; when the movements of its governors, in the
words of the historiographer of London, would in-

fluence the whole body of the public, its offices expel a church from its site, and emulate the palaces of emperors; when their determination, according to Richard Cobden, would affect all the markets in the world; and the representatives of commerce in the east, and the pioneers of trade and civilization in the west, watch earnestly and anxiously the proceedings of the directors of the Bank of England. " I happened to be travelling in Turkey and Greece, in the spring of 1837," said this gentleman, in his evidence on Banks of Issue, " and I saw in the little island of Syra, the Greek merchants there, with their telescopes in their hands, looking out anxiously for the arrival of a vessel from Trieste, giving an account of the proceedings of the Bank of England, as a merchant on the Exchange at Manchester would watch for the arrival of the mail to know what the next step to be taken by the Bank directors would be; and we know that in the message of the President of the United States, in 1837, and in the addresses of some of the governors of the states, New York in particular, the Bank of England was not only mentioned by name, but a considerable space given to the discussion of its policy." On the 1st of January, 1735, the marble statue of the founder of the Corporation, by Cheere, which the reader has probably often seen, was placed upon its pedestal, and a volley fired by the servants of the Bank, in honour of the founder.

The following is a translation of the inscription:

"FOR RESTORING EFFICACY TO THE LAWS,
AUTHORITY TO THE COURTS OF JUSTICE,
DIGNITY TO THE PARLIAMENT,
TO ALL HIS SUBJECTS THEIR RELIGION AND LIBERTIES,
AND
FOR CONFIRMING THESE TO POSTERITY
BY THE SUCCESSION OF THE ILLUSTRIOUS HOUSE
OF HANOVER
TO THE BRITISH THRONE,
TO THE BEST OF PRINCES, WILLIAM III.,
FOUNDER OF THE BANK,
THIS CORPORATION, FROM A SENSE OF GRATITUDE,
HAS ERECTED THIS STATUE,
AND DEDICATED IT TO HIS MEMORY,
IN THE YEAR OF OUR LORD, MDCCXXXIV.,
AND THE FIRST YEAR OF THIS BUILDING."

This is a graceful homage to the man who was the origin of its greatness. It is a testimony of more worth than the engraven marble which records a conquest. It is a tribute of higher honour than the brass by the way side which tells of goodly cities sacked. The past age did not, even the present may not, fully appreciate this, but the progressive spirit of the times renders it certain, that, at some future period, the name of William III. will be regarded with more honour as the founder of the Bank of England, than as the soldier who fought in the trenches at Namur, or the statesman who organized the grand alliance of European powers against the house of Bourbon.

The inefficiency of the police a century ago is a matter of history. It is difficult to say whether murders or robberies most abounded. The records of the period bear witness that both were committed with comparative impunity; that "highwaymen" who were then peculiar to the time, flourished in all the gay *insouciance* which arises from a precarious mode of existence. The literature of the day is full of allusions to them; and an opera, commemorating the heroism of one of the fraternity, was performed on the stage, and applauded by lords and ladies until it became a fashion. Amid these scenes of crime, that of robbing the mail was a favourite occupation, as it not only required, but also rewarded, boldness. These robberies grew to such a height by 1738, that the post-master made a representation to the Bank upon the subject; and the directors, in consequence, advertised an issue of bills, payable at seven days sight, "that in case of the mail being robbed, the proprietor may have time to give notice."

In 1742, the period for the reconstruction of the Bank charter had arrived. The renewal of the privileges of the Company created the usual consideration of what amount might be gained by the state in payment, and of how hard a bargain might be made with the Corporation when compelled to sue for a favour. The latter were obliged to buy, and the Government determined to sell at as high a price as practicable. The loan of one million six hundred thousand pounds, without interest, was required by the state, too frequently a hard task-master in its transactions with the Corporation.

It was effected by blending this sum with the previous loan of £1,600,000, at six per cent., and the united sum of £3,200,000 bore the diminished interest of three per cent. In compensation, the exclusive banking privileges were renewed, till August, 1764. By this act " persons forging, counterfeiting, or altering any bank note, bill of exchange, dividend warrant, or any bond or obligation under the Bank seal, shall suffer death :" and also, " the Company's servants, breaking their trust to the Company, shall suffer death."

Another danger arose with the times. Since the run on the Bankers, when the States' Admiral swept our commerce from the Thames, and menaced our strongholds, London had been free from the danger of invasion. The rebellion of 1715 had been quelled with ease ; but that which followed in the memorable year of 1745, was impressive from its picturesque features, while it was dangerous only from the paralytic fear which seized the nation. It has ever been a feature in the history of the Bank, that, although not, strictly speaking, a government establishment, it has always been a point of attack for the political rabble, in times of tumult; while, during crises which should only affect the state, doubts have been thrown on its credit, and senseless clamour made for its gold. That which is now to be related was one of the most important periods of its career. The relation may be considered prolix ; but a mere announcement that, in the year 1745, a great demand for gold occurred, would be as uninstructive as uninteresting. The adventurous daring which occasioned it, the panic which seized peer as well as peasant, the moral and the mental features of the period, are all necessary to explain why the directors of the Bank of England were compelled to have recourse to stratagem to meet the demands made upon their specie.

The expedition of Charles Edward was as romantic as it was remarkable. Landing in the wilds of Moidart, attended by only seven devoted gentlemen, he succeeded in striking a terror throughout England. The prize for which he struck was a kingdom. The spirit with which he contended was worthy the prize. His march was one scene of triumph. From highland to lowland, from barren height and fertile vale, he gathered strength, until, with a solitary guinea in his pocket, the gallant adventurer entered the fair city of Perth. From Perth he passed on to the capital of Scotland; and the old walls of Holyrood, the antique palace of the Scottish monarchs, resounded once more with the sounds of joy. The lofty loyalty of the people of Scotland responded to the claims of the unfortunate house, and the tartan of the clan Stuart waved a joyous welcome from street and square of the city of palaces. The person of the Pretender, his chivalrous adventure, his princely bearing, won him "golden opinions." Men fought for him. Women embraced him.

At Doune some Scottish lasses kissed his hand; and one, with the romantic enthusiasm of girlhood, begged permission to kiss the royal lips. The favour was graciously granted by the young Chevalier, who, taking the loyal lady in his arms, " kissed her blushing face, from ear to ear;" to the great vexation, adds Chambers, of the other ladies who had been contented with a less liberal allowance of his princely grace. These things are related because they prove the great devotion evinced throughout Scotland, and explain why, with a mere handful of men, Charles Edward had, even then, struck a panic into the commercial heart of England. When, therefore, Carlisle had capitulated, when Penrith was invested, and Manchester, with its thirty thousand inhabitants, "was taken by a serjeant, a drummer, and a girl," the English were seized with dismay. London expected, in two or three days, to witness the triumphant entry of the rebel army, the seizure of her treasure, and the plunder of her citizens. The adherents of the young adventurer had printed his declaration to the people of Great Britain, and throughout the capital, in the highways and byeways, in the streets of the town, in the dwellings of its inhabitants, were these declarations mysteriously spread. Men found them in their houses; they were placed under their doorways; they penetrated the sanctuary of their homes. It was a time of great rejoicing for the staunch Jacobite. It was a period of dread for the loyal and peaceable citizen. Consternation obtained throughout the capital. The Duke of Newcastle, Secretary of State for the War department, whose name was said, by Sir Robert Walpole, to be perfidy, shut himself in his closet for three days to decide on his conduct, uncertain whether he should support his monarch or declare for the prince. The first catholic peer of the realm was ready to join the invader. The inhabitants fled to the country with their most precious effects. The king caused his valuables to be removed to a yacht by the tower, and was prepared to effect an escape. A proclamation was issued for a general fast. A run commenced upon the Bank, for which the directors were not prepared; and there appeared every prospect of its destruction. The funds fell; the quotations of the day do not shew so great a decline as might have been expected; but the probability is that they were but nominal.

The second article of the manifesto issued by the pretender, stated, that though the national debt "was contracted under an unlawful government, and was a most heavy load unto the nation, yet his father would take the advice of his parliament." This was deemed small comfort for the fundholders, who placed no faith in the honesty of a senate, called upon to act in a period of convulsion, under an arbitrary Stuart. The sins of the sire were visited upon the children. The seizure of the money in the mint by the first Charles, and the shutting up the Exchequer by his dissolute son, were remembered to the injury of their descendant.

But more alarming news was in store for the citizens. The town of Derby, only one hundred and twenty miles from the capital, was occupied by the rebels. The magistrates had fled in terror. London, with all her treasure, was temptingly exposed. The alarm of the citizens magnified the reports, and the reports increased in proportion to the alarm. During the whole of one day passed in Derby, the Highlanders fought for precedency in getting their claymores sharpened at the shops of the cutlers. The habitants of London looked on the rebels as wild men, coming from the depths of interminable forests, where they dwelt in caverns, and lived on human flesh. Mothers wept over their children; and substantial traders exaggerated the alarm that spread throughout the shops and the counting houses of the great city. With these prospects the merchants outvied each other in liberal subscriptions, which, while they were recorded as the fruits of loyalty, were really the offspring of fear.

The day on which the news arrived that the rebels were at Derby, was known in London as Black Friday. The gates of the city were shut. The train bands were placed on duty night and day. The guards were ordered out. The Tower was closed before its time. The shops were unopened; and no business was done excepting at the Bank. Many of the inhabitants collected their valuables, and fled from the country. The Stuarts had always been partial to obtaining money by the strong hand, and Charles Edward had imitated the profitable example. The Londoners had heard of £5000 raised in Glasgow; of heavy contributions levied in Manchester; of £2500 procured in Derby; with minor sums in other places; and they watched with almost breathless interest the advance of the Pretender, in full expectation of similar results.

The effect upon the national Bank was as usual. Its interests were involved in those of the state; and the creditors flocked in crowds to obtain payment for their notes. The directors, unprepared for such a casualty,—who could have foreseen that a few thousand men would overrun half England?—had recourse to a justifiable artifice. The Chevalier Johnston, whose evidence was collected immediately after the battle of Culloden, says, that the Bank only escaped bankruptcy by a stratagem. Payment was not refused; but the Corporation retained its specie, by employing agents to enter with notes, who, to gain time, were paid in sixpences; and as those who came first were entitled to priority of payment, the agents went out at one door with the specie they had received, and brought it back by another, so that the *bona fide* holders of notes could never get near enough to present them. "By this artifice," says the Chevalier, somewhat quaintly, "the Bank preserved its credit, and literally faced its creditors." The wisdom of the artifice was witnessed in its effect. The London merchants, with honourable promptitude, called a meeting of their body at Garraway's Coffee House. They expressed their confidence in the Bank Corporation, and agreed to receive its notes in payment. The following was their resolution, and deserves to be recorded:

"We, the undersigned, merchants and others, being sensible how necessary the preservation of public credit is at this time, do hereby declare that we will not refuse to receive Bank notes in payment of any sum of money to be paid to us; and we will use our utmost endeavours to make our payments in the same manner."

26th Sept., 1745.

The feeling which dictated this resolution was very general, as, by four o'clock in the afternoon, it was signed by one thousand one hundred and forty merchants, large traders, and proprietors of the public funds. History records the retreat of the young Pretender from Derby, the news of which stopped the run, and brought confidence to the homes of the citizens. The policy of Charles Edward has been questioned. Doubtless a march upon the capital would have been worthy the noble prize for which he contended; and it is the opinion of many that he must have been successful. This might have been the case; but it is scarcely probable that the religion which gave William the English crown would

have submitted once more to the despotic sway of a
Stuart; and still less is it to be imagined that the
Stuart would have forgotten those dreams of absolute
power which had driven him from the throne, and
still lingered with him in the mock monarchy of
St. Germain's. It must have been another period of
fear and dread to the supporters of the Bank. Had
Charles Edward reached the capital, a levy on it would
have been his first act; and that levy would have been
in proportion to his own power, the hatred which
he bore it for supporting the revolution, and the
rapacity of the exiled house. The danger passed
away with the crisis. The adventurer lost his only
chance of a crown; and commenced a disastrous
retreat, which was closed by his escape from Scotland.
Confidence was once more restored. The shops were
re-opened. The citizens grew suddenly brave. The
courtiers grew doubly loyal. The vigour of the people
returned; and London was a scene of rejoicing. Commerce resumed its pristine strength; and the only
memorials which remained of the past panic, were to
be found in the punishment of those misguided men,
who, under a sense of duty, had supported the scion
of their ancient monarchical race.

The particulars which led to this panic have been
fully recounted; for it is the last instance of a run
occasioned solely by the fear of invasion; and the
last time that Englishmen lost faith in their
political institutions, or sought to empty their

bankers' coffers from fear of foreign or domestic warfare.

The following anecdote, given by Mr. Ireland, who says he received it from an authority not to be doubted, is, if true, curiously illustrative of the evil spirit which, only a century ago, influenced public bodies. It is probably a partial statement.

"It is well known that, in the year 1745, on account of the domestic confusion which prevailed in the northern part of this island, Bank notes were at a considerable discount. The notes, however, which were issued by Child's house, as well as those of Hoare and Co., still maintained their credit, and were circulated at par.—The Bank directors, alarmed at the depreciation of their paper, and attributing it to the high estimation in which the house of Messrs. Child still remained, attempted, by very unfair artifices, to ruin their reputation. This plan they endeavoured to accomplish by collecting a very large quantity of their notes, and pouring them in all together for payment on the same day. Before the project was executed, the Duchess of Marlborough, who had received some intimation of it, imparted the information to Mr. Child, and supplied him with a sum of money, more than sufficient to answer the amplest demand that could be made upon them. In consequence of this scheme, the notes were sent by the Bank, and were paid in their own paper; a circumstance which occasioned considerable loss to that corporation; their paper being circulated considerably below par. Perhaps this anecdote will be confirmed by the well known circumstance of the hostility of her Grace to the administrators of that trust." The precision with which this account is given, must be accepted as a reason for its insertion. It is, however, most difficult of belief, that any body of honourable men would act so disgraceful a part. The story has, in all probability, arisen out of some financial operation, the object of which was perverted by the opponents of the Bank, because it was beyond their comprehension.

The rebellion was scarcely over, when the Government were compelled to apply once more for assistance. The cost of the war, which had been fiercely contested with France, in order to preserve the integrity of the Hanoverian Electorate, together with the expenses attending the invasion, had pressed heavily on the resources of the state.

The ministers endeavoured to meet their difficulties by opening a public subscription, in 1746 ; but the monied interest did not respond. The great support given to the credit of the Bank by the mercantile community, had been thoroughly successful, and the company were enabled to offer that assistance, which the state found it difficult otherwise to procure. One million was advanced to Government, at four per cent. interest ; and the court of proprietors authorized the directors to draw up proposals for converting £986,000, held by them in Exchequer bills, into an annuity, at four per cent; and for creating new stock to the same amount. The proposal was accepted, and an act passed to authorise it. A call of ten per cent. was made upon the proprietary; and the Bank capital increased to £10,780,000. Even at this late period, some of the proprietors neglected to answer the call; and the directors sold a sufficient amount of their stock, (about £12,000,) to produce the required sum.

In 1746, the capital, on which the Bank Stock proprietors divided, amounted to £10,780,000. In a little more than half a century, it had been more than octupled, so great had been the prosperity of the Corporation. The dividends had varied with the success; and though at one period ten and a half per cent. for the half-year was paid, the average amount was greatly below this; and in 1746, the half-yearly dividend had fallen to two and three quarters. The value of money, also, which had been so enormous, previous to the new establishment, had been reduced considerably. At first, the rate of discount was from four and a half to six per cent.; and a less amount was charged to those who kept accounts with the Bank; inland bills being discounted for them at four and a half, and foreign bills at three per cent.; while six per cent. was charged for bills of all kinds to other persons. The rates of discount were afterwards equalized, and varied from four to five per cent., till 1775, when the latter sum was fixed upon, at which it remained till 1822. This reduced value of money was advantageously experienced by Government, receiving the same benefit in 1745, for three per cent., for which, before 1690, they had paid twenty-five to thirty per cent. It has not been considered necessary to detail on each occasion the rise or fall of the dividends, given to the proprietary, as a clearer and more comprehensive view may be obtained in the appendix.

Another reduction of the interest on the national debt was effected in 1750; a meeting of the Corporation was called at Merchant Tailors' Hall, at which the proposals of the ministry were acceded to, and three instead of four per cent. agreed to be received on £8,486,800 of the government debt. In addition, the Company consented to advance a sufficient amount to pay off the dissentients; and to raise this they established a "Bank circulation." As the amount to be required was uncertain, books were opened to the public, and any individual was allowed to enter the sum he proposed to lend, in case it should be called for. When the books were closed, the Bank had the power of calling for all or any part of the sum so subscribed. Two shillings per cent. was to be paid on the amount proposed, and four pounds per cent. on the sum advanced. The payment required by government for those who did not consent to the reduction, amounted to £1,190,041 16s. 1d. For this sum, Exchequer bills, bearing interest at £3 per cent., were received in exchange.

The course of this history will not record the many transactions in which the Bank have been concerned for government in the creation of stock. The year 1752, in which the foundation of the present "three per cent. consols" was laid, is, however, sufficiently interesting to attract attention. This stock was thus termed from the balance of some annuities, granted by George I., being consolidated into one fund with a three per cent. stock formed in 1731. The amount of this security at the present time is upwards of 360 millions, to so large a superstructure has it grown from a small foundation. The same observation will also apply to the year 1757, when the stock, which had borne four per cent. interest till 1750, and from that period paid 3½, was reduced to 3 per cent.; from this operation the name of the "three per cents. reduced" is derived. This stock is much smaller than the former, as it amounts to little more than £123,500,000.

A correspondent of the "Gentleman's Magazine" gives the following particulars of the external appearance of the Bank in 1757. "When I came to London, and lived near it, it was comparatively a small structure, almost invisible to passers by, being surrounded by many others, viz., a church called St. Christopher le Stocks, since pulled down; three taverns, two on the south side, one (the Fountain) in Bartholomew Lane, facing the church there, just where the great door of entrance is now placed, and about fifteen or twenty private dwelling-houses. Visitors are sometimes shown in the bullion office the identical old chest, somewhat larger than a common seaman's, also the original shelves or cases, where the cash, notes, papers, and books of business were kept; and well are they preserved, as pregnant vouchers no less of the Bank's pristine simplicity and confined exertions, than of the amazing rapidity of its modern extension, and almost boundless accommodation of the monied interest and commercial world."

CHAPTER X.

THE FIRST FORGED NOTE—LEGAL DECISION—ISSUE OF NOTES—
NEW CHARTER—GREAT PANIC AND FAILURE OF BANKERS IN
1772—THE GORDON RIOTS—CONFUSION OF THE PEOPLE—SUSPEN-
SION OF TRADE IN THE CITY—ATTACK ON THE BANK—ITS
REPULSE—BEHAVIOUR OF WILKES—EXTRAORDINARY SERIES OF
FORGERIES—DETECTION OF THE FORGER—HIS FATE—MORLAND
THE PAINTER—LIBERALITY OF THE DIRECTORS.

THE day on which a forged note was first presented
at the Bank of England, forms a memorable era in its
history. For sixty-four years the establishment had
circulated its paper with freedom ; and during this
period no attempt had been made to imitate it. He
who takes the initiative in a new line of wrong doing,
has more than the simple act to answer for ; and to
Richard William Vaughan, a Stafford linen-draper,
belongs the melancholy celebrity of having led the
van in this new phase of crime, in the year 1758.
The records of his life do not show want, beggary,
or starvation urging him, but a simple desire to seem
greater than he was. By one of the artists employed,
and there were several engaged on different parts of
the notes, the discovery was made. The criminal

had filled up to the number of twenty; and deposited them in the hands of a young lady to whom he was attached, as a proof of his wealth. There is no calculating how much longer Bank notes might have been free from imitation, had this man not shewn with what ease they might be counterfeited. From this period forged notes became common. The faculty of imitation is so great, that when the expectation of profit is added, there is little hope of restraining the destitute or the bad man from a career which adds the charm of novelty to the chance of gain. The publicity given to the fraud, the notoriety of the proceedings, and the execution of the forger, tended to excite that morbid sympathy, which, up to the present day, is evinced for any extraordinary criminal. It is, therefore, possible, that if Vaughan had not been induced by circumstances to startle London with his novel crime, the idea of forging Bank notes might have been long delayed, and that some of the strange facts to be related would never have occurred.

The same year was also memorable for a judgment passed by the Lord Chief Justice, in connexion with some notes which were stolen from one of the mails. The robber, after stopping the coach and taking out all the money contained in the letters, went boldly to a Mr. Miller, at the Hatfield post-office, who unhesitatingly exchanged one of them. Here he ordered a post-chaise with four horses; and at several stages passed off the remainder. They were, however, stopped at the Bank, and an action was brought by the possessor to recover the money. The question was an important one ; and it was decided by the law authorities, "That any person paying a valuable consideration for a Bank note, payable to bearer, in a fair course of business, has an undoubted right to recover the money of the Bank." The action was maintained upon the plea that the figure 11, denoting the date, had been converted by the robber to a 4.

In 1759, Bank notes, to a smaller amount than £20, were first circulated ; and the directors commenced issues of £15 and £10, to meet the necessity experienced by the community.

In January, 1764, the Charter, granted to the Bank in 1745, had nearly expired, and the question of its renewal was again agitated. The customary process of extension, that process which has procured a good price from the Corporation for all the favours granted, was once more under consideration. The terms on which Government consented to place the exclusive power of the Bank again in its possession, were sufficiently onerous. By this agreement, the Directors were to advance cash for Exchequer bills to the amount of one million, at three per cent. interest, till the year 1766, when the bills were to be discharged. They were also to pay £110,000 ; and for this they were to receive neither interest nor repayment. In consideration of these sums, they were to continue a body corporate, with all their advantages, till the redemption of the debt, due to them by Government; and one year's notice, from the first of August, 1786. By the same act, it was made felony, without benefit of clergy, to forge powers of attorney, or other authorities, for receiving dividends, transferring or selling stock, or for personating the proprietors of any stock, for such purpose. The falling in of the Bank Charter at this period was a piece of great good fortune to the Government. A successful, but costly war had pressed upon the nation. During this contest, important islands had been conquered; great battles gained; forts, castles, and fortified cities had yielded to our prowess. Twelve millions had been acquired in plunder; and captured standards were borne in triumph to St. Paul's, amid the shouts of assembled multitudes. The navy of France was annihilated. Spain loathed a contest which produced only reverses. Portugal was anxious for peace. The fall of the French colonies was consummated at Martinique. The empire of the East had been wrested from French sway; and conquests, rivalling those of the "great captain" accomplished by a youth bred to a writing desk. France was exhausted. The treasury of the "great nation" was empty. The plate of "the most christian king" was converted into money; and England triumphed in a treaty which consolidated her strength; which gave her a great pre-eminence among the nations; which added to her name a splendour she has since retained, and which the confidence of her ministry in the resources of the country, and the assistance of the Bank of England, greatly tended to produce. The expenses pressed heavily upon the people. A loan, therefore, of £3,000,000, with an absolute gift of £110,000, were no unimportant addition to those sources, which had been drained by the glorious, and successful, seven years' war.

A new crime was discovered in 1767. The notice of the clerks at the Bank had been attracted by the habit of William Guest, a teller, picking new from old guineas, without assigning any reason. An indefinite suspicion—increased by the knowledge that an ingot of gold had been seen in Guest's possession—was attracted ; and although he asserted that it came from Holland, it was remarked to be very unlike the regular bars of gold, and that it had a considerable quantity of copper on the back. Attention being thus drawn to the behaviour of Guest, he was observed to hand one Richard Still some guineas, which he took from a private drawer, and placed with the others on the table. Still was instantly followed; and on the examination of his money, three of the guineas in his possession were deficient in weight. An enquiry was immediately instituted ; and forty of the guineas in the charge of Guest looked fresher than the others upon the edges, and weighed much less than the legitimate amount.

On searching his home, four pounds eleven ounces of gold filings were found, with some instruments calculated to produce artificial edges. Proofs soon multiplied; and the prisoner was found guilty. The instrument with which he had effected his fraud, of which one of the witnesses asserted it was the greatest improvement he had ever seen, is said to be yet in the mint, a memento of the prisoner's capacity and crime.

In June, 1772, one of those panics occurred with which London is unhappily so familiar. On the 10th of the month, Neale and Co., bankers, in Threadneedle Street, stopped payment. Other failures resulted in consequence; and throughout the city there was a general consternation. The timely interposition of the Bank, and the generous assistance of the merchants, prevented many of the expected stoppages, and trade appeared restored to its former security. It was, however, only an appearance; for, on Monday, the 22nd of the same month, may be read, in a contemporary authority, a description of the prevailing agitation, which forcibly reminds us of a few years ago. "It is beyond the power of words to describe the general consternation of the metropolis at this instant. No event for fifty years has been remembered to give so fatal a blow to trade and public credit. An universal bankruptcy was expected. The stoppage of almost every banker's house in London was looked for. The whole city was in an uproar.

Many of the first families were in tears. This melancholy scene began with a rumour that one of the greatest bankers in London had stopped ; which afterwards proved true. A report at the same time was propagated that an immediate stop of the greatest must take place. Happily this proved groundless ; the principal merchants assembled, and means were concerted to revive trade and preserve the national credit."

The resumption of payment by many houses, at first compelled to bend before the storm, is in singular contrast with the following event, which took place in France three years previously. The extract is from the " Gentleman's Magazine." " A considerable banker at Paris having a draught brought to him from a public office in that city for a large sum, which he could not answer, after cramming down the draught into a loaded pistol, called to the gentleman who brought it, and telling him, ' This, Sir, is the way that persons who have no money pay bills that are due,' instantly clapped the pistol to his ear, and shot himself dead."

Although the crisis had passed in England, the spirit of " launching into rash and boundless projects in commerce," says Macpherson, " which were to be supplied by artificial credit, and the madness of towering speculation in the public funds, spread all over Europe. The evil, which had reached its height in England in 1772, burst out on the continent in the end of that, and the beginning of the following year, with such an extensive crash, that there seemed to be an universal wreck of credit throughout Europe, to the amount of ten millions sterling. In this time of general distress, a happy mixture of generosity and prudence in most leading nations, though without any previous concert, averted many of the fatal consequences, and prevented the mischief from spreading. The Dutch merchants, where the evil was greatest, acted with their usual commercial wisdom. The bank of Stockholm gave support to every house of real responsibility ; and the Empress of Russia gave credit to the British merchants at Petersburgh, by giving them a credit on her own banker, for such sums as they needed." The cloud soon passed away for the sunshine, and commercial faith took place of commercial distrust.

It is worthy of notice that the circumstances to which allusion has been made, were the first instances of the failures of bankers in London ; and this may excite wonder when it is seen, by the following extract from " Anderson's history of commerce," that firms often traded upon capital somewhat incommensurate with the importance of their transactions. " At the breaking up and dividing the profits of an eminent partnership many years ago of a private city banking house, which for many years had divided a profit of several thousands, on valuing all the real stock of the partnership, the whole did not amount to above three or four hundred pounds, consisting entirely of shop instruments and furniture."

In this year, an action, interesting to the public, was brought against the Bank. It appeared from the evidence that some stock stood in the joint names of a man and his wife; and, by the rules of the Corporation, the signatures of both were required before it could be transferred. To this the husband objected; and claimed the right of selling without his wife's signature or consent in any form. The Court of King's Bench decided in favour of the plaintiff, with full costs of suit; Lord Mansfield declaring that "it was highly *cruel and oppressive* to withhold from the husband his right of transferring." The words italicized were unnecessary. One object of the Bank is the attainment of the public good. It is, however, a prejudice which attaches itself to juries—and sometimes even to judges—to view with jaundiced eyes the proceedings of large corporations; and for this reason the verdicts occasionally given are only compatible with a very small reasoning power, or a very extensive vindictive feeling.

In 1773, an act was passed making it death to copy the water mark of the Bank note paper; and, in order to prevent imitation, it was enacted that no person should prepare any engraved bill or promissory note containing the words " Bank of England," or " Bank post bill," or expressing any sum in white letters on black ground in resemblance of "Bank paper," under the penalty of imprisonment for six months. By an act, passed in 1775, notes of a less amount than twenty shillings were prohibited; and two years afterwards, by the 17th George III., the amount was limited to £5.

On Friday, the 2nd of June, 1780, commenced those riots which form so disgraceful a portion of the English history, and which, had it not been for the resolute daring of the London citizens, might have been fatal to the Bank. On that day, a large body of men, calling themselves the "Protestant Association," headed by Lord George Gordon, a nobleman whom some termed a fanatic, and others a fool, but who was, in truth, a mixture of both, with the great merit of being in earnest, assembled, about half-past two, before the houses of Parliament, to make a demonstration against a bill in favour of Catholicism, then in progress; and to present a petition against it. After uttering a loud shout, more expressive of animal strength than moral power, the arbitrary authority of an excited populace was exercised. They obliged the members of both houses to put blue cockades in their hats, and to call out "No Popery." Some were compelled to take whatever oaths they chose to administer; and some were personally abused in the full insolence of unchecked power. Twice they attempted to force an entrance into the senate house. The Archbishop of York was saluted with hisses, groans, and hootings. Lord Bathurst was kicked;

and Lord Mansfield buffeted. The watch of the
Duke of Northumberland was stolen by this " No
Popery" immaculate mob. The gown of the Bishop
of Lichfield was torn off; and the Bishop of Lincoln
was compelled to escape in disguise. Lords Townshend and Hillsborough were sent into Parliament
without those important appendages of gentlemen,
their bags, while their hair, hanging loosely in unpic-
turesque disorder on their shoulders, conveyed a
vivid picture to the assembled senate of the " majesty
of the people." The coach of Lord Stormont was
destroyed ; and his lordship only saved from personal
damage by the appeal of a gentleman who harangued
the mob into temporary good humour. Lord Boston
was so long in the power of the populace, that the
peers, with some remnant of that chivalric feeling
which bade one knight couch his lance against a
multitude, proposed to sally forth to the rescue, and
were only prevented by his lordship's timely escape
from the rudeness of the rioters. The mob, after
finding their favourite petition rejected by the large
majority of 192 to 6, dispersed to various quarters
of the town, where they effected all the mischief compatible with an absence of danger.

The following day, Saturday, was comparatively
quiet, but on Sunday, acting upon the proverb, " the
better the day the better the deed;" the crowd gave
vent to an ignorant fanaticism, by destroying the chapels and homes of the catholics. The insignia of the

worshippers of the ancient faith was insulted; the pulpits destroyed; the missals burned; and the altars desecrated. Nor did they, in the purity of their protestantism, forget to seize the images of silver and vessels of gold, which lay temptingly exposed to view. The military were inactive, and the magistracy ceased to be a terror to evil doers.

Scenes such as these; the reports which, from time to time, greatly alarmed the directors of the Bank; the information that large masses of men, uncontrolled save by their own passions, were destroying all that they approached, must have greatly affected the friends of the Corporation. The knowledge that the military were useless; that there was no efficient power to protect their building; that an application for a regiment would be futile; and that, therefore, their defence must rest on their resources, greatly added to their responsibility.

Monday saw tallow chandlers' shops, and Catholic chapels, alike attacked. The organs of destruction were in active play, and their owners would not be disappointed. Tuesday witnessed the military out to protect the senators; but it also witnessed a peer of the realm wounded, his carriage demolished, and his life with difficulty saved. The cry soon arose "to Newgate;" and at six o'clock, street, square, and lane, saw serried masses of fierce and desperate men rushing to the work of destruction. It was a popular cry; who, among that wild and violent crowd, did not hate and dread the very name. The furniture of the Governor was piled in a heap and burned. The building was fired, and the criminals, made worse by their residence, were released to join their brethren in crime. From Tyburn to Whitehall, the shops were shut ; business was suspended at all places save the Bank ; and the courts of law were abandoned. The houses of Sir John Fielding and Justice Cox were destroyed. The children of the Prime Minister were taken from their beds and placed on the table of the horse- guards. Fragments of the Catholic chapels were borne in triumphal procession, and the *detenus* of the new prison were liberated. The elegant mansion of Lord Mansfield was consumed, and with a barbaric contempt of literature, his library, the labour of a life, was thrown into the flames, while three hundred soldiers stood calmly by, and witnessed its destruction. As the day closed, a spectacle almost grand, save from its cause, was witnessed. From prison and from private building,—from Catholic chapel and Catholic dwelling house,—in every quarter of the great metropolis, rolled clouds of smoke, from which pillars of fire arose with a sad and almost solemn sublimity. In one night the flames of six-and-thirty fires created a wild and fearful illumination.

With such desolation and fury reigning unchecked, the Bank of England was sure to feel and pay for its importance. It is only to be attributed to the thoughtlessness of the mob, that this establishment was not attacked when the defence was insufficient for its protection. When the news came, that the rioters, headed by a man on horseback, caparisoned with the trophies of Newgate, were on their way, the governor was absent; he soon reached his post however, and preparations were made for their reception.

The old inkstands were cast into bullets; a strong force was placed within, while the military awaited their arrival without the walls. The officers of the establishment were called upon to assist, and another force was placed on the roof, to fire upon the assailants if they entered. Every possible arrangement was made for the defence of a building, far more important to the credit of the country than any in the capital. If the mob could have penetrated through all this force, the loss would have been immense. But the citizens of London had formed a volunteer corps; and with the military, who had shaken off their lethargy, distinguished themselves in defending the Bank. When the rioters,—fierce in the exercise of their mad passions, and fierce in the possession of uncontrolled power, saw the display made by the Directors, their attacks were feebly conducted. It was one thing to destroy an unresisting Catholic gentleman's property; it was another to attack a body of resolute men. It was one thing to fire a prison, and another to receive the fire of disciplined soldiers. Wilkes is said, on this occasion, to have rushed out during the pauses which occurred in the attack, and dragged some of the ring-leaders from their fellow-rabble. A witness of the scene says, "When the ministers trembled and remained inactive, when the magistrates durst not venture out of their houses, he was seen presenting himself before that unprincipled rabble, and braving death, in order to preserve the Bank, which they were about to pillage. Prayers, representations, and threats, he successively made use of, and even carried his intrepidity so far as to seize some of the ring leaders. This bold and patriotic action, in such circumstances, restored to him the favour of his sovereign, who had borne him for twenty years a mortal hatred." It is added, that Wilkes received the thanks of the Council for his conduct during the riots. The first fire of the military repulsed the mob; their second attempt was unsuccessful; nor did they hazard a third. Several were killed, and many wounded in the skirmish.

"Had the Bank," says the "Annual Register," "been the first object of their fury, there can be little doubt but that they would have succeeded; and what the consequence would have been, let any rational mind figure to itself."

It seems, indeed, little short of a miracle, that a place like the Bank should have been so long relieved from attack. It was probably owing to a want of organization among the rioters; for a leader, who failed to obtain possession of the sinews of war, must have been very unworthy the name. At any rate, it was a remarkable salvation of private property and public credit. But the most vivid representation of the danger which the Bank of England had happily escaped, is to be found in the following particulars of the appearance of the city, after the riots. "The metropolis presented in many places the image of a city, recently stormed and sacked; all business at an end; houses and shops shut up; the Royal Exchange, public buildings, and streets possessed and occupied by the troops; smoking and burning ruins, with a dreadful void and silence, in scenes of the greatest hurry, noise and business." The cause of all this riot, the scion of the ducal house of Gordon, proved the durability of his love for protestanism, by professing the Hebrew faith; his last hours embittered by the dread of his remains being interred in any other than the sepulchres of the ancient people of Israel.

Since the danger which the Bank so happily escaped, a military force has been placed nightly in the interior of the establishment. A dinner is provided for the officer on guard and two friends. "A snug, plain excellent dinner it is," says Mr. Weir, in "Knight's Pictorial London," brought daily from one of the best taverns in the neighbourhood. The store which the guards set by this dinner, excellent though it be, speaks volumes for the ennui which broods over the period during which they are stationed at the Tower. Some time ago, a regiment of the line was marched into the Tower, and the battalion of guards withdrawn. All the other duties of the place were gladly and unreluctantly given up to the new comers, with the solitary exception of the inlying piquet at the Bank. The duty might have been given up ; but to relinquish the dinner was impossible. And, on this account, so long as the Tower remained denuded of the presence of the guards, the Bank piquet regularly detailed from the far west end, duly and daily threaded the crowded Strand, passed under Temple Bar, jostled over Fleet Street, scrambled up Ludgate Hill, rounded St Paul's, and over Cheapside, erst the scene of tournaments, charged home to the Bank of England. The cynosure of attraction to the weary sub on duty— the magnet which drew him to encounter this long and toilsome march, and worse, the incarceration of four-and-twenty mortal hours within the walls of the Bank, was not the ingots piled within these walls— his high spirit disdained them ; not the bright eye of city maid or dame, these must now be sought in the suburbs ; it was the substantial savoury fare of the city—the genuine roast beef of Old England, and the city's ancient port, far surpassing the French cookery and French wine of St. James's."

The proclamation of peace in 1783 was indirectly an expense to the Bank, although hailed with enthusiasm by the populace. The war with America had assumed an aspect which with all thinking men crushed every hope of conquest. It was therefore amid a general shout of joy, that on Monday, 1st

October, 1783, the ceremonial took place. A vast multitude attended, and the people were delighted with the suspension of war. The concourse was so great that Temple Bar was opened with difficulty, and the Lord Mayor's coachman was kept one hour before he was able to turn his vehicle. The Bank only had reason to regret, or at least not to sympathize so freely, with the public joy. During the hurry attendant on the proclamation at the Royal Exchange, when it may be supposed the sound of the music, and the noise of the trumpet, occupied the attention of the clerk more than was beneficial for the interest of his employers, fourteen notes of £50 each were presented at the office, and cash paid for them. The next day they were found to be forged, and there was no mode of discovering the person who had defrauded the establishment.

The losses occurring to the Bank from forged notes and other fraudulent documents, were commensurate with the greatness of its transactions. Many of these were mixed up with much of the romance of life ; the attempts of some were successful through great good fortune ; others were detected at once ; while many, by their dexterity, either defied discovery or baffled the Bank for years. It is one of the latter which will now be related. Constant references are made in the journals of the time to some unknown power which defrauded the Bank of England ; of some mysterious agent who laughed at precautions, and escaped exposure; of new modes of robbery which, from time to time, startled alike both clerks and directors. Such is the story now to be related; too dramatic for the stage, and too startling for an appearance of probability.

Charles Price was one of those men whose whole abilities are employed in defrauding. At the age of seventeen he left his home to seek a fortune; and threw himself on the world with the determination to live by it. He soon learned to play many parts. Now a comedian; and now a gentleman's servant. At one time a rogue, and the companion of rogues; and then a fraudulent brewer or a fraudulent bankrupt. Great talent was employed in enormous crimes; and great evil was the result. After trying his hand as lottery-office keeper, stock-broker, and gambler, he attained sufficient importance to grace a work entitled "The Swindler's Chronicle." From this the step was easy to the "Newgate Calendar;" and he embarked in a bold, skilful, and resolute career of fraud on the Bank. His only confidant was his mistress. He practised engraving till he became proficient. He made his own ink. He manufactured his own paper. With a private press he worked his own notes; and he counterfeited the signatures of the cashiers, until the resemblance was complete. Master of all that could successfully deceive, he defied alike fortune and the Bank directors; and even these operations in his own house were transacted in a disguise sufficient to baffle the most penetrating.

About the year 1780 a note was brought to the Bank for payment. So complete were all its parts ; so masterly the engraving ; so correct the signatures ; so skilful the watermark, that it was promptly paid ; and only discovered to be a forgery when it reached a particular department. From that period forged paper continued to be presented, especially at the time of lottery drawing. Consultations were held with the police. Plans were laid to ensure detection. Every effort was made to trace the forger. Clarke, the Forrester of his day, went, like a sluth-hound, on the track ; for in those days the expressive word "blood-money" was known. Up to a certain point there was little difficulty ; but beyond this the most consummate art defied the ingenuity of the officer. In whatever way the notes came, the train of discovery always paused at the lottery-offices. Advertisements offering large rewards were circulated ; but the unknown forger baffled detection, at the expense of the Corporation.

Among other advertisements in the "Daily Advertiser," in 1780, might be seen one for a servant ; to which an answer was sent by a young man, in the employment of a musical instrument maker, who, some time after, was called upon by a coachman, and informed that the advertiser was waiting in a coach to see the candidate for the situation. The young man

went; and was desired to enter the conveyance, where
he saw a person with something of the appearance of
a foreigner, sixty or seventy years old, apparently
troubled with the gout, as some yards of flannel were
wrapped around his legs. A camblet surtout was
buttoned round his mouth; a large patch placed over
his left eye; and nearly every part of his face was
concealed. He affected much infirmity; and a faint
hectic cough; and invariably presented the patched
side to the view of the servant. After some
conversation, in the course of which he represented himself as guardian to a young nobleman of
great fortune, the interview concluded with the en-
gagement of the applicant; and the new servant was
directed to call on Mr. Brank—the name by which
he designated himself—at 29, Titchfield Street, Oxford
Street. At this interview Brank inveighed against his
whimsical ward for his love of speculating in lottery-
tickets; and told the servant that his principal duty
would be to purchase them. After one or two meetings, at each of which Brank kept his face muffled,
he handed a £40 and £20 Bank note; told the
servant to be very careful not to lose them; and
directed him to buy lottery-tickets at separate offices.
The young man went, fulfilled his instructions, and at
the moment he was returning, was suddenly called
by his employer from the other side of the Street,
congratulated on his rapidity, and then told to go
to various offices in the neighbourhood of the Royal

Exchange, and purchase more shares. To do this £400 in Bank of England notes were handed him, and the wishes of the mysterious Mr. Brank were satisfactorily effected. These scenes were continually enacted. Notes to a large amount were thus circulated; lottery-tickets purchased; and Mr. Brank, always in a coach, with his face studiously concealed, ready on the spot to receive them. The surprise of the servant was somewhat excited; but had he known that from the period he left his master to purchase the tickets, one female figure accompanied all his movements; that when he entered the offices, it waited at the door, peered cautiously in at the window, hovered around him like a second shadow, watched him carefully, and never left him until once more he was in the company of his employer, that surprise would have been greatly increased. Again and again were these extraordinary scenes rehearsed; again and again were lottery tickets procured; and again and again was the servant allowed only to see the patched side of his master's face. At last the Bank obtained a clue, and the servant was taken into custody, his simple statement disregarded, and his person incarcerated. The directors imagined that at last they had secured the actor in so many parts; that the flood of forged notes which had inundated the establishment would cease. Their hopes proved fallacious, and it was found that " old Patch " had been sufficiently clever to baffle the Bank directors

The house in Titchfield street was searched ; but Mr. Brank had deserted it. The servant was discharged from custody with a present of £20 ; the advertisements re-appeared ; rewards were again freely offered ; but in vain. The extraordinary Mr. Brank remained as inaccessible as ever, and the forgeries as usual became more plentiful about the period of the lotteries. But the mind of this man—a master in the art of crime—invented a new method of fraud. In 1785, the public prints report the following. " On the 17th of December, £10 was paid into the Bank, for which the clerk, as usual, gave a ticket to receive a Bank note of equal value. This ticket ought to have been carried immediately to the cashier, instead of which the bearer took it home, and curiously added an 0 to the original sum, and returning, presented it so altered to the cashier, for which he received a note of £100. In the evening, the clerks found a deficiency in the accounts ; and on examining the tickets of the day, not only that but two others were discovered to have been obtained in the same manner. In the one, the figure 1 was altered to 4, and in another to 5, by which the artist received, upon the whole, near £1000." The contriver of this ingenious fraud proved to be the same individual who had so long baffled the police ; but in a short time his career was closed. One of the notes, given in pledge for costly articles of plate, with which he graced expensive entertainments, was traced to the silversmith, and after innumerable names, innumerable lodgings, and innumerable disguises, the end of Charles Price was fast approaching. With great ingenuity he procured the destruction of his implements, through the agency of his mistress, notwithstanding the acuteness of the police. The assurance of this man in the safety of his transformations had been complete. It has been seen that his accomplice in crime watched the person he employed, while Price was waiting close to the spot. Had any suspicious appearance occurred at the lottery-office, she would immediately have given a signal to Price, who would have torn off his dress as old Patch, and appeared in his own character. He seems to have been thoroughly known as "Patch," (from the covering over his eye,) but his identity with Price, the lottery-office keeper and stock-jobber, was not suspected. His end was worthy his life. He employed his son to procure the necessary implements of destruction; and on the following morning he was found hanging. A jury sate upon the body, on which the old barbaric custom was enacted; and midnight witnessed the lonely cross-road receive the remains of the forger.

The desire of the directors to discover the makers of forged notes, produced a considerable amount of anxiety to one whose name is indelibly associated with British art. George Morland—a name rarely mentioned but with feelings of admiration and regret—had, in his eagerness to avoid incarceration for debt, retired to an obscure hiding-place, in the suburbs of London. The description of Allan Cunningham is vivid. " On one occasion," says this biographer, " he hid himself in Hackney; where his anxious looks and secluded manner of life induced some of his charitable neighbours to believe him a maker of forged notes. The directors of the Bank despatched two of their most dexterous emissaries to enquire, reconnoitre, search, and seize. The men arrived, and began to draw lines of circumvallation round the painter's retreat; he was not, however, to be surprised; mistaking those agents of evil mien for bailiffs, he escaped from behind as they approached in front, fled into Hoxton, and never halted till he had hid himself in London. Nothing was found to justify suspicion; and when Mrs. Morland, who was his companion in this retreat, told them who her husband was, and showed them some unfinished pictures, they made such a report at the Bank, that the directors presented him with a couple of Bank notes of twenty pounds each, by way of compensation for the alarm they had given him."

CHAPTER XI.

LEGAL OPINION—ABOLITION OF TALLIES—FORGERY—EXTENSION OF THE CHARTER—OPINIONS OF LORD NORTH—INCREASE OF CAPITAL—LEGAL DECISION CONCERNING FORGED NOTES—STAMP DUTIES—NATIONAL DEBT—CURIOUS ANECDOTES—FRAUD AND FORGERY—UNCLAIMED DIVIDENDS—DISTRESS OF 1793—ISSUE OF EXCHEQUER BILLS—LOYALTY LOAN.

UP to the year 1780, Bank stock was transferred to legatees without the interposition of executors. The opinion of Lord Eldon seems undecided as to the justice of altering this arrangement. "I have always doubted," he said, "whether the legislature, who meant to give a peculiar value to stock in the life of the party, did not also mean that he should have the power of devising it; and that it should go to the devisee, not through the executor or administrator, but by the effect of the devise; and that it should go to the executor or administrator only in fault of the devise directed by the statute." It is now settled that it passes to the executor, the assent of whom is necessary before the legatee can receive.

In 1783 an act was passed which arranged for the

abolition of tallies. The word has been so often used, that the following description may not prove uninteresting. " A tally is a cleft piece of wood, used to score an account upon by notches, and was given at the Exchequer to those who pay money there upon loans. Another part was called the counterfoil, or counter-stock, and was kept by an officer of the Exchequer. The first contractors were authorised to transfer their interest by endorsements on these tallies, and the endorsements were entered in the Bank books. The entries in the books were only to inform the government to whom the dividends were payable, the right of these persons depending on the tally." The act passed in 1783 abolished tallies for a better method of transacting business, and they are now only known by tradition.

The notes of a banking establishment are always liable to imitation; and as the paper of a national bank circulates as freely as coin, it is not surprising that men of desperate hopes have successfully attempted to gain by fraud that which they were denied by fortune. From time to time the public records bear testimony to this; and so numerous did the forgeries become, that it will be only the more important or the more curious with which the patience of the reader will be tried.

John Mathison was a man of great mechanical capacity, who, becoming acquainted with an engraver, unhappily acquired that art which ultimately proved his ruin. A yet more dangerous qualification was his of imitating signatures with inconceivable accuracy. Tempted by the hope of sudden wealth, his first forgeries were the notes of the Darlington bank. This fraud was soon discovered ; and a reward being offered, with a description of his person, he escaped to Scotland. There, scorning to let his talents lie idle, he counterfeited the notes of the Royal Bank of Edinburgh, amused himself by negotiating them during a pleasure excursion through the country, and reached London, supported by his imitative talent. Here a fine sphere opened for his genius, which was so active, that in twelve days he had bought the copper, engraved it, fabricated notes, forged the water mark, printed, and negotiated several. When he had a sufficient number, he travelled from one end of the kingdom to the other, disposing of them. Having been in the habit of procuring notes from the Bank, (the more accurately to copy them,) he chanced to be there when a clerk from the Excise-office paid in 7000 guineas, one of which was scrupled. Mathison, from a distance, said it was a good one. " Then," said the Bank clerk, on the trial, " I recollected him." The frequent visits of Mathison, who was very incautious, together with other circumstances, created some suspicion that he might be connected with those notes, which, since his first appearance, had been presented at the Bank. On another occasion, when Mathison was there, a forged note of his own was presented, and the teller, half in jest and half in earnest, charged Maxwell, the name by which he was known, with some knowledge of the forgeries. Further suspicion was excited ; and directions were given to detain him at some future period. The following day, the teller was informed that " his friend Maxwell," as he was styled ironically, was in Cornhill. The clerk instantly went ; and under the pretence of having paid Mathison a guinea too much on a previous occasion, and of losing his situation if the mistake were not rectified by the books, induced him to return with him to the Hall ; from which place he was taken before the directors, and afterwards to Sir John Fielding. To all the enquiries he replied, " He had a reason for declining to answer. He was a citizen of the world, and knew not how he had come into it, or how he should go out of it." Being detained during a consultation with the Bank solicitor, he suddenly lifted up the sash, and jumped out of the window. On being taken and asked his motive, if innocent, he said " it was his humour."

In the progress of the enquiry, the Darlington paper, containing his description, was read to him, when he turned pale, burst into tears, and saying he was a dead man, added, "now I will confess all." He was, indeed, found guilty only on his own acknowledgment, which stated he could accomplish the whole of a note in one day. It was asserted at the time, that. had it not been for this confession, he could not have been convicted. He offered to explain the secret of his discovery of the water mark, provided the Corporation would spare his life; but his proposal was rejected, and he paid the penalty of his crime.

The charter of the Company, being within five years of its expiration, was discussed in 1781. The experience of years had proved that the renewal of the privileges was only to be obtained by payment. The ministry of 1781 were not likely to be less urgent than their predecessors. The position of Great Britain, also, was somewhat precarious. Mr. Alison says of the period: "French diplomacy acquired the lead in Europe: the dreams of the philosopher were exchanged for the skilful combinations of experienced statesmen: Russia, Sweden, Denmark, were united in a hostile league; America, Spain, and France, in an armed confederacy against Great Britain: the combined fleets rode triumphant in the British Channel; and, however strange it may sound to modern ears, it is historically true, that England was more nearly subdued by the wisdom of Louis XVI. and the talent of Vergennes, than by the genius of Napoleon and the address of Talleyrand." To maintain such a war, money was absolutely necessary; and once more the authorities were called on to bargain with a necessitous State. The first charter had been expressly granted by William, in return for the loan of £1,200,000. On its extension, in 1697, no payment was asked in return. The services of the Bank were felt because they were novel; and they were acknowledged because they were felt. The great financier of that day, Mr. Montesquieu, with the "wise Lord Godolphin," were, in the first flush of gratitude, sufficiently honest to enunciate a principle, which they were equally honest to act upon. They, with other great men of the day, declared in 1696, "that the establishment and prosperity of the Bank were so much a national benefit, that they were of opinion, that *no fine ought to be expected for a renewal*, but that the Company should always be supported and cherished by the public." The Directors had learned by experience, however, that statesmen's views, like lover's vows, are mutable. The terms they proposed for an extension of the charter, for twenty-five years, were a loan of two millions for three years, at three per cent. Vehement opposition was the result. Some objected to the amount of payment; others resisted the principle of a renewal. It is, indeed, surprising, that so moderate an offer was accepted. The remarks of Lord North, however, betray how much the money was required. "I propose to pay off two millions of Navy debt with the two millions now offered; a debt which has ever hung like a millstone round the neck of public credit." The whole of this speech is worth recording, for it marks in strong and energetic language, the opinion which this statesman entertained of the services of the

Corporation. "The Bank, by prudent management, by judicious conduct, wise plans, and punctuality in establishing its credit, had contributed very essentially to promote national credit; a matter equally advantageous to this country at home and abroad. It might be said by some, if the present Banking Company will not give more, institute a new company. They knew not the solid advantages resulting to the public from its connexion with the present company. They were not aware of the dreadful consequences that might attend the attempt to incorporate a new one. And were it possible, how materially might the national credit be affected from many years elapsing before a new company could establish its character and credit in so eminent a degree as the present Bank. So dreadful would be the consequence of breaking up the present Bank, that he hoped never to hear of a new company. From being the Banker of the public, the Bank undoubtedly derived advantages : but the public derived advantages equally considerable from the important accommodation which the Bank afforded. It had given him great satisfaction to hear, that, in consequence of the bargain being in agitation, not a Navy bill was to be bought ; if so, it had already produced one great effect."

Sir George Saville said, that " the noble Lord had spoken of the connection between the public and the Bank, as if he had been describing conjugal love, and enlarging upon the affection of a man and his wife.

He desired to know if the public were about to take a new wife; whether it was fair to say, your great grandfather married the great grandmother of the young lady without a fortune; your grandfather also married her grandmother without a fortune; your father married her mother with a small fortune; and therefore you ought to marry the daughter with a very trifling increase of portion? It was much fairer for the public to say, ' Aye, indeed, were my ancestors so improvident? I will not copy their example. The young lady's father is grown rich, he can afford to give his daughter a good fortune, and a good fortune I will have, or I will not marry the young lady.' "

Mr. Ewer, Governor of the Bank, declared that the proposition of the directors was such as he could meet on public ground. He thought the Bank offered fairly and handsomely, when they tendered the public a loan of two millions, at three per cent. interest, for three years.

After some further debates the proposals of the Bank were accepted; and the bill renewing the charter for twenty-six years passed into a law.

In 1781 a general court was held at the Bank to inform the proprietors that Government had consented to renew the charter on the terms stated; and in the same year the proprietors held a general meeting to determine the question of increasing the dividend from $5\frac{1}{2}$ to 6 per cent. It may be assumed that this was against the wishes of the directors, as it was carried by ballot. On the following day they met to confirm the vote, and to make a call of 8 per cent. on the capital, which was thus increased to £11,642,400. A new question arose this year, and was tried by a special jury before Lord Mansfield. From the period of the first forgery the paper of the Bank of England had been abundantly imitated. The legal liability of the directors to cash these notes soon became an important point; and a case was tried in which, though it was proved that the cashiers' names were so artfully copied that it was almost as difficult to own as to deny them, yet, being also proved that the notes for which payment was sought had not been issued by the Bank, a verdict was given which effectually destroyed the hopes of those who held them. It appears strange that any one could be found to press such a claim. We believe that the directors of the Bank of Austria pay without demur the notes forged in imitation of those issued by them. But this must be a question of policy, and not of justice, as it is impossible to contend that the managers of any bank should pay notes which are formed out of their establishment, which do not bear the signatures of their officers, and for which they have received no consideration.

An act for enlarging the Stamp duties was passed in June, 1783. By this the notes and bills of the Bank were exempted from its operation, in consequence of the company engaging to pay £12,000

yearly for the privilege ; the government allowance
of £562 10s. per million, for managing the national
debt, was reduced to £450. Of this, which has
usually been regarded as a moral rather than a
physical weight, a curious estimate was made in
1788. The debt was calculated at 242 millions,
and divided into £10 notes ; 512 of which weighing
one pound, the whole debt amounted to 47,265lbs.

During a great part of 1782, and part of 1784, the
cash and bullion in the Bank were very low. The
drain proceeded from the great extension of commerce which followed the peace ; and so large was
the export of merchandize, that the circulation could
scarcely support it. But it was evident to the
directors that the return of the amount of the
exports would amply compensate for the preceding
diminution. Without therefore consulting the
Ministry, they took the bold step of refusing to
make advances on the loan of 1783. Their judgment proved just. By an alteration in the exchanges
their anxiety was relieved, and the soundness of
the circulation restored.

There are many trifles which an anxious search
into contemporaneous documents has brought before
the writer. A few of these will be given before
proceeding to the most important periods of the
history of the Bank. Some are curious in themselves ; others possess an interest from their allusion
to the times ; and all are more or less in connexion

with an account of the Bank. Thus we read in a magazine of 1796, it was calculated that the average balances of the banking houses, including the Bank of England, amounted to £100,000 each; and that the interest of £11,665,440 on the national debt, was one shilling in the pound on £233,308,800, the annual income of the country.* The following is a curious instance of the "vile use" to which Bank notes may occasionally be placed, from ignorance of their value. A gentleman who had missed his path in Hertford, rode up to a cottage for directions. Here, with an old ballad stuck against a broken window pane, was a bank note for £20. The aged couple to whom it belonged could neither read nor write, and were overjoyed at the money of which they had been in ignorant possession.

The fascinations of fraud must be great. Half the ingenuity which is experienced in deception, or half the talent which persons of damaged reputation employ to gain a living dishonestly, could not fail to win wealth, repute, and the world's applause.

In 1780, a gentleman of eminence in the mercantile world, was grieved by the contents of a letter which he received from a correspondent at Hamburgh, the post-mark of which it bore. From the statement

* Mr. W. Ray Smee, in his pamphlet on the income tax, in 1846, after some elaborate calculations, estimates the present income of Great Britain at 488 millions.

it contained, it appeared that a person most minutely described, had defrauded the writer, under extraordinary circumstances, of £3000. The letter continued to say, information had been obtained that the defrauder—the dress and person of whom it described—was occasionally to be seen on the Dutch Walk of the Royal Exchange. The object of the writer was to induce his correspondent to invite the party to dinner; and by any moral force which could be used, compel him to return the money; adding, that if he should be found amenable to reason, and evince any signs of repentance, he might be dismissed with a friendly caution and five hundred pounds, as he was a near relation of the writer. As the gentleman whose name it bore was a profitable correspondent, the London merchant kept a keen watch on the Dutch Walk, and was at last successful in meeting, and being introduced to the cheat. The invitation to dine was accepted; and the host having previously given notice to his family to quit the table soon after dinner, acquainted his visitor with his knowledge of the fraud. Alarm and horror were depicted in the countenance of the young man, who, with tones apparently tremulous from emotion, begged his disgrace might not be made public. To this the merchant consented provided the £3000 were returned. The visitor sighed deeply; but said that to return all was impossible, as he had unfortunately spent part of the amount. The remainder, however, he proposed to yield instantly, and the notes were handed to the merchant, who, after dilating upon the goodness of the man he had robbed, concluded his moral lesson by handing a cheque for £500 as a proof of his beneficence. The following morning the gentleman went to the banker to deposit the money he had received, when, to his great surprise, he was told that the notes were counterfeit. His next enquiries were concerning the cheque, but that had been cashed shortly after the opening of the bank. He immediately sent an express to his Hamburgh correspondent, who replied that the letter was a forgery; and that no fraud had been committed upon him. The whole affair had been plotted by a gang, some of whom were on the continent, and some in England.

From a pamphlet, published a quarter of a century ago, the following description of the probable origin of country banking is presented.

Banking in the country, like that in the metropolis, first originated among the more opulent and respectable class of traders and merchants. In every town, and in many villages, there existed, prior to what were afterwards termed Banks, some trader, manufacturer, or shopkeeper, who acted, in many respects, as a banker to the neighbourhood. The shopkeeper, for example, being in the habit of drawing bills on London, and of remitting bills there, for the purpose of his own trade, and receiving also much money at his shop, would occasionally give gold to his customers,

taking in return their bills on the metropolis ; which
were mixed with his other bills, and sent to his London correspondent. Persons who were not customers,
being also found to want money for bills, or bills for
money, the shopkeeper was led to charge something
for his trouble, in accommodating them ; and the
trade of taking and drawing bills being thus rendered
profitable, it became an object to increase it. For the
sake of drawing customers to his house, the shopkeeper, having yet, possibly, little or no view to the
issuing of bank notes, printed " the Bank," over his
door, and engraved these words on the checks, on
which he drew his bills.

It may be assumed also to have been common,
before country banks were established, for the principal trader in a town to take at interest some of
the money of his neighbours, on condition, however,
that he should not be required to give it back
without notice. The money thus deposited, or
borrowed by him, might either be thrown into his
trade, or employed in discounting bills soon to
become due ; but the latter would evidently be the
most safe and prudent way of investing it.

The transition from this capacity to that of the
modern country banker is so obvious, that it is not
necessary to trace it through the several grades by
which it was made. It was some time, however,
before the practice of issuing notes payable to bearer
on demand, was adopted, and which only became

general in the interval between the French and American war. The country was then in a state of great prosperity, confidence was high, commerce and trade had gradually extended, the income and expenditure of individuals had augmented, and every branch of the banking business naturally enlarged itself. An increase had been made in the number of London bankers; and some of them took active measures to encourage the formation of small banks in the country, with a view to the benefit expected from a connexion with them.

These new establishments having taken place, various country traders, who had before made use of their own correspondents in London, fell into the practice of transacting their business with the metropolis, through the medium of their country bankers, with whom they kept their cash. The country banker drew largely on a London banker on the account of the country trader, and the London banker was willing to execute the extensive country business which he thus acquired, in consideration of a much lower commission than had before been paid by the several country traders to their separate correspondents in London, who had been, for the most part, London merchants.

Such are the most material facts in the origin and progress of the provincial banks, and the general substitution of a paper for a metallic currency. They naturally grew out of the circumstances of the country, and are an effect of the division of labour, which takes place in every opulent community.

In 1789 an ingenious fraud was perpetrated by Francis Fonton, a clerk in the establishment, one of those men whose real sin is covered by an appearance of sanctity. Having been requested by a friend to purchase £50 stock, Fonton gave him a forged receipt, and induced him, in addition, to sign a transfer for £450, under the idea that it was an acceptance of the £50. He remarked to a friend shortly after his conviction, that "he had taken care of his soul, and did not mind what they did with his body;" which was dealt with according to law.

On the 15th December, 1790, Mr. Pitt made his first attempt upon the dividends of those fund-holders who had allowed them to remain unclaimed. In 1727, the balance of this fund was £43,000: in 1752, £60,000; in 1774, £292,000; in 1776, £314,000; and in 1789, £547,000. In consequence of these accumulations Mr. Pitt proposed to take all, excepting a floating balance of £50,000, to be left in the hands of the Bank. It caused indignation not usual in collective bodies to spread through the bank stock proprietary; courts were held at which the proposition was denounced, counsels, opinions stated, speeches uttered which blended national insecurity with the seizure of the unclaimed dividends, and the destruction of public faith with the invasion of the corporation coffers; and all with that earnest eloquence which is born of invaded rights, or diminished purses. But the measure was introduced into parliament, and the opposition became more energetic. The fine mind of Burke was employed in ridiculing the proposal, and the great Whig leader argued strenuously against its injustice. Meetings of the proprietors were again held, and the conduct of Mr. Pitt reprobated in no measured terms. It was called " so miserable a financial operation that the world would think we were at the end of our resources." A proposal was made by the governor to lend £500,000, without interest, until the unclaimed dividends should be less than £600,000, on condition of an abandonment of the claim. The prescient mind of Mr. Pitt, which saw the improbability of their decrease, induced him to accept the proposal, and thus ended the first attempt upon the unclaimed dividends. It is probable that the Bank proprietors regarded them as the property of the corporation, and this may account for the lively interest excited at the prospect of their removal. The question appears a very simple one. In the absence of a claimant they belonged either to the Bank or to the State: if to the Bank, it must have been by special agreement. As mere paymasters of the Government they could not possess the slightest claim. It was an accumulated fund which belonged to the Government, in the absence of the owner. It is, however, impossible to read the objections raised against the Government, for demanding their own property, without wondering at the party spirit which could warp the clear views of statesmen like Mr. Fox and Mr. Burke, and induce them to oppose a claim, the justice of which was indisputable. In 1791, in consequence of this question being mooted, a list of those persons entitled to unclaimed dividends was first published. It has proved in many cases a benefit of the utmost importance, and should be circulated to the greatest possible extent, as it is probable that at the present moment many creditors of Government are languishing in poverty, from an ignorance of their just claims.

In 1793 an act was passed protecting the Governor and Company from any penalty on account of their having advanced, or advancing in future, any sums of money in payment of bills of exchange, not charged on any branch of the revenue. In the same year the East India Annuities were placed under the management of the Bank; and in the following year the Government of Ireland negociated a loan, with an option to the subscribers of receiving their dividends and transferring their stock in London. The management of such dividends and transfers was undertaken by the directors of the Bank, and the agreement received the sanction of

Parliament. In 1795 the corporation commenced an issue of £5 notes.

During the year 1793, one of those seasons of distress, which occur from time to time, shed a gloom throughout England. A period of peace had produced great apparent prosperity. From the American war to the French revolution, England had enjoyed a state of profound repose. The eminently commercial minds of the people had employed this period in extending the trade, and in seeking fresh employment for the accumulating capital. Building, machinery, and inland navigation, employed part of it; and the augmented business of the country demanded new banks ; which, by the additional facilities they gave to commerce, tended greatly to improve it. For eight or nine years, it had progressively increased; but at the end of 1792, wide commercial misery spread throughout England. " On Tuesday evening, the 19th February, 1793," says Chalmers, "the Bank of England threw out the paper of Lane, Son and Fraser ; and next morning they stopped payment, to the amount of almost a million of money. This great failure involved the fate of several very substantial traders."

Merchants with ample but unavailable funds were compelled to bend before the storm   Bankers of unquestionable solidity ceased payment under the influence of the panic. Every man was suspicious of his neighbour. The value of property seemed annihilated in the doubt and dread of the people. Gloomy apprehensions seized on all; and those who had money preferred rather to hoard than to risk it. The country banks were the greatest sufferers; and the ruin they experienced spread like a plague among the interests which had trusted them. They had pushed their notes eagerly into circulation, and were the chief cause of the great drain of cash from the Bank of England, which exceeded any demand of the kind for more than ten years. Upwards of one hundred country banks failed. Mr. Tooke considers the distress of this period to have been exaggerated; but the failure of so many banks must have involved an incalculable amount of misery.

- Chalmers believes the whole mischief to have arisen from the increased number, and reckless operations, of the country banks, one of which was in nearly every market town. Of these establishments, 204 out of 279 issued what were termed optional notes, payable either in the metropolis or in the country. "They came oftener," he says, "and in greater numbers, to London, than were welcome in the shops of London. These notes became discredited, not only in proportion as the supply was greater than the demand, but as the banks were distant and unknown. The projects and arts by which those notes were pushed into the circle of trade were regarded with a very evil eye by those who, in this management, saw great imprudence in many, and a little fraudulence in some.

When suspicion stalked out to create alarm, and alarm ran about to create panic, more than 300 country banks in England sustained a shock."

The alarm grew so universal, that government were compelled to take notice of the applications made for assistance. The restoration of confidence was an important point : Mr. Pitt, therefore, called a meeting at his private residence, to consider the propriety of a parliamentary advance of exchequer bills, on sufficient security, to those persons by whom the pressure of the times was felt. Various opinions were broached ; and, after a lengthened discussion, it was resolved, that a meeting should be held at the Mansion house, to consider the plan proposed by the minister. Here another discussion ensued, which ended in the unanimous adoption of a resolution, "that the interposition of parliament was necessary, and that an issue of exchequer bills was the best practical remedy."

The position of trade at this juncture was unquestionably critical. The discredit of the country paper had produced a deficiency of the circulating medium, and mercantile transactions were greatly impeded by it. The bankers, anxious to retain their own credit immaculate, kept larger sums in their possession than was necessary, so that a considerable part of the circulation was withdrawn ; and those merchants who required discounts on long-dated bills, found a difficulty in procuring them. Houses, with sufficient securities to meet all their creditors, and probably leave an overplus of hundreds of thousands, were compelled to suspend payment. Manufacturers could neither dispose of their goods nor raise money on them. The two great chartered banks of Scotland felt the difficulty. Those of Glasgow, Paisley, and Greenock had ceased to discount to any extent, as their notes were returned for gold, and their power crippled. On these, and similar grounds, a committee recommended that five millions should be advanced in Exchequer bills, on security approved of by the commissioners, or on the deposit of goods of double the value of the sums advanced. The effect of this measure was immediate and universal. The capitalists, who had held back when help was required, came forward directly government proffered its assistance. " The very first intimation of the intention of the legislature," says Macpherson, " to support the merchants, operated all over the country like a charm, and in a great degree superseded the necessity of the relief, by an almost instantaneous restoration of mercantile confidence." Out of the five millions voted, only £2,202,200 were advanced, which was all ultimately repaid; and though two hundred and thirty-eight persons were assisted, only two became bankrupt. By the end of the year, confidence was restored, and the facilities for raising money were as usual. A drain upon the gold of the Bank, arising from these causes, commenced in June, 1792, and lasted till the following March. The Bank increased their discounts ; and the amount of cash and bullion gradually arose until it reached the amount from which it had commenced declining.

A writer of the present century, now no more, but one whose losses in American securities were a great gain to literature, wrote with his unequalled pen, " The warlike power of every country depends on their three per cents. If Cæsar were to reappear on earth, Wettenhall's list would be more important than his " Commentaries ;" Rothschild would open and shut the Temple of Janus ; Thomas Baring, or Bates, would probably command the tenth legion; and the soldiers would march to battle with loud cries of scrip and omnium, reduced, consols, and Cæsar." The following fact is some testimony of the truth of these remarks of the witty Canon of St. Paul's. In 1796, the wealth of England was demonstrated in an extraordinary degree. The correspondence of Lord Malmesbury has proved that Mr. Pitt was always willing to enter into a negociation for peace. The French directory, however, fancying that the riches of England were evaporating, were reluctant to come to terms. The belief spread throughout the country that this arose from an opinion that the resources of England ·were nearly exhausted, and Mr. Pitt determined to avail himself of the feeling, by demanding a loan of £18,000,000. The following were the terms proposed : " Every person subscribing £100 to receive £112 in five per cent. stock, to be unredeem-

able unless with the consent of the owner, until the
expiration of three years after the present five per
cents. shall have been redeemed, but with the option
of the holder to be paid at par, at any shorter period,
not less than two years from the conclusion of the
definitive treaty of peace." On the first day of December the subscription opened. The Bank subscribed
one million, and each of the directors £400,000.
The first day saw five millions subscribed, and in
the second the subscription reached nearly twelve
millions. The anxiety continued on the third; and
on the following Monday, the names received from
the country were added before the opening of the
doors, when, so great was the crowd, that numbers
could not get near the books, but called out to their
more fortunate brethren to enter their names. In
an hour and twenty minutes the subscription was
filled. " So great and so general," says Mr. Weir,
" was the desire to subscribe, that the room was a
scene of the utmost confusion. Persons continued to
come long afterwards; and a vast number of orders
were sent by post, which were too late to be executed.
It is a curious fact that the subscription for this
enormous sum was completed in fifteen hours and
twenty minutes. The loan, from the stimulus of
national excitement under which it was raised, was
called " the Loyalty Loan."

CHAPTER XII.

A HISTORY of the cessation of cash payments, in 1797, would be incomplete without a sketch of the political events which tended to produce it. Thirty years of peace, thirty years of social, moral, and physical progress, have enabled the present generation to judge calmly of the events of half a century ago.

Up to the year 1789, the spirit of the times was monarchical. The existing European dynasties possessed great, and, in many instances, irresponsible power. That power was wielded harshly. The great lesson had yet to be learned, that the real strength of a king is the love of his people. In that year, the upheavings of the moral earthquake, which was to create a change in all the institutions of Europe, were felt in Paris. At first, a generous love of liberty pervaded the nation; and the inhabitants of England

sympathised with their neighbours. But anarchy
succeeded to revolution; the capital was convulsed;
the reign of terror followed; and they who had been
loudest in their applause, were the most rapid in their
recantation. "Even in its first hours it showed a
thirst for slaughter," says Dr. Croly, "which stamped
its nature. The acclamations of Europe, which, struck
with its sudden vigour, its lofty protestations, and the
bold rapidity of its strides over the wrecks of feu-
dalism, had followed its early progress, soon died
away; men could not wade after it so deep in gore.
Still it rushed on, flinging aside at every step some
portion of that jesuitical mask which it first wore;
hourly rending away, with a more contemptuous hand,
some fragment of those ties which allied it to the
common families of nations; until at length it scaled
the steps of the throne, tore down its unfortunate
possessor, and, with the guillotine for its footstool,
and the populace for its ministers, seated itself in full
supremacy of ruin."

England, with the English nation, felt the shock;
a desire for political change spread throughout the
country. But the people witnessed the thirst for
blood which seized their neighbours, and the sound
English heart recoiled from the horrors of the guillotine, from the barbarities of the convention, and
from the reign of terror. The powers of the Continent were stricken with alarm, and united to quench
the democratic fury of the republic. But the energy

of the French citizens pervaded the soldiery; and they sent the invaders in confusion from the soil of France. From this period a fierce and expensive war shook Europe to her centre ; and England bore the burthen. In six months, William Pitt concluded seven treaties, and six subsidies ; and France saw her territories invaded by three hundred and fifty thousand of the most warlike troops in Europe. But the pressure fell fearfully upon the people of Great Britain. The national debt was doubled ; the national taxes were increased ; the national industry was checked ; and, more dangerous than all, national credit was difficult to maintain. Gold grew scarce throughout the country ; bullion fled from the Bank coffers ; and the Corporation, urged by William Pitt, strained credit, means, and almost character, to support the government of which he was the leader. It was, indeed, a question of national existence. A dishonourable peace might have been obtained ; but no true Englishman thought of that. It was a question also of existence for the Bank, whose life was bound up with that of the state.

It is not too much to say that the Bank Directors were the support of the country's credit. Bills for which no forethought of the ministry could provide, were met by them. Sudden emergencies of the state were never disregarded by them. The credit of the treasury was maintained ; the army and the navy were supported by them. They acted as generous bankers to the government ; and bore the displeasure of their proprietary, to whom, had they been disposed to be selfish, they might have pointed, while they exclaimed, " We do perceive here a divided duty." They were the nerves and sinews of the state.

This is no overcharged picture, drawn by a partial testimony. The evidence of the bankers, and other great men of the city, vouch for it. The letters of William Pitt verify it. The censure of some of the proprietary, who shortsightedly preferred a large dividend, to the salvation of their country, proves it.

But the Court of Directors were not passive tools. Because no remonstrances appeared, it is not to be concluded that none were made. On the 15th January, 1795, two years before the cessation of cash payments, they came to a resolution, to inform the Chancellor of the Exchequer, " it was their wish that he would settle his arrangements for the present year, so as not to depend on any further assistance from them : and that the stipulation for the future advances for payment of Treasury bills of Exchange, be strictly adhered to, as they could not allow it to exceed £500,000." On 16th April, the Governor and Deputy-Governor, were requested by the Court "to wait on the Chancellor of the Exchequer, and express their uneasiness at being in advance for so long a period, of from one and a half to two millions on the Treasury bills." It was added, " The court cannot allow any disbursement, exceeding £500,000 ; and

they request the Chancellor of the Exchequer to order
the same to be paid." On the 5th of June, a note
from the Governor and Deputy Governor informed
Mr. Pitt, that though he had promised the advance on
the Treasury bills should not exceed £500,000, yet
they were in advance on them £1,210,015; that by
next week it would be £168,467 ; and they hoped he
would give directions in future to prevent it." On
the 30th July, it was resolved, " That the Governor
and Deputy-Governor request the Chancellor of the
Exchequer to adopt some other mode of paying the
Treasury bills ; and that the court is determined to
order their cashiers to refuse payment of all bills
whenever the advance shall amount to £500,000."

The only reply from Mr. Pitt was a request for
a further accommodation, on the credit of the
consolidated fund, which the court refused to
sanction until they had received satisfaction on the
topic of the treasury bills, and requested Mr. Pitt
to enter into a full explanation on this subject,
which was not even touched upon in his letter.
This resolution being communicated, Mr. Pitt wrote
to the Governor and Deputy-Governor, on the 12th
August, that "they might depend upon measures
being immediately taken for the payment of one
million, and a further payment to the amount of
one million, being made in September, October,
and November, in such proportions as might be
found convenient. But, as fresh bills might arrive,

he was under the necessity of requesting a latitude
to an amount not exceeding one million." About
the same period the Court "desired the Governor
and Deputy-Governor would express their earnest
desire that some other means might be adopted for
the future payment of bills of exchange drawn on
the treasury." On the 8th of October, Mr. Pitt
was desired to reimburse the Bank one million,
conformably to his agreement, together with two
millions and a half lent him on the consolidated
fund. On the 23rd October the Governor mentioned to the Chancellor that he had heard there
might be annexed to a proposed loan, one of
£1,400,000 to the Emperor of Germany. Mr. Pitt
replied that he had not at present the most distant
idea of it. The Governor said "he received the
answer with pleasure, thinking as he did that
another loan of that sort would go nigh to ruin
the country." The Governor also acquainted Mr.
Pitt that there was a drain on the cash, which
was likely to continue while the bills from abroad
were drawn on the treasury.

There is no servility in these communications.
They are such as any honourable body, jealous of
its own credit, and desirous of the country's reputation, could not fail to make. But their appeals
grew more serious. On the 18th November "the
Governor informed Mr. Pitt that gold was £4 2s.
per ounce, that the daily large drains of specie

from the Bank filled the minds of the directors with serious apprehensions, and that he must not rely on any aid from them." In a communication of 20th November, the Governor repeated to Mr. Pitt the "absolute determination of the Court to have the advance on the treasury bills quite cleared off," and that it would be utterly out of the power of the Court to make the advance on the vote of credit. On the 28th January, 1796, the Governor informed the Court that £201,000 treasury bills would fall due for payment at the Bank, on 3rd February, and that the sum now in advance was £1,157,000. The Court came to the bold resolution "That the Governor give directions to the cashiers not to advance any money for the payment of these bills, nor to discharge any part of the same; unless money shall be sent for the same."

To this resolution the directors adhered, and for once the Chancellor of the Exchequer, after dwelling on the great inconvenience it would cause him, said, "he would arrange his affairs so as to provide the money in time for the payment of the treasury bills." Compulsion like this was not very pleasing to the "heaven-born Minister;" and on 12th February, 1796, Mr. Pitt made the following ominous remark, in reply to a communication from the Governor: "It lay with the Court of Directors to judge whether they chose to accommodate the public or not."

About the commencement of this year it was

proposed to raise a loan in Germany, for the Emperor, to be assisted by a guarantee from the English parliament. It was soon discovered, however, that the loan might as well be procured in England, as the guarantee would have nearly the same effect as raising it in this country. The directors were alarmed at the prospect of the gold diminishing, and came to the following resolution : " It is the opinion of this Court, that if any farther loan or advance of money to the Emperor, or any other foreign state, should, in the present state of affairs, take place, it will in all probability prove fatal to the Bank of England. The Court of Directors do therefore most earnestly deprecate the adoption of any such measure, and they solemnly protest against any responsibility for the calamitous consequences that may follow thereupon."   On the 20th of July Mr. Pitt wrote a letter to the Governor. The following is an abstract of some of the most marked sentences, and demonstrates the importance attached by Mr. Pitt to the advances for which he asked :

"I shall consider it as a great accommodation." " I am also under the indispensable necessity of expressing my earnest hope that the Court will be induced to make a present advance of £800,000 on the consolidated fund." " I shall also be obliged to request a further advance of £800,000 on the same security in August."   The conclusion is re- markable.   " It gives me much concern to be obliged to apply for an accommodation to so large an extent ; but I cannot too strongly represent how necessary it is for the public service." One week only after this he wrote even more ardently, with a request for assistance, stating, " He felt it an indispensable duty to represent to them in the most earnest manner that it would be impossible to avoid the most serious and distressing embarrassments to the public service," unless his request could be complied with. This appeal was met by the resolution that the " Court do agree to advance, for the service of the public, the sum of eight hundred thousand pounds, on the security of the exchequer bills."

But the almost solemn tone of the letter from Mr. Pitt alarmed the directors, and they resolved " that this Court do expect, that the Chancellor of the Exchequer will give a promise that a new mode of paying the treasury bills shall be adopted immediately on the meeting of parliament, as this Court will not continue discharging them any longer." It was also accompanied by the following memorial : " The Court of Directors of the Bank of England, fully sensible of the alarming and dangerous situation of the public credit of this kingdom, and deeply impressed by the communication made to them by the Right Honourable William Pitt, are very willing and desirous to do every thing in their power to support the national credit; but in complying with the request made them by the Right Honourable

William Pitt, they think they should be wanting in their duty to their proprietors, and to the public, if that compliance was not accompanied with the following most serious and solemn remonstrance, which, for the justification of their Court, they desire may be laid before his Majesty's cabinet:—

"They beg leave to declare, that nothing could induce them, under the present circumstances, to comply with the demand now made upon them, but from the dread that their refusal might be productive of a greater evil; and nothing but the extreme pressure and exigency of the case can in any shape justify them for acceding to the measure; and they apprehend that, in so doing, they render themselves totally incapable of granting any further assistance to government during the remainder of this year; and unable even to make the usual advances on the land and malt for the ensuing year, should those bills be passed before Christmas. They likewise consent to this measure, in a firm reliance that the repeated promises, so frequently made to them, that the advances on the Treasury bills should be completely done away, may be actually fulfilled at the next meeting of Parliament, and the necessary arrangements taken to prevent the same from ever happening again, as they conceive it to be an unconstitutional mode of raising money, what they are not warranted by their charter to consent to, and an advance always extremely inconvenient to themselves."

This important declaration should be remembered. It marks strong good-will on the part of the directors towards the country, which government should always have borne in mind. On 31st January, 1797, the Governor and Deputy-Governor waited on the Chancellor of the Exchequer, to represent to him how uneasy the court were at their large advances, and to require that some effective measure should be immediately taken for the payment. On the 10th February, the Committee, startled at the prospect of a loan of one million and a half for Ireland, a great part of which would be made in specie, resolved to ask a reduction of the following advances to government:

Arrears of advance on Land and Malt, 1794	£337,000
Do. . . . . . . do. . . 1795	491,000
Do. . . . . . . do. . . 1796	2,392,000
Exchequer bills on vote of credit	968,000
Do. on Consolidated fund, 1796	1,323,000
Treasury bills paid	1,674,645
	£7,185,645
Arrears of Interest	400,000
	£7,585,645

This statement was immediately placed before Mr. Pitt, accompanied with a desire that the sums specified might be repaid, or arranged before the settlement of the Irish loan, which was then contemplated. On the 18th of the same month, the governor was requested by the directors to assure Mr. Pitt that this loan " would most probably bring them under the necessity

of shutting up their doors." On the 21st, a minute
of the meeting of the court expressed the conviction
impressed upon them "by the constant calls of
bankers from all parts of the town, for cash, that
there must be some extrordinary reasons for this
drain."

It is impossible to read these communications, and
not remark the assistance afforded to the state,
through a series of years.   That Mr. Pitt was fully
sensible of it, is proved by the proposition he made to
the House, to give bank notes the guarantee of the
national security.   As it was a crisis in the history of
the corporation, caused solely by the advances made
to government, so it could only be removed or reme-
died by the Chancellor of the Exchequer, in his public
character.   It is due to this gentleman to say, that
he did not shrink from the responsibility, but met the
galling fire with which his opponents assailed him
with great gallantry.   The fine rhetoric of Mr. Fox,
the wit and the eloquence of Mr. Sheridan, were all
borne with an equanimity that resulted equally from
the possession of a great mind and a great majority.

While these proceedings were pending, other causes
were also in active operation.   The drain of bullion
continued.   From month to month the Bank found
its stock decreasing.   From month to month the
directors were alarmed by the foreshadow of that
which afterwards overtook them.   Whether the plan
they adopted to avert the difficulty was advisable,

is an open question. In 1795 they began to limit their discounts. On the last day of that year the Court of Directors came to the following resolution, which was ordered to be placed in the discount office :

"Bank of England, 31st December, 1795.

"Pursuant to an order of the Court of Directors, notice is hereby given,

"That no bills will be taken in for discount at this office, after 12 o'clock at noon, or notes after 12 o'clock on Wednesday.

"That in future, whenever the bills sent in for discount shall on any day amount to a larger sum than it shall be resolved to discount on that day, a *pro rata* proportion of such bills in each parcel as are not otherwise objectionable, will be returned to the person sending the same, without regard to the respectability of the party sending in the bills, or the solidity of the bills themselves.

"The same regulations will be observed as to notes."

The diminution of gold; the price of bullion compared with the value of coin; the alarm occasioned by the position of the country, still maintaining its doubtful struggle with an unscrupulous enemy; the expensive operations of the war, which demanded extensive loans, and the subsidies to foreign powers, which carried the gold out of the country; must be accepted as reasons for the diminution of discounts, which preceded the panic of 1797. Many competent persons have been persuaded that the decrease of the circulation from 1795, so far from preventing what is popularly known as a run on the Bank, possessed a contrary tendency. They asserted that, by reducing the requisite issue, and diminishing the general accommodation, a pressing demand for specie was occasioned. This idea is supported by the fact, that, from March, 1792, to June, 1793, there was a drain of cash and bullion considerably larger than in the same period during the crisis ; but instead of lowering, the directors raised the amount of their discounts, and an almost immediate result was an increase of cash and bullion. There was then, however, no distrust in our political relations. The French revolution had not assumed the appearance which, in 1797, shed a gloom over all the continent, nor were Government called upon to subsidize half the powers of Europe, for the sake of checking an universal anarchy. Another cause tended to alarm the people. A man named Thomas Paine possessed a certain degree of unenviable notoriety. In 1796 he wrote an inflammatory pamphlet, termed " The decline and fall of the English system of finance," in which he attempted to prove that the cellars of the Bank of England " could not contain so much as two millions of specie; most probably not more than one million." The following is a part of the reasoning by which he arrived at this false conclusion. After arguing that there could not be more than sixteen millions of gold and silver coin in England, he thus proceeds: "But admitting there be sixteen millions, not more than a fourth part thereof can be in London, when it is considered that every city, town, village, and farm house in the nation must have a part of it; and that all the great manufactories, which most require cash, are out of London. Of this four millions in London every banker, merchant, tradesman, in short every individual, must have some. He must be a poor shopkeeper indeed who has not a few guineas in his till. The quantity of the cash therefore can never, on the evidence of circumstances, be so much as two millions; most probably not more than one million." The same writer then endeavoured to prove that the total amount of bank notes in circulation amounted to sixty millions. These assertions, speciously supported, and put forward at a time when the national anxiety was extreme, produced considerable effect amongst those who required support in their faith in the Bank. It was the small holder of bank notes who most needed encouragement, and it was the small holder to whom this pamphlet was addressed, and who was most particularly affected by it. At the very period when it was pronounced that there was most probably only one million of specie in the Bank, and sixty millions of notes in circulation, it was afterwards proved that the specie was about three, and the circulation only from nine to ten millions. But the mere assertion that sixty millions were circulating, with only one million of cash to meet the payment, must have produced a want of confidence in the people of England, by many of whom the author was regarded as an authority. The public mind, indeed, was altogether agitated. Towards the close of 1796, and the commencement of 1797, fears of an invasion were very prevalent. Rumours of descent on various parts of the coast were freely propagated. The public were in so feverish a state that they were inclined to believe all they heard, and those possessed of public securities became anxious to receive gold in exchange. The occasion was a pressing one. The position of the directors was most responsible. The well-being of the commercial state was at issue. The drain of cash continued, and the dwindling coffers were difficult to replenish. In March, 1796, the stock of bullion was £2,972,000. By June it had fallen to £2,582,000. In September it lowered to £2,532,000. In December it was £2,508,000 ; and on 25th February, 1797, it had fallen to £1,272,000.

Thus diminished and diminishing the directors had but one course to pursue. The government, which had reduced their means, was alone capable of supplying a remedy. The Chancellor of the Exchequer was, therefore, made acquainted with their present position, and with their fears for the future ; and to his judgment was left the proposal of a plan to obviate the evil. It does not appear that any proposition was made by the Bank directors, but that their danger was simply placed before him. On the 24th of February the deputy governor, with one of the directors, waited on him, to ask how long the Bank might venture to pay cash before he would think it necessary to interfere. Mr. Pitt replied that it was a matter of great importance, and that he must be prepared with some resolution to bring before the council, for a proclamation to stop cash payments at the Bank. At the same time, he added, it would be necessary to appoint a committee of enquiry into their affairs. No objection was offered to this proposition. On the contrary, it was intimated that every assistance would be rendered.

In addition to foreign force, domestic treachery was justifiably feared. Corresponding societies, Friends of the People, and Jacobin societies, were spreading a poison and a pestilence through the minds of the nation. It was well know that a number of discontented men would gladly hail the appearance of a French fleet off the English coast. Ireland was approaching an open insurrection. Disaffection had seized upon our seamen. The Nore witnessed an open mutiny. The only defence from invasion appeared to fail the country ; and men knew not where the evil would pause, or how far the seeds of treason were spread, when that navy, which was familiarly and affectionately termed "the wooden wall of Old England," forsook the nation in its dark and perilous hour.

The fire-side of the yeoman heard these things; and a vague oppressive terror agitated the beautiful homesteads of England. The difficulties of the great London Bank, the dissatisfaction of the metropolis, the fear of invasion, the disaffection at the Nore, were exaggerated in journals and reported in villages, and a feverish desire to hoard manifested itself. The small tradesman took his notes to the banker, and kept the specie in his house, until the aspect of the times was determined. The cottager heard the report, caught the infection, and followed the example. The country banker grew anxious; and sent for gold rather in proportion to his fears than his necessities. The London banker applied to the Bank of England upon the same principle; and thus the gold of the Corporation became unnecessarily decreased. The inhabitants of the remote parts of the empire are always prone to needless alarm. Their information is more vague, their judgment less cultivated; they are more easily acted on by reports than the dwellers in large cities; and thus a great portion of the notes were presented through the groundless fears of an ignorant impulse.

CHAPTER XIII.

ORDER IN COUNCIL—SUSPENSION OF CASH PAYMENT—MEETING OF THE MERCHANTS—PARLIAMENTARY DEBATES—ISSUE OF DOLLARS—ENLARGED DISCOUNTS REQUIRED—THE RESTRICTION ACT PASSED—ISSUE OF ONE AND TWO POUND NOTES—BANK OF FRANCE—THE REST—RENEWAL OF THE CHARTER—OPINION OF MR. PITT AND OTHER MINISTERS.

THE evening of Saturday, the 24th February, 1797, was a gloomy period for most of the merchants and traders of London. More than all must the directors of the Bank have felt their important and responsible position. They had seen during the week a heavy demand made on their diminished cash. They had marked their small stock of bullion decreasing day after day. They had witnessed and participated in the dismay which preyed upon the people. They knew that the demand would continue unless some method could be adopted to check it; and they felt that the period had arrived when, for the first time in their history, they must altogether cease payment of their notes; for the first time since 1697 they must fail in meeting the demands of their creditors. On the following day, Sunday, a cabinet council was held at Whitehall ; and it is said that the only occasion on which the monarch violated the sabbath was this great one. He attended the council at this important crisis ; and the presence of royalty gave a high sanction to the proceedings. Immediately after the meeting, the members of the government met the governor, deputy governor, Mr. Thornton, and Mr. Bosanquet in Downing Street, to inform them of the result of their deliberation, when the following resolution was communicated.

At the Council Chamber, Whitehall, Feb. 26, 1797.

By the Lords of his Majesty's most honourable Privy Council.

" Upon the representation of the Chancellor of the Exchequer, stating that, from the result of the information which he has received, and the enquiries which it has been his duty to make, respecting the effect of the unusual demands for specie that have been made upon the metropolis, in consequence of ill-founded or exaggerated alarms in different parts of the country, it appears, that unless some measure is immediately taken, there may be reason to apprehend a want of sufficient supply of cash to answer the exigencies of the public service, it is the unanimous opinion of the Board, that it is indispensably necessary for the public service that the directors of the Bank of England should forbear issuing any cash in payment, until the sense of Parliament can be taken on that subject, and the proper measures adopted thereupon for maintaining the means of circulation, and supporting the public and commercial credit of the kingdom at this important conjuncture; and it is ordered that a copy of this minute be transmitted to the directors of the Bank of England; and they are hereby required, on the grounds of the exigency of the case, to conform thereto, until the sense of parliament can be taken, as aforesaid."

On Monday morning, the 27th of February, at the earliest period of commencing business, the office was crowded. Bullion was vociferously demanded. The notes of the Bank were eagerly proffered in exchange for gold. The notice of the previous day was placed conspicuously in the hall; but men will not easily see that to which it is their interest to be blind. Officers were in waiting to repress any indecent ebullition of feeling. Copies of the order in council were distributed; and the announcement of the suspension of specie payments, passed off as quietly as its nature would allow. To pacify the natural alarm, the following notice was freely circulated, and advertised in all the daily papers.

"Bank of England, February 27th, 1797.

"The Governor, Deputy-Governor, and Directors of the Bank of England, think it their duty to inform the proprietors of Bank stock, as well as the public at large, that the general concerns of the Bank are in the most affluent and prosperous situation, and such as to preclude every doubt as to the security of its notes. The Directors mean to continue their usual discounts for the accommodation of the commercial interest, paying the amount in bank notes; and the dividend warrants will be paid in the same manner."

The rumour that the Bank had stopped payment spread throughout London. Those persons who were unacquainted with business looked upon it as tending to universal ruin. The better informed saw the importance of the proceeding; and with them there was every effort made to support the credit of the Corporation.

Notwithstanding the terror which possessed the less instructed portion of the community; notwithstanding the severe language which Mr. Fox used in the house, when he said that " the measure had destroyed the credit of the Bank," that for the " first time since the revolution, an act was done which struck at the foundation of the public credit by seizing the money belonging to individuals;" notwithstanding his triumphant question of " What can restore that public credit? " it appeared as if, now that the blow was struck, a feeling of security was produced, which the mercantile community had long required. For, notwithstanding these things, notwithstanding even the oratory of Mr. Sheridan, of which the Chancellor of the Exchequer remarked, " it would be atrocious arrogance in him to attempt to answer what it would be unpardonable arrogance to attempt to understand;"

a great authority of that day, Mr. Henry Thornton, said before a committee of the House of Commons, "I conceive the distress for sometime preceding, and especially for two days before, to have been so great, that the relief given by the discounts on the Monday more than compensated, in the minds of most of the mercantile world, for any alarm occasioned by the stoppage." Throughout the evidence of this gentleman, the conviction that the Bank should have increased its circulation instead of diminishing it was constantly expressed. The question yet remains unsettled. On the day succeeding the suspension, the discounts were augmented; and the feeling of security which has already been mentioned confirms the opinion of Mr. Thornton.

A meeting of the merchants was promptly called; and, on the 27th of February, they proved their desire to support the credit of the Bank by voting the following:

"Resolved unanimously,—that we, the undersigned, being highly sensible how necessary the preservation is of public credit at this time, do most readily hereby declare, that we will not refuse to receive bank notes in payment of any sum of money to be paid to us; and we will use our utmost endeavours to make all our payments in the same manner. The "Gentleman's Magazine," speaking of the above, says, "We never remember to have witnessed a more loyal meeting;" four thousand of the best names in the city were soon attached to this resolution. On the following day, a paper, nearly similar, which was published by the Lords of the Privy Council, tended greatly to relieve the public mind ; and confidence, to some extent, was restored.

On the 25th of February, the discounts were reduced to one-fourth of the sum at which they stood in the beginning of the year ; and the decreased accommodation of the Bank compelled a similar decrease in the discounts of the private banker. This joint restriction, at the very crisis when an increase was desirable, tended to augment, if not to produce, the demand for cash. The advances made to Mr. Pitt, were specially asserted by the Governor to have originated the embarrassments. The voluminous correspondence, which has been abridged, amply proves that it was of the utmost importance for the bank directors to be relieved from the incessant claims of the Chancellor ; the urgent tone of their letters, and the earnest personal appeals of their representatives, are only to be equalled by the demands of Mr. Pitt. But the energy of his applications to the loyalty of the directors, almost demonstrates that the continuance of their advances was imperatively required for the safety of the commonwealth. Many of the practical men, besides Mr. Thornton, summoned before the Committee of the House of Commons, considered the great diminution of discounts as the cause of the run upon gold ; and thus, indirectly, blamed the policy of the Bank. It must be remembered that the directors were in a critical position. An embarrassed Government urged them to make advances for the safety of the country. Extensive mercantile operations demanded extensive discounts. To meet both demands, was, in their opinion, imprudent. Every reason which could operate tended to the former. The extracts from the correspondence with the Chancellor of the Exchequer, prove that it was no servile wish to court a powerful friend, but a positive necessity, wrung from them by the pressure of the application.

In the evidence before the secret committee, Mr. Walter Boyd says: "I attribute the drain chiefly to that line of conduct which, I believe, the directors of the Bank have pursued since the month of December, 1795, when they announced to the public, by an advertisement, certain changes in the quantity and manner of conducting their business of discount." "The diminution of discounts has diminished the powers of commercial houses, and diminished the value of public securities." Mr. Henry Thornton remarked, "It was the want of Bank notes, and not of guineas, that had been felt, and no anxiety seemed to be entertained in the city if Bank notes were brought into circulation, respecting the manner of contriving to effect the smaller payments." On another occasion this gentleman expressed his conviction, that, if the quantity of Bank notes had remained as they were, or without any material alteration, the inconvenience would have resulted, though in a less degree, as the increased transactions of commerce required an increased circulation. This gentleman also stated that an enlarged number of notes, proportioned to the occasion for them, would prevent a demand for guineas; but if fewer notes were issued than the mercantile world required, it would occasion a demand for gold.

The measure had now to be justified and reported to the House of Commons. On the evening of the day that this announcement was issued to the public, Mr. Pitt brought down a message from his Majesty, to the " experienced wisdom and firmness of his parliament." At the same time he announced his conviction that the resources of the Bank were most abundant, and proposed, as an aid to public faith, to give the security of the state to its engagements. The rhetoric of Mr. Fox, and the oratory of Mr. Sheridan, were employed to reprobate the course of the ministry: but rhetoric and oratory are feeble assailants when truth and justice are opposed to them. On the following day the message was taken into consideration, and a motion carried for a committee to ascertain the affairs of the Company. Mr. Fox again attacked the policy of Mr. Pitt with vehement eloquence, and in the same speech gave due credit to the conduct and importance of the Bank. He added: " The effect of this measure I will not describe by saying that it has impaired—

that is but a weak word—it has destroyed the credit of the Bank." "For the first time since the revolution an act has been done in the King's name which has struck at the foundation of the public credit, by seizing the public money, belonging to individuals, deposited in the public treasury of the public creditor." No time was lost by the committee; and on the 3rd of March they reported "that the total amount of demands on the Bank on the 25th February, was £13,770,390, and that the total amount of funds (not including £11,686,800 due from government,) was £17,597,280; leaving a surplus of £3,826,890, exclusive of the government debt."

The necessity of an issue of notes under £5 being greatly felt by the commercial interest, an act was passed by the 3rd of March, authorising it; and by the 10th of the same month notes for £1 and £2 were ready for delivery. The country bankers also circulated notes under £5, owing to the repeal of the act passed in 1777.

The report of the secret committee had satisfied the minds of the most doubtful, but among the less informed branches of the community great uneasiness continued. Some anxiety was therefore relieved when the following, bearing date the 6th of March, appeared. "In order to accommodate the public with a further supply of coin for small payments, a quantity of dollars, which have been supplied by the Bank, and stamped at the Mint, are now ready to be issued at the Bank, at the price of 4s. 6d. per dollar, and a further quantity is preparing."

A discovery was made, however, in time to prevent the issue. It was found that 4s. 6d. would be 2d. under their value in the market as bullion; and this great error was rectified by the following notice on the 9th of March. "In consequence of its appearing to be the general opinion that the dollars will be more conveniently circulated at the rate of 4s. 9d. than at that of 4s. 6d., notice is hereby given, that dollars are now ready to be delivered at 4s. 9d. per dollar." The dollars were Spanish, and bore a small king's head stamped on the Spanish king's neck.

The debates in the senate attracted attention; and the public mind, ready to start at shadows, was depressed by the language of the opposition. The enemies of the ministry had sought to depreciate the value of Bank paper; the announcement, therefore, that dollars would be issued in exchange, created great satisfaction to the holders of notes. On the first morning appointed for their delivery the office was crowded with applicants; the cashiers saw the public several deep waiting for dollars; the usual striving and struggling which, to the present day, distinguishes the claim for cash was acted, and many had to wait some hours before they could be supplied. The knowledge that the Bank was filled with claimants increased the alarm of others. The following days witnessed the same scene; but as there appeared no hesitation in supplying all the applications, and as there seemed no want of the metal, the claims soon abated.

The report of the committee gradually produced its proper effect; and the call for dollars decreased every day. In less than a month the demand was measured by the wants and not the fears of the people; and on the 31st of October, 1797, these dollars, of which 2,325,099 had been issued in eight months, were called in. Since their circulation a large number had been imported into the country, and stamped in resemblance of those sent from the Mint. When the latter were paid in, it was almost impossible to distinguish the true from the false, and after some vain and futile attempts to do so, the Bank were compelled to receive, without discrimination, all stamped dollars at 4s. 9d.

Notwithstanding the increased accommodation granted to the mercantile interest on the 27th of February, and stated by Mr. Thornton to have more than balanced the distrust occasioned by the cessation of payments in specie, it appears to have been generally considered that the increased amount of business demanded enlarged discounts. A meeting, therefore, at which the principal merchants attended, took place at the London Tavern. Mr. Alderman Lushington presided; and some resolutions, of which the following are the heads, were agreed to. " That the accommodation afforded by the Bank of England, in discount of bills and notes, is inadequate to the present extended commerce of the country." "That without an extension of the circulating medium of the kingdom, by discount of mercantile bills and notes, the general commerce of the country will be exposed to the most serious, immediate, and alarming evil." "That the recent mark of confidence reposed in the Bank of England by the respectable association for receiving their notes, notwithstanding the Order of Council of 26th of February, has given the merchants and traders a fair claim to reasonable and necessary accommodation."

On the 24th March another meeting was held, at which it was resolved, "That in the opinion of this meeting, the capital employed in the export and import trade of Great Britain, has amounted, on an average of the last six years, to forty-five millions per annum ; and that there is always two months' supply of this merchandize in the custody of the merchants and traders, and that a discount accommodation to such proportion may be afforded without risk, backed by this security." These resolutions were forwarded to the directors of the Bank ; but the reply was not considered satisfactory. On the following week a third meeting was held, at which it was resolved, "that though well satisfied with the sentiments expressed by the Bank, they considered that the practice of discounts should be extended upon the scale mentioned at the previous meeting."

The reply of the Bank directors to these resolutions was to the effect that they declined pledging themselves to any specific sum ; that though they were perfectly apprised of the larger discounts required by the trade of the country, it would be impossible to meet the views expressed in the resolutions until government had paid off a considerable portion of the debt due to them. But should this occur, they would have a greater latitude, and feel strongly inclined to avail themselves of it in favour of the merchants.

On the 3rd of May, nothwithstanding the great opposition made, and the blame thrown on government, "The Bank restriction Act" was passed. This, which is the 37th Geo. III., is entitled "An Act for continuing for a limited time the restriction contained in the minute of council of 26th of February, 1797." By it the Bank directors were not permitted to issue cash, except for sums under twenty shillings. But if any person lodged specie in the Bank, he might be repaid to the extent of three-fourths of the sum lodged, if it exceeded £500. The directors were also allowed to advance to the bankers any sum not exceeding altogether £100,000. They were also permitted to lend £25,000 each to the Bank, and Royal Bank of Scotland. The act was only to remain in force till the 24th of June. On the 22nd of that month, however, another was passed continuing the restriction of cash payments until one month after the commencement of the following session ; and in

November a third act was passed, limiting it to the somewhat indefinite period of six months after the conclusion of the war.

On the 17th of November, a report from the committee of secrecy was ordered to be printed, of which the following is an abstract. The total amount of outstanding demands on the Bank on the 11th of November was £17,578,910, while the funds for discharging the same (not including £11,686,800 due from government,) was £21,418,460. The bankers and traders, who might have claimed three-fourths of their deposits in cash, had only demanded one-sixteenth. Notwithstanding, however, all these favourable circumstances, the committee concluded by saying, " they were led to think it would be expedient to continue the restriction" from the political circumstances of the period.

The last act was deemed politic by the Government; but a court of proprietors was held in the same month ; and Mr. Raikes, after saying, that by the Report of the Secret Committee, there was a net balance in favour of the Bank, exclusive of the government stock of £3,839,000 ; added, that the Bank was in so affluent a state, as to be ready to pay all the demands on it in specie, whenever called upon. The consent of the proprietors was also asked for advancing the amount on the land and malt tax of £2,750,000, which was unanimously agreed to.

By the act passed in November, the power of paying in cash was taken from the hands of the directors. The ministers, viewing it principally in a political light, and regarding the war, which was then furiously raging, as one which was almost as doubtful as it was determined, adopted the policy, which, whatever its faults, led to, if it did not produce, some of the finest results which ever inspired the pen of the historian. Let it be remembered that, during the whole of the time, prohibitory of cash payments, we were waging a fierce but eminently triumphant contest, with a memorable spirit and with a memorable man. The spirit was that of the French revolution; the man was Napoleon Buonaparte. Let us remember also that, during the existence of that system, which has been so much censured, we were alone in the contest with him, whose name was for many years synonymous with success. The thunders of the Vatican were silenced. The military pride of Prussia was humbled. The power of Austria lay prostrate at his feet. Russia embraced the universal conqueror. England stood alone in her resolute defiance. She strengthened the weak, and encouraged the wavering. Wherever the free spirit of a people arose, her gold gave strength to their arms; her wisdom enlightened their councils. Her navy swept the seas and crippled the commerce of her adversary. And when her unconquerable resolution once more stirred the prostrate powers of Europe, when, through her exertions " the little island of St. Helena confined him for whom a world was once too small," the law passed in 1797 was in active existence. These things are not written to defend, they are only penned to mitigate the wrath which has been poured upon the Bank Restriction Act. Extraordinary events require extraordinary measures, and our history from 1797 to 1815 is unsurpassed in the annals of nations.

The haste with which the one and two pound notes had been executed, together with the ease with which they were received by the public, produced extensive forgeries. In January, 1799, the Bank advertised that all notes of the above amount, dated before July, 1798, might be received in cash, or exchanged for new notes, and that all odd sums not exceeding £5, might be received in specie. The first fruits of the restriction on cash payments occurred this year, as the proprietary received a bonus of ten per cent. on their capital in Five per cents., 1797.

It is curious, and sometimes not uninteresting, to notice in what manner other establishments have acted under similar circumstances. In January, 1814, the national bank of France experienced a demand for bullion. The star of Napoleon was on the wane : the climate of Russia had destroyed the confidence in his success. He was engaged in a desperate strife with those he had so often subdued ; and the conviction was felt that the glory had departed from him. The holders of the notes of the French bank, uncertain how far a change of dynasty might affect them, went eagerly to require payment in gold; until £600,000 only remained. With the sanction of the Emperor, the bank determined not to pay more than £20,000 a day, and to effect this the prefect of police announced that no one might apply for gold, unless he should be the bearer of a number, to be supplied him by the mayor of his quarter.

It has already been seen that the government were constantly pressed for money, and in 1798 an act was passed to legalize voluntary contributions for carrying on the war. Merchants and manufacturers vied with each other in subscribing. A temporary office was erected under the east piazza of the Royal Exchange, to receive contributions. The Bank of England offered £200,000; the city of London gave £10,000. The place was filled with all classes and conditions, eagerly crowding to contribute. £300,000 were remitted from India, with the promise of a similar annual repetition during the war; and upwards of two millions, exclusive of this sum, were contributed to support the dignity of the empire against the aggressions of the enemy.

The question of preserving the Rest, was disputed in 1798, by a portion of the proprietors. The maintenance of a reserved capital has been argued in another place, and time has tested its wisdom. A

strenuous exertion was however made by Mr. Allar-
dyce, who published a quarto volume, and called
courts of proprietors to his aid, to compel the division
of this fund. The question is a simple one; and
as the proprietor derives part of his half-yearly
interest from the reserved capital, while the value
of the stock is in some proportion to it, he has no
just cause of complaint. Should such a proposal
ever be carried out, the price of the stock would
be deteriorated, and the dividends would vacillate
as they did a century and a half ago. A great fraud
like that of Astlett, or a series of colossal forgeries
like Fauntleroy's, might engross the whole of the half-
year's profits, and send the proprietors from their half-
yearly meeting, discontented and without a dividend.

The reasons which actuated Mr. Samuel Thornton, then Governor, and the Court of Directors,
to moot the renewal of the charter at so early a period
as 1800, when it had twelve years to run, are to
be found in the acknowledgment that they considered
it a favourable moment, because Ministers, pressed
by the expenses of the war, were disposed to accept
terms which, under more favourable auspices, would
be rejected. For more than a hundred years the name
of Thornton appears in the list of the direction, and the
house of Thornton constantly occupied an important
mercantile position. During the governorship, therefore, of such a man, with whom the capacity of direction
was almost hereditary, there was every chance of the

Bank receiving its due proportion of justice from the Government. The period also was propitious. The services rendered by the Bank to the state had been so important that Mr. Pitt, in all his pride of place, was compelled to acknowledge their necessity. They were so recent that they could not be forgotten. The ministry to which they had been rendered were still in power, and still compelled to seek assistance; and, to crown all, the undeniable fact that the Bank had stopped payment through its endeavours to aid government, was in the remembrance of every one. These, then, were claims to a just consideration, the remembrance of which was calculated to lead to a fair and favourable result. The reasons assigned by Mr. Thornton in the House of Commons were to the following effect. That the first overtures had come from the governor and directors, because they were convinced that a renewal at such a period would prove of utility to the Bank and the country. A motion had been made for the establishment of a rival bank. Meetings had been held; endeavours had been made; pamphlets had been written in its support; and the renewal of the charter would be the most effectual check to so idle a measure.

But no considerations have ever prevented a ministry from making a good bargain with the Bank. It has grown into a habit; and custom is too often a cloak for injustice. In 1708, when the charter was renewed for twenty-two years, the renewal was paid for with a loan of £400,000 without interest, and the cancelling of a million and a half of Exchequer bills. In 1713, when found expedient to extend it for a further ten years, the Bank undertook in return to circulate nearly a million and a quarter more of these bills. In 1742, on a renewal of twenty-two years, £1,600,000 were lent without interest in perpetuity. The year 1764 witnessed an equal exertion of the screw; and for a further extension of a similar period £110,000 were paid, and one million lent to government. In 1781, a loan of two millions for three years was claimed for the same service. That statesmen regarded these agreements with the eyes of traders is evident from a remark of Mr. Grenville, that " he thought the last-named contract a good bargain for the nation." But is this the light in which such matters should be regarded? Is it worthy a great nation to fly to a corporate body in the hour of need, and, when met honourably and liberally with the requisite supplies, to turn round and bargain like a miser with its benefactor? Is it befitting the character of a great statesman to make a Company pay a tax for their charter, and then, in the time of panic and peril, demand increased assistance, which carries danger and distress with it? The government either have no right to claim payment for the privileges they grant, or they have no right peremptorily to demand further assistance. It has been already seen that Mr.

Montague and Lord Godolphin were decidedly of opinion "that no fine ought to be expected for a renewal." This is the principle they propounded; but this is not the principle upon which their successors have acted.

For the renewal of the charter, in 1800, the Bank proposed to lend three millions for six years, without interest; a right being reserved to them of claiming repayment at any time before the expiration of six years if consols should be at or above eighty per cent. In the event of such repayment they were to allow six per cent. per annum on the sum repaid for such part of the six years as might remain. This proposal was deemed liberal by Mr. Pitt, who considered the profits to amount to six or seven hundred thousand pounds "on dry calculation," and not the actual gain, which would probably be much more. In return for this payment, Mr. Pitt expressly enumerated, among the advantages to be enjoyed, and for which they made the government a remuneration, that of holding the public balances in their possession. This minister stated that "the public had derived great assistance by the aid of the Bank, and would do so again under any similar pressure." Such was the opinion of William Pitt—such was the persuasion of Lord North—such was the declaration of Mr. Grenville—at the renewal of each successive charter. Yet at each period a heavy sum has been claimed; and in the present instance six or seven hundred thousand pounds were paid by the proprietors of the Bank of England for the privilege of benefiting the people of Great Britain; and it will be seen at a later period that the state made a further claim upon the Bank many years before the charter had expired.

CHAPTER XIV.

The circulation of £1 notes proved conducive to a
melancholy waste of human life. Considering the
advances made in the mechanical arts, they were
rough and even rude in their execution. Easily
imitated, they were also easily circulated ; and from
1797 the executions for forgery augmented to an extent
which bore no proportion to any other class of crime.
During six years prior to their issue there was but one
capital conviction : during the four following years
eighty-five occurred. This great increase produced
enquiry, which resulted in an act " For the better pre-
vention of the forgery of the notes and bills of
exchange of persons carrying on the business of
bankers." By this, some stringent penalties were

denounced against offenders ; and a notice to the following effect was published in September, 1801 :—
" All the one and two pound notes issued by the Bank
of England, on and after the 1st of August, will, to prevent forgeries, be printed on a peculiar and purposely
constructed paper; consequently, those dated 31st
July, or any subsequent day, will be impressed upon
paper manufacture, with waved or curved lines."

It will be seen, at a later period, that this endeavour
to repress crime fell sadly short of the necessity,
owing to the great truth which now begins to possess
the minds of our legislature, that punishment is not a
sufficient preventive ; but that to teach men to be
good is more effectual than to punish them for being
bad.   The extinction of human life continued.   The
English criminal laws, those laws which were said to
be written in blood, and which were the remains of
the old feudal spirit that disregarded the life of the
serf, at first found supporters among the class which
suffered from the evil.   So long as the law was left
to take its course, and no voice was heard, save that
of the victim, the justice which hung a man for a one
pound note was unquestioned ; while those who read
in the daily press of the punishment of the offenders,
rejoiced in it as an evidence of increasing civilization ;
and thanked heaven, as they sate down to their well-
stored tables, that they had been preserved from so
great a crime.   Nor was it for a long period after that
of which we write that the eyes of men were opened

alike to the sinfulness and inutility of capital punishments.

A second bonus was made in 1801 to the proprietors of bank stock, who received £5 per cent. upon the capital, in navy five per cents. To the artizan and to the stipendiary it was a time of much distress. By the latter a period of scarcity is, perhaps, most keenly felt, from the necessity of supporting an appearance in keeping with his position, and from the dangerous ease with which he can procure credit. A magazine of this year says, " of all the modes of relief, that which was adopted by the Bank directors, in their conduct towards their servants, is entitled to the highest praise, and furnishes an example every way worthy of imitation. They made a very liberal addition to the salaries of their numerous clerks and other servants."

In the year 1802, a peace, which, unhappily, proved only temporary, known by the name of the " peace of Amiens," was concluded. The war, which had deprived England of the blood of some of her bravest citizens, and reduced the national treasure to the verge of bankruptcy, was supposed to be over. The empire once more saw a prospect of the enjoyment of peace ; and men, tired with "war and rumours of war" sick at heart of the announcements of great battles won and lost, and more than all, dissatisfied at the rapid increase of taxes which accompanied laurels by land and supremacy by sea, began to think that a cessation from so costly a game would be agreeable. Though gilded by many victories; though triumphant in Egypt; and though the battle of the Nile had spread a rejoicing throughout the land; England had witnessed too many reverses not to hail anything like peace with gladness. On the Continent Napoleon had been everywhere successful; and when the preliminaries were ratified on 10th October, 1801, the most enthusiastic tokens of delight were exhibited throughout England.

By the act of November, 1797, the payment of cash was restricted to within six months after the conclusion of the war. It became therefore necessary in April, 1802, to increase this limit. The reasons assigned by Mr. Addington, in the House of Commons, were " that it would be inexpedient to increase the circulation of guineas, as the exchange was against this country, and for several months guineas had been purchased with a view to exportation. For three or four years the credit of the Bank had undergone no diminution. Bank notes were received cheerfully and readily; and when the Bank was allowed to call in notes of £1 and £2 to the amount of £800,000, only £400,000 were claimed in specie. The motion was opposed on the ground that the very mention of it was a word of terror, and that since the restriction in 1797, the forgeries of bank notes had increased so alarmingly, as to require seventy additional clerks to be employed merely in detecting them, that within that very year no less than thirty or forty persons had been executed for the crime. To this it was replied, that in Liverpool bank paper was preferred to cash ; that the credit of the Bank had increased, and that no petitions had appeared against it." The motion was carried, and the Bank restricted from paying cash before 1st March, 1803.

The first instance of fraud, in the present century, to a great amount, was perpetrated by one of the confidential servants of the Corporation. In the year 1803, Mr. Bish, a member of the Stock Exchange, was applied to by Mr. Robert Astlett, Cashier of the Bank of England, to dispose of some Exchequer bills. When they were delivered into Mr. Bish's hands, he was greatly astonished to find not only that these bills had previously been in his possession, but that they had been also delivered to the Bank. Surprised at this, he immediately opened a communication with the directors, which led to the discovery of the fraud, and the apprehension of Robert Astlett. By the evidence produced on the trial, it appeared that the prisoner had been placed in charge of all the Exchequer bills brought into the Bank, and when a certain number were collected, it was his duty to arrange them in bundles, and deliver them to the directors, in the parlour, where they were counted, and a receipt given to the cashier,

This practice had been strictly adhered to; but the prisoner, from his acquaintance with business, had induced the directors to believe that he had handed them bills to the amount of £700,000, when they were only in possession of £500,000. So completely had he deceived these gentlemen, that two of the body vouched by their signatures for the delivery of the larger amount.

He was tried for the felonious embezzlement of three bills of Exchequer, of £1,000 each. A fatal objection was, however, raised by the counsel of Mr. Astlett, and the Bank failed in their endeavour legally to establish his guilt. Though the prisoner was acquitted in this instance, he was detained in custody, until the directors could cause a civil process to be issued against him. From this plan they departed, however; and on the renewal of the sessions Astlett was again tried for the criminal offence. The indictment charged him this time with the felonious embezzlement of property and effects of the Bank of England. He was found guilty, with the reservation of some points of law, which were left for the decision of the twelve judges. In the following year Mr. Baron Hotham said the objections had been ably and legally discussed, and that the judges were of opinion that " the prisoner, having been found guilty of the embezzlement, was subjected to the pain of death."

This sentence, however, was not executed; and Mr. Astlett remained a prisoner in Newgate for many years.

At the next half-yearly meeting of the proprietors it became necessary for the Governor to state that a loss had been sustained through Mr. Astlett of £320,000, £78,000 of which the directors hoped to recover. It was announced that this would make no alteration in the dividend, although it amounted to nearly the entire interest of the half-year. The Governor then said that the directors were not to blame for the malpractices of Mr. Astlett, who had succeeded in making away with the effects of the Bank by inter-lineations, and by calling out false sums, when the property was regulated. A very satisfactory explanation was given, by which it appeared that the directors had relied on Mr. Astlett's character and long fidelity. Under all circumstances it was stated that it would have required a supernatural power to have at first detected him.

Although the Governor stated that the defalcation would make no difference in the dividend, it was probably preventive of a bonus. Upon the capital stock of the company the fraud would have amounted to two-and-a-half per cent., and as this was the only year between 1798 and 1807 (with the exception of that when the charter was renewed) which passed without the declaration of a bonus, there can be little error in assigning the crime of the cashier as a cause of the omission.

In February, 1803, the Bank Restriction Bill was again proposed by Mr. Addington. The uncertainty of the peace enjoyed by the nation, the knowledge that the restless spirit of the first French Consul was planning schemes of conquest, and an extension of territory, incompatible with the liberty of England, was undoubtedly one great reason. In addition, a three years' scarcity had compelled us to seek a supply of grain from the continent; and for this purpose twenty millions of bullion had been sent out of the country within that period. An additional large drain of cash for our army and navy also appeared to render a return to specie payments almost impossible, as, in the opinion of Mr. Addington, we ought to wait the operations of a flourishing commerce, to bring back some proportion of this vast amount. A bill, therefore, limiting the suspension of specie payments to six weeks, after the commencement of the ensuing session, was passed. The wisdom of the arrangement was soon seen. The stipulations of the treaty of Amiens had never been fulfilled by Buonaparte. The attempt to control by treaties the man who never made one but with the view of violating its provisions proved fallacious. During the short period which the truce lasted, antagonistic feelings were operating in England, and a violation of justice was witnessed in the transactions of the first Consul of France, which obviously tended to destroy the existing peace. His insidious foment-ation of the quarrels of the Swiss, and his insolent assumption of the character of arbiter, his interfe-

rence with St. Domingo ; his treacherous conduct to
"Toussaint, the most unhappy man of men !"
tended to nourish the dislike with which Napoleon
was universally regarded by the English. The feelings
of the rival nations were soon kindled into rage.
Foul, and even false assertions, were made on both
sides of the channel. The press of London and Paris
attacked and recriminated, and the ruler of France
lowered the personal dignity which he usually so
sternly maintained, by prosecuting a royalist emigrant,
for an offensive libel. But that which marked the
insecure nature of the truce of Amiens was the
discovery of persons, chiefly military, in the act of
performing Buonaparte's directions to make exact
plans of the harbours and coasts of the United
Kingdom. The indignation of England, hitherto
somewhat suppressed, burst forth like a torrent. The
treachery of France was openly and vehemently denounced. The press and the Parliament alike spoke
the voice of the people. The government openly announced that the French were recruiting their armies,
and increasing their fleet, and that it was necessary
for England to adopt the same course. At length
the storm burst forth which was to desolate Europe.
The ambassador was recalled from Paris; and on
the 18th May, after a short and uncertain peace of
fourteen months, war was again declared.

The commencement of hostilities rendered a return
to cash payments impracticable. The English govern-

ment was well aware that this country would be
called upon, by whatever allies she might form, for
pecuniary support. Her great commercial prosperity,
the vast stake she had in preserving her independence,
and with it that of the great nations of Europe,
rendered England the most important enemy of
France. But it was her gold which chiefly made
her dangerous. The sinews of war possessed by her
caused her demonstrations to be regarded with
anxiety, enabling her to treat upon independent terms
with the enemy, when the remainder of Europe
crouched obsequiously before him. It was necessary,
therefore, to reserve her specie as much as possible,
to meet the expenses of the contest; and in 1803
a bill was introduced, postponing cash payments until
six months after a definitive treaty of peace. "Nor
was this done," said Lord Hawkesbury, "either at
the request or suggestion of the Bank directors, as
government had brought it forward solely from a
conviction of its necessity." In the debate which
occurred the Chancellor of the Exchequer remarked,
" that it was very much to the credit of the Bank,
that it had not abused the discretion given it, with
a view to its own private profits."

The scarcity of silver had been severely felt for
some time prior to 1804, and the Bank issued
dollars of five shillings. " These dollars," says Mr.
Gilbart, " had on the obverse side an impression of
his Majesty's head, and the following superscription :

' Georgius III., Dei Gratia Rex ;' and on the reverse side, the impression of Britannia, and the following, ' Five shillings dollar. Bank of England, 1804.' " In the same year, a bill was introduced to prevent the tokens issued by the Bank from being counterfeited ; and though, in the course of the debate, the directors were accused of wishing to grasp one of the privileges of the sovereign, the bill was carried. Of these coins 1,419,484 were issued.

The restriction placed upon the Bank by government was naturally productive of increased profits. Although the Chancellor said " that to its honour it had not availed itself of the disposition of the act, to issue a quantity of paper exceeding its amount of capital," yet the absence of treasure in its bullion office was a sufficient reason for the bonus which was annually presented to its proprietary, and which was renewed in 1804, 1805, and 1806, at the rate of five per cent. in cash upon the capital in each year ; and in 1807 they received the agreeable announcement that the dividend would be raised from seven to ten per cent. free of income tax, at which rate it remained until 1822. At the declaration of the bonus in 1806, a proposal was made by one of the court, and carried unanimously, that the gratuity to the directors should be doubled. The amount of income received by these gentlemen for their devotion to the interests of the proprietary, has always been regarded by them of small moment compared with the importance of the position, and the circumstance is therefore only noticeable as an evidence of an estimation of their services.

In 1696, it was arranged that the same recompence to the governor, deputy governor, and directors, which had been presented them by an order of the court in 1695, should be continued annually. In accordance with this, £200 per annum had hitherto been received by the governor and deputy governor, and £150 by each of the directors; but, by the new arrangement, the former have since continued to receive £400, and the latter £300 per annum.

In 1806, the three millions which the Bank had advanced to the state in payment of the charter of 1800 became due. In the ordinary course of events, this sum should have been returned, or an increased rate of interest allowed. The government, however, thought differently, and prevailed upon the Bank to renew the loan at three per cent., until six months after the ratification of peace. An additional sum, therefore, of nearly five hundred thousand pounds, may be added to the price paid by the Company for the renewal of its charter.

The war had been costly to the government. The star of Napoleon was yet in the ascendant. Threats of invasion were boldly uttered by the French. Vast efforts were made in England to meet them. Five hundred men of war traversed the seas, ventured into the enemy's harbour, destroyed his navy, and crippled his flotillas. The officers of the Bank formed a volunteer corps. On every hill-top throughout the island, beacons blazed, and sentinels watched. The spirit of the citizen soldiery was awake, and Europe saw the tradesman leave his shop, the merchant his counting house, and the clerk his desk, to attest that the ancient spirit of England still survived to maintain the freedom bequeathed to the land. The fine coalition organized by Mr. Pitt had been crushed. The Emperors of Russia and Germany witnessed their armies cut to pieces and their hopes defeated, from the heights of Austerlitz, and England mourned the death of that great man who had roused the states of Europe to a sight of their national degradation. The continuation of a loan of three millions, therefore, at an interest far below the market value, was of some importance. It is, perhaps, to the same causes, together with others, hereafter to be mentioned, that the Bank of England was made the object of a searching enquiry at a later period. The energy with which the ambition of Buonaparte had been met by the government of Great Britain, the knowledge that the commerce of this country, together with her insular position, rendered her calm, self-possessed, and defiant, while the remainder of Europe either courted him or was crushed by him, produced from the conqueror that fiercest of feelings, an impotent longing after vengeance. With the vain hope of destroying our supplies of corn from the Baltic, the entrance of

British ships was prohibited into any of the ports or rivers of Prussia ; and in November, 1806, from the captured city of Berlin, was issued a decree, declaring the British islands in a state of blockade. France was without a navy ; the maritime power of England was pre-eminent ; and the insolence, therefore, of such a proclamation can only be measured by its impotence. The chivalrous spirit which has from time to time shone from the anarchy of war, and which, in our own days, we have seen exemplified in the noble conduct of Mehemet Ali, was absent in Napoleon Buonaparte. But the blow aimed by him in his Berlin decrees was more mischievous to French commerce than to English enterprise. In all the seaports of France the contraband trade was at a premium. In vain from the heart of conquered nations did he launch his imperial edicts. English merchandize was requisite, and English merchandize was borne in triumph through the Custom-houses of France to the homes of her people. The only difference between illegal and legal traffic being that, in the former, the profit was made by the contrabandist, and in the latter by government. In addition to this our capitalists sought other fields ; and the energy which, to some extent, was depressed in one, was more determined and successful in its attempts after another market.

In 1808 a Committee was appointed to enquire into several branches of the public expenditure ; the accounts of the Bank of England were examined with the view of decreasing the emoluments. Since 1786, when the charge upon each million of the public debt had been reduced from £562 10s. to £450, no change had occurred. The national debt, which then was £224,102,424, and for the management of which £100,846 were paid, amounted in January, 1807, to £550,441,314 on which £265,818 were received by the Bank, in addition to the original £4,000 and £1,898 on £4,000,000, bought from the South Sea Company.

The difficulty of the Finance Committee was great in procuring some satisfactory criterion by which to arrive at a fair conclusion. The South Sea House, which received £582 13s. 6d. for each million, was the nearest; but the small amount of stock was a reason for so large a sum being paid. The charges of the Bank of Ireland had been fixed by the rate which was paid to the English Bank, and to argue from that would be very like arguing in a circle. The management of the public debt in America afforded some illustration; but there was one material difference in the banks of the United States merely undertaking the payments of the dividends, while the transfers were managed at the public offices. For this cause, and from the limited number of the stock-holders, (at that period about 15,000,) the risk and expense of the American could not be brought into comparison with the English Bank. This was some-

what unfortunate; for the Finance Committee might
have urged the fact that the American Bank
charged nothing for their trouble, with full force
upon that body, on the profits of which they were in
judgment.

Under these circumstances, they had recourse to the
Corporation itself for information. "Assuming as an
incontrovertible proposition," says the report, "that
in proportion as the business becomes enlarged, a
moderate commission on a large business produces a
greater proportionate profit than a higher rate on one
more confined, it is obvious that a charge of allowance
reasonable upon 20 or 25 millions, becomes profuse
and extravagant upon five hundred millions. The
increase in the establishment of the Bank, which
has been rendered necessary by the augmentation
of this branch, consists principally in the number
of the clerks; of whom the whole number employed in the public business exclusively or principally, was, in 1786, 243; in 1796, 313; and in
1807, 450; whose salaries, it is presumed, may be
calculated on an average, at between £120 and £170
for each clerk; taking them at £135, which exceeds
the average of those employed in the South Sea
House, the sum is £60.750
at £150   .   .   .   .   .   .   67.500
    170   .   .   .   .   .   .   76.500
either of which two last sums would probably be
sufficient to provide a superannuated fund.

Incidental Expenses and Sundries, about £15,000
Additional Buildings and Repairs 10,000
Law Expenses, and Losses by Frauds and Forgeries . . 10,000

On this penurious calculation, the Committee proceeded to state that the whole increase of officers who transacted the business, was in the previous eleven years 137, the annual expense of whom might vary from £18,449 to £23,290, the addition to the other permanent charges being probably about one-half, or two thirds of that sum, while the increased allowance for management in the last ten years, was more than £155,000." The conclusion at which the Committee arrived, was recommendatory of a reduction of the profits. After stating that the Bank, "over and above the charges of management, are accustomed to receive allowances from the public of £805 15s. 10d. per million, for receiving contributions for loans ; and £1,000 for contributions to the lottery, and that they have the benefit of holding all the money for half-yearly dividends, besides having the cash for the navy and army service," they concluded by stating that "it is deserving the attention of Parliament, whether a further reduction of expense cannot and ought not to be made upon this branch of public expenditure."

The reason which appeared most plausible was the large amount of deposits committed by the government to the keeping of the Bank, to meet the expenses of the war. In 1800, Mr. Pitt alluded to this balance as affording some right to an interest in the annual profits of the company. These balances were, however, entirely optional. It suited the purpose of the state to choose so secure a depository as the national Bank; it was a cause of expence to the latter; and the claim of Mr. Pitt to participate in the profits, appears about as reasonable as the demand of any wealthy individual to share in the yearly returns won by the sagacity of his banker, because he has, to meet his own views, deposited a large sum in the hands of the latter. The real origin of the committee was the spirit which could not bear to see the Bank directors give bonus after bonus to their proprietors, or increase their dividend from seven to ten per cent. without longing to participate. This is apparent in the following extract: "The annual and temporary bonus of £5 per cent. which the Bank have for some successive years added to their accustomed dividends of seven per cent., and the recent augmentations of their regular dividends to ten per cent., exclusive of property tax; the rise also in the market price of their stock, which, having sold in 1786 from £156 to £172 per. cent., now sells at £230, are strong circumstances in confirmation of the large increase of their profits." These profits the government desired to grasp, but they were only attainable by mulcting the establishment in an indirect way.

The unclaimed dividends were another source of gain recommended by the committee which was perfectly justified in the report, that as they amounted, on the 8th of July, 1806, to £986,573, the sum of £800,000 might be honourably claimed.

It has long been the custom to regard the Bank as indebted entirely to the state. The profit on the management of the national debt is pompously announced. The gain arising from the paper circulation secured by the Bank charter is proclaimed as an additional revenue. The interest also arising from the government balances is not forgotten. But let it be remembered that there are other and strong claims for the Bank. At the period of the Finance Committee, its capital, of more than eleven millions, was lent at the low interest of three per cent., and on this an annual payment of £230,000 was derived from the Company for the charter. Advances were also made to the extent of £2,750,000 on the annual land and malt taxes, at four per cent., and this produced a profit to the country; while the three millions advanced for six years, and continued when this period had expired, at the interest of three per cent., was another mode of payment for the patronage of government. The Bank also deducted the property tax from the public dividends, and paid it into the Exchequer without charge, by which means delay was obviated, and the expense of collection saved.

The only point of the report, independently of the unclaimed dividends, which bore the semblance of justice, was its conclusion, when, after pointing out in

what place the establishment was most vulnerable,
and where it might be most easily assailed, it stated,
"The accommodations derived by the public from
its connexion with the Bank, have been carried on
some years to a very large amount ; and it must
always be considered as an object of the greatest
consequence to maintain the permanence of an establishment of such opulence and credit, which has
contributed so materially to extend commercial prosperity, and to maintain the public faith of the
country. Your committee cannot conclude their
report without bearing testimony to the favourable
disposition so often manifested on the part of the
Bank towards the public service ; and they entertain
no doubt of the same readiness to accede to any
equitable arrangement that may be proposed under
the present circumstances."

The report of the committee was followed by an
application on the part of Mr. Spencer Percival,
proposing a reduction in the rates of management,
a further advance of £500,000 of the unclaimed
dividends, and a loan without interest of three millions, until six months after the conclusion of the
war, or the payment of £150,000 per annum for the
same period, urging, however, the superior benefit
to be derived by the public from the former. The
following extract from a letter, the last written on
the occasion by the Chancellor of the Exchequer,
embraces the arrangement as it was concluded :

" I have proposed, first, that the Bank shall now advance, out of the unclaimed dividends in their hands, the sum of £500,000 for the use of the public, in addition to the sum already advanced out of that fund, provided that the amount of such dividends remaining in the Bank shall not be reduced below £100,000.

2ndly. That for the management of the public debt the Bank shall henceforth be allowed as follows : £340 per million per annum upon the debt, whenever it may amount to 400 millions, and not exceed 600 millions, £300 per million per annum on the amount of any debt unredeemed above 600 millions. The said 600 millions continuing in such case to be managed at the aforesaid rate of £340. £450 per million per annum on the debt when it may exceed 300 millions, and not amount to 400 millions.

3rd. That the Bank shall, on or before the 5th April next, advance for the public service in the present year, three millions, by way of loan, without interest. The principal to be secured by Exchequer bills."

At a meeting of Bank proprietors in January, 1808, the proposals were read by the governor, and after some explanations unanimously agreed to. The following was their purport : " That £500,000 should be withdrawn from the fund appropriated for unclaimed dividends, for the use of the public. That an alteration should take place in the rate of the

management which would be a saving to the government of £70,000 per annum; and that three
millions sterling should be advanced to the state,
without interest, the payment to be secured by Exchequer bills, to be made payable from the signing
of a definitive treaty of peace."

These resolutions, after some debate, were agreed
to, and the object of the finance committee gained.
The interest on the three millions, at five per cent.,
till the conclusion of the war, amounted to about
one million sterling.

The name of Abraham Newland, that name by
which the notes of the Bank were often indicated, is
familiar to most readers. In 1807 he retired from
the office of chief cashier, after a service of more
than half a century. His last act was to decline
the pension which the liberality of the directors
offered. The same year he died; and as a specimen
of the fortunes which were occasionally amassed in
the service of the establishment, it may be mentioned
that his property amounted to £200,000, besides
£1000 a-year landed estates. It must not be supposed that this was saved from his salary. During
the whole of Mr. Newland's career, the loans, which
during the war were made almost yearly, and occasionally oftener, proved very prolific. A certain
amount of them was always reserved for the cashier's
office (one parliamentary report names £100,000), and
as they generally came out at a premium, the profits

were great. The family of the Goldsmiths, then the leaders of the Stock Exchange, contracted for many of these loans, and to each of them he left £500, to purchase a mourning ring. From some remarks in the papers it may be gathered that the large funds of Mr. Newland were occasionally lent to these gentlemen, to assist their varied speculations. It was also the subject of frequent allusion in the pamphlets of the period; and as those who know the least are frequently the most confident, there was not much ceremony used in the strictures passed upon Mr. Abraham Newland.

The odium thrown upon the Bank for the many deaths which have taken place for forgery, must necessarily find some palliation in the subtlety of those who entered into the dangerous traffic. It was in truth a trade. The notes were frequently sold at so much in the pound, and, as in the instance about to be related, they were often sent into the foreign market. In 1808, Vincent Alessi, a native of one of the Italian states, went to Birmingham, to choose some manufactures likely to return a sufficient profit in Spain. Amongst others he sought a brass founder, who showed him that which he required, and then drew his attention to "another article," which he said he could sell cheaper than any other person in the trade. Mr. Alessi declined purchasing this, as it proved to be a forged Bank note; upon which he was shown some dollars, as fitter for the Spanish market. These also were declined, although it is not much to the credit of this Italian, that he did not at once denounce the dishonesty of the Birmingham brass founder. It would seem, however, from what followed, that Mr. Alessi was not quite unprepared, as, in the evening, he was called on by one John Nicholls; and after some conversation he agreed to take a certain quantity of notes, of different value, which were to be paid for at the rate of six shillings in the pound.

Alessi thought this a very profitable business, while it lasted, as he could always procure as many as he liked, by writing for so many dozen candlesticks, calling them Nos. 5, 2, or 1, according to the amount of the note required. The vigilance of the English police, however, was too much even for the subtlety of an Italian; he was taken by them, and allowed to turn king's evidence, it being thought very desirable to discover the manufactory whence the notes emanated.

In December John Nicholls received a letter from Alessi, stating that he was going to America, that he wanted to see Nicholls in London, that he required twenty dozen candlesticks, No. 5; twenty-four dozen No. 1; and four dozen No. 2. Mr. Nicholls, unsuspicious of his correspondent's captivity, and consequent frailty, came forthwith to town, to fulfil so important an order. Here an interview was planned, within hearing of the police officers. Nicholls came with the forged notes. Alessi counted up the whole sum he was to pay, at six shillings in the pound, saying, " Well, Mr. Nicholls, you will take all my money from me." " Never mind, sir," was the reply, " it will be all returned in the way of business." Alessi then remarked that it was cold, and put on his hat. This was the signal for the officers. To the dealer's surprise and indignation he found himself entrapped, with the counterfeit notes in his possession, to the precise amount in number and value that had been ordered in the letter. Thus Mr. Nicholls found his business suddenly brought to a close, and the brisk trade in imaginary candlesticks finished, to the infinite welfare of the public.

In 1809, also, the public were made aware that a traffic in one, two, and five pound notes, had existed for some time to a most alarming extent. The Bank of England had long known of these forgeries, and had been successful in detecting many of the delinquents. A traffic so large had never before been discovered. It was positively sworn that forged notes might be bought in " sufficient quantities to load a jackass." Those which reached the Bank were detected at a glance. The signatures of some cashiers who had long been dead were on many, while others bore only Christian names. From these inconsistencies, and the bad colour of the paper, they were chiefly circulated in parts remote from the metropolis. Not the less, however, was it the duty of the directors to detect the culprits, thirteen of whom were taken in one day, through a clever contrivance of the officers ; and notes to the amount of £10,000 seized on the premises. The paper had been retailed by poor ignorant people, few of whom could write or read, at from five to ten shillings in the pound. Birmingham was the fountain head whence they flowed, and Wales and Scotland the parts where they were principally passed. The idea was prevalent among all, that if the forged notes were not actually found in their possession they could not be convicted ; a delusion quickly dispelled, to the cost of these unhappy men.

CHAPTER XV.

BY the regulations of the mint, the price of standard gold was £3 17s. 10½d per ounce. In 1809, however, it rose to £4 9s. and £4 12s. in the market. The Bank paper was correspondingly depreciated. The enemies of the Corporation proclaimed that this arose from the over issue of its notes. Some attributed it to the war, which occasioned a large exportation of gold. Others, again, thought these opinions wrong, and that it arose from something else, which would correct itself; only, as Mr. Henry Thornton remarked, " it had not yet done so." All agreed that it would be advisable to enquire into its origin, and Mr. Horner moved for accounts relative to the circulation. From this arose the famous Bullion Committee. The following is a portion of the report.

"The directors of the Bank of England have exercised the new and extraordinary discretion reposed in them since 1797, with an integrity and regard to the public interest, according to their conceptions of it, and, indeed, a degree of forbearance, in turning it less to the profit of the Bank, than it would easily have admitted of, that merit the continuance of that confidence, which the public has so long and so justly felt, in the integrity with which its affairs are directed, as well as in the unshaken stability and ample funds of that great establishment."

The result of the deliberations was made known in the following words.

"That there is at present an excess on the paper circulation, of which the most unequivocal symptom is the high price of bullion, and next to that the low state of the Continental Exchanges ; that this excess is to be ascribed to the want of a sufficient control in the issues of the Bank of England, and originally to the suspension of cash payments, which removed the natural and true control." "Your Committee, therefore, report it as their opinion, that the circulating medium of this country ought to be brought back, with as much speed as is compatible with a wise caution, to the original principle of cash payments, at the option of the holder of bank paper. Your committee have understood, that remedies or palliatives of a different nature have been prescribed : such as a compulsory limitation of Bank advances and discounts, during the suspension ; or a compulsory limitation of the bank dividends, by carrying the surplus to the public account. But such schemes, in addition to other reasons, would be objectionable, as a most improper interference with the rights of commercial property. According to the judgment of your Committee, no sufficient remedy for the present or security for the future can be pointed out, except the repeal of the law which suspends the cash payments of the Bank of England."

"In effecting so important a change, some difficulties must be encountered; and there are some contingent dangers to the Bank, against which it ought most strongly to be guarded. But they may be provided for, by restoring to to the Bank the charge of conducting and completing the operation, and by allowing the Bank an ample period for conducting it. To the discretion, experience, and integrity of the directors of the Bank, parliament may safely entrust the charge of effecting that which it may determine upon as necessary : the directors of that great institution, far from making themselves a party with those who have a temporary interest in spreading alarm, will take a much larger view of the permanent interests of the Bank, as indisputably blended with those of the public."

The Committee concluded by recommending the lapse of two years previous to removing the restriction, and an issue of notes for less than £5, for a short time after the return to cash payments.

The state of commerce in Great Britain demanded serious attention in 1811. Considerable distress existed. The markets in South America, the Brazils, and other parts, had been opened to English adventure. Great hopes were entertained, and great ventures made. Extensive exports took place to those countries, and to the West India Islands, which, not meeting with a ready sale, ruined the shippers, and prevented them from paying the manufacturers, who had the bills returned upon them.

No sooner is a new sphere of operation opened, than the manufacturing interest appears to lose its usual keen discrimination. The thoughtful energy which ordinarily characterises it, degenerates into an unwholesome excitement, and a spirit, not of trade, but of speculation, ensues. It was thus with these exportations. In a few weeks more goods were sent out to Buenos Ayres and the Brazils than had been consumed there in the previous twenty years. The warehouses were filled with the most valuable produce. On the arrival of fresh cargoes there was no space to contain them ; and while the brain of the exporter was filled with visions of eager purchasers, and of cent. per cent. profits, his merchandize lay exposed to the winds and the waves on the beach, with every chance of depredation and of damage. Exquisite services of China and of cut glass were forwarded to those who had been accustomed to the primitive horn, or to the yet more natural cocoa-nut shell; and as golden mines formed the invariable accompaniments of the Brazils in the fancy of the English trader, tools, with a hammer on one side and a hatchet on the other, were sent out, under the idea, says Mr. Mc Culloch, from whom this information is collected, " that the inhabitants had nothing more to do than to break the first stone that they met with, and then cut the gold and diamonds from it." If the old jest of sending out warming-pans to Jamaica be untrue, it is at least certain that, at this time, the people of that warm climate were presumed to be proficients in the use of skates, as some of the speculators sent out this article with an eagerness that could only be surpassed by their ignorance. The effect on the merchant and the artizan is obvious. Some manufactories were closed. Half the operatives were dismissed from others. In many the workmen found their wages reduced ; and the mischief thus fell upon the class which were least able to support it. Tho merchants who had exported beyond their capital were gazetted. In many instances it was known that they would pay in full; but in the mean time master and man were alike depressed. The prices of goods fell 40, 50, and 60 per cent. Want of confidence was also keenly felt. Some of the Scotch Banks contracted their business, contented with retaining their capital, in preference to running any risk in the pursuit of profit. This, although only a few acted so, added to the misery in that country.

A meeting of the merchants of London was con-
vened, which, after entering into a specification of the
causes of the distress, concluded by recommending a
loan of Exchequer bills.

The attention of Parliament was drawn to the
subject. An advance of six millions was authorised
by them on the principles which had guided the loan
of 1793, in sums of not less than four thousand
pounds. Few houses, however, could give the requisite security, owing to the decreased value of merchandize ; and bankruptcies were numerous.

On the 6th of May, 1811, Mr. Horner brought
forward his resolutions founded on the report of the
Bullion Committee, with a view to produce a resumption of payments in specie. The speech has been
happily eulogised by Lord Brougham as a finished
model of eloquence applied to such a subject. Anxious
that his speech should not appear to blame the Bank,
Mr. Horner gave it a testimony which, from a mind
so well versed in monetary subjects, is worth recording. " No man who has ever attended to the
distresses which, in various parts of our history, war
has produced, can doubt for a moment that from the
Bank of England, not only the government but the
commercial credit of the country, has received the
most important assistance. It is to that assistance
alone, so beneficially rendered on so many trying
occasions, that in the prospect of similar exertions
and efforts on the continent we can look for support.

The interests of the Bank of England, therefore, form a great and integral part of the public credit of the state." The debate occupied several sittings. The opinions which were propounded were as various as opinions upon the currency have ever been ; and the resolutions were lost by a vast majority.

The publication of the Bullion report was stated to have produced mischievous consequences. Napoleon's decrees, which had been levelled at our commerce, and had forbidden the importation of any English manufactures, had not effected the anticipated result. The enterprize of Great Britain sought other ports ; her gold still subsidized her opponents; her energy remained uncrushed ; her enduring courage proved on many well-fought fields that she was as fearless now, as when, centuries before, she met her ancient enemy on his own soil ; or, at a later period, battled with him beneath the shadow of the pyramids. Despairing of success, and finding himself more injured than injuring, the ruler of France was on the point of abandoning his anti-commercial policy. Subsequently, when he read the declaration of the depreciation of our currency, the necessity of returning to specie payments, and the mischiefs inflicted on this country by its paper not being convertible into cash, he persevered with increased energy.

On the 13th of May, 1811, Mr. Vansittart brought forward and carried his celebrated resolutions, to the effect, that the price of gold had advanced, but that

the value of bank notes was not depreciated. The
debate is worthy perusal, from its occasionally indecorous scenes and strange language; nor will the reader's
patience be much tired by the following specimen of a
speech, made upon the currency, in the great delibera-
tive assembly of the national council. The speaker
was a Mr. Fuller, who said, "I don't like this business
at all. I think it is a humbug. There is no depreciation, or I know nothing about the matter. I can't
understand how they would make out that there is any
depreciation of the currency. No sir, this is all the
attempt, this is all the system of the base faction, the
cowardly faction, who are undermining the credit of
the country. Yes, sir, the faction that originates
everything malevolent to ———; but, sir, I go to other
things. Some gentlemen say, sir, the guinea was once
worth 20s. It is now worth 21s., and some say it is
worth 24s. Why, then, if this be the case, why not
say so? Why not speak out? Why not raise the
guinea at once to 24s. I don't pretend to puzzle myself with these things ; but I say, let the country be
firm; let the country keep up the credit of its currency, and all will go well. There are various reports
as to what goes with the gold; some say it has disappeared ; and some say it has been hoarded on the
sea coast, in order to send it off by the first boats that
come, to take it to the continent. No matter for that.
What should hinder us from having a circulation of
our own, that nobody can take from us. The people

would make no objection, they would take anything for money; they would take tallow candles for change if they would not melt in their pockets. If we once adopt this plan, we may defy the enemy as long as we like. We can make coin of leather or oyster-shells; and if we can only keep up its credit for a year, we shall have Buonaparte on his knees at the end of it. He, that tyrant, the Emperor of France himself, will be in despair of ruining us. I wish I could see a gentleman here. I mean, Mr. Speaker, I wish I could see a gentleman in his place that was here the other night, when we were talking about playhouses. A great man, a noble person, sir, I would have given him a hundred playhouses. Sir, he always came forward, he always spoke when there was a mutiny; when there was a riot; wherever, in short, the country was in danger, he forsook his party and spoke his mind.* He would have put down this mean conspiring set, sir. I wish to set my face against the whole scheme. It grieves me to see the time of the house taken up night after night. It grieves me to see so much labour and sweating about this bullion report. Why sir, it wo'nt make a bit better appearance in the papers than that nonsensical dispute between you and me."†

* Mr. Sheridan was the individual alluded to.

† Mr. Fuller here referred to a recent scene of indecorous altercation, in which he, being heated with wine, had attempted to throw a chair at the Speaker, on which account he was committed to the custody of the Serjeant-at-arms.

Mr. Fuller was probably what is termed a " a thick and thin " man.   Sir John Sinclair followed in a speech which tended to prove the advantages of a paper issue, from the great prosperity at home and success abroad ; intimating, at the same time, an idea that the metallic phrensies of the Bullion Committee might be cooled to advantage in the Thames, the Tweed, or the Shannon.

This year was remarkable for a letter of Lord King, addressed to his tenantry.   So open an attack upon the issues of the Bank could not be passed over in silence.   It excited great censure from one party, and praise from another, and occupied the attention of the legislature no less than that of the people.   It ran as follows :

" By lease dated 1802, you have agreed to pay the annual rent of————in good and lawful money of Great Britain.   In consequence of the late depreciation of paper money, I can no longer accept of any Bank notes at their nominal value in payment for satisfaction of an old contract.   I must therefore desire you to provide for the payment of your rent in the legal coin of the realm : at the same time, having no other object than to receive payment of the real intrinsic value of the sum stipulated by agreement, and being desirous to avoid giving you unnecessary trouble, I shall be willing to receive payment in either of the manners following, according to your option.

" 1st. By payment in guineas.

" 2nd. By a payment in Portugal gold coin, equal in weight to the number of guineas requisite to discharge the debt.

" 3rd. By a payment in Bank notes of a sum sufficient to purchase, at the present market price, the weight of standard gold requisite to discharge the rent. The alteration of the value of paper money is estimated in this manner. The price of gold in 1802, the year of your agreement, was £4 per ounce; the present market price is £4 14s., arising from the diminished value of paper: in that proportion an addition of £17 10s. per cent. in paper money will be required, as the equivalent for the payment of rent in paper.

" KING.

" N.B. A power of re-entry and ejectment is reserved by deed in case of non-payment of rent due. No draft will be received."

This notice was too important and significant to escape animadversion. It struck at the very root of the declaration that Bank notes retained their original value, and was therefore warmly debated in the Upper House. But the descendant of the illustrious Locke was not a man to be daunted from the path he had chosen. He boldly defended his circular, asserted the depreciation of the Bank note, and maintained the superior value of the metal. It appears by the following extract from the " Morning Chronicle " of

1802, however, that the idea of his lordship had previously occurred to others:

"Thursday being the general licensing day for victuallers in the parish of St. Martin's-in-the-fields, the publicans received previous notice that they must pay the usual licenses in hard cash, as no Bank of England notes would be taken."

If this paragraph may be relied on, the claim of novelty is lost to Lord King. The difficulty was, however, met by Lord Stanhope proposing a resolution declaring it illegal to receive or give more than 21s. for a guinea, or less than 20s. for a one pound note.

"The Bank," said the Earl, "is one of the bottom planks of the ship of England, and woe be to us if we permit it to be bored through." Lord Holland defended Lord King, and said that it was a most judicious act, as he was only doing that which the claims of himself and his family demanded ; and that he acted according to the law of the country. Lord Grenville eulogized the character of Lord King, his public spirit, his great information, the remarkable extent of his acquaintance with the subject discussed, and spoke of his private virtues, and his general bene-volence of disposition. Among other remarks Lord King said, " I saw no course left but to give up my property, or hold it at such value as the Bank, in its good pleasure, might put upon it, or to avail myself of the means which the law yet affords me for its preservation."

When produced before the Lower House, a warm discussion was created. Opinions, varying as much as the views of the speakers, were enunciated. It was said by some that the Bank note had not depreciated at all : it was asserted by others that it had decreased immensely. Some honourable members avowed their belief that if the bill should pass, the glory of England would pass with it ; while others expressed their conviction that it was the only chance the country possessed of maintaining its greatness. Many took the opportunity of prophesying that which time has proved to be false; while others contented themselves with contradicting their opponents, and uttering oracular sayings, more distinguished for vagueness than for wisdom.

The resolution was materially altered by the ministers, and only about five lines left unchanged of his lordship's bill, which, however, retained its purport and original intention.

Lord King, on the third reading, asserted that the law would create additional mischief, and great inconvenience ; that landlords would now refuse to grant leases ; that the bill could not effect its object, or retard the depreciation of bank notes. Lord Eldon gave his powerful sanction to the act, and declared that the claim of Lord King, in the letter of the latter to his tenantry, was oppressive and unjust, and that the bill was necessary to prevent such grievous wrong. The following forms part of his speech : " The Restriction Act of 1797 interfered so far with individual contracts as to say that a debtor should not be arrested, if he tendered his debt in bank notes ; the justice of that enactment has never been disputed, and it is now to be said, that a tenant shall have his goods or stock seized, because he cannot pay in gold, which is not to be procured? Let us suppose a young professional man, struggling with the world, who has a rent to pay of £90 per annum, and who has £3000 in the Bank, in the three per cents. His lordship demands his rent in gold, but the Bank refuses to pay the tenant his dividend in gold. Would not the tenant have a right to say, ' as a public creditor I am refused any other payment than in bank notes ; but here is a legislator—one of those by whose act of Parliament I am thus refused to be paid except in bank notes—insisting upon my paying him his rent in gold, which I cannot procure; and because I cannot procure it my goods are to be distrained !' Would not this be a grievous oppression? Surely so long as it should be expendient to continue the Cash Suspension Act of 1797, this present bill must become a part of it : for otherwise there would be no equality in the situation of different contracting parties, nor would equal justice be dealt out to those who had an equal claim to it; as there could be no justice in leaving the tenant, who had tendered bank notes, exposed to be distrained upon by his landlord, whilst the debtor in other cases, who had tendered bank notes, was exempt from arrest. I am peculiarly situated with respect to this question, having the official care of twenty-five millions of the property of his Majesty's subjects, and without the means of enforcing the payment of any part of that sum except in bank notes."

The bill, which was limited to the 25th of March, 1814, passed, and enacts " that the taking of gold coin at more than its value, or Bank notes at less, shall be deemed a misdemeanour."

A protest was entered, as " manifestly tending to the compulsory circulation of a paper currency; a measure necessarily productive of the most fatal calamities." Lord Holland added, that " he made it also, because, in his judgment, the repeal of the Cash Suspension Act was the only means which could cure the yet greater calamities which were impending, from the present state of the circulation of the country."

At one period in 1811 the market price of gold touched £5 11s., and the Bank note sunk to 14s. A regular traffic was maintained; guineas were bought at a premium, and Bank notes sold at a discount. In spite of Lord Stanhope's Act, the traffic continued. While the mint coined, there were always exporters ready to take advantage of the exchanges; it was, indeed, according to one of the members, only a contest which would tire first. " The havoc which the depreciation had made with all the dealings of men," says Lord Brougham, " was incalculable. Those who had lent money when the currency was at par, received the depreciated payment, and lost thirty or forty per cent. Those who had granted leases received only two-thirds of their interest, and were liable to be paid off with two-thirds of their capital." The following will give some idea of the necessity of the restrictions which had been so often placed on specie payment. "Buonaparte," says Knight's History of England, " never took the field without carrying an immense military chest with him, and this chest, from obvious motives of convenience, was always filled and replenished with gold. On starting on a campaign the French officers, and even those of the soldiers who had money, were all eager to convert it into gold, some of which was carried with them, and some secreted at home. In France, all cautious persons accumulated all the gold specie they could, to conceal and keep it for the evil hour. Nearly all over the continent the insecurity of property and the dread of forced contributions, and of less regular plunder, had induced the habit of hoarding and hiding; and gold was bought up and sought for at a constantly increasing price, to be buried in the earth or concealed in secret recesses. In this matter, as in others, Europe was returning to her ancient barbarism, or to the condition of the despotic nations of the earth, where so large a proportion of the precious metals is constantly withdrawn from circulation and kept hidden. In 1812 and 1813, as much as six Spanish dollars could be obtained in any part of the Mediterranean for an English guinea. With such a temptation to send gold abroad, it was not likely that English traders and speculators should be prevented from sending gold to the best market. Even in England, Scotland, and Ireland, the practice of hoarding specie, during the whole of this revolutionary war, was far from being uncommon. Again, every English officer, traveller, or merchant that went abroad, endeavoured to carry with him some gold, as a *corps de reserve*, in case of capture by the enemy, or of other accident. Through all these causes united, a guinea, half a guinea, or seven shilling piece had become a rare sight in Great Britain."

A rise of ten per cent. in the current value of the stamped dollar took place in the same year. In consequence of the advance in the price of gold, the dollars circulated by the Bank sold for more as bullion than their rate as coin. To remedy this evil, a notice was published by the directors, that they would receive all Bank dollar tokens at the rate of 5s. 6d. each, instead of 5s. The same notice advertised that for the future they would be issued from the Bank at the increased price. Some of the members of the House of Commons animadverted strongly upon this announcement; but they were silenced by the reply of Mr. Manning, one of the directors, " that the arrangement would cost the Bank fifty thousand pounds; and put as much into the pockets of the public." In the latter part of the year, in conse-

quence of great inconvenience experienced from the
absence of small change, the Bank issued large
quantities of silver tokens at 5s. 6d., 3s., and 1s. 6d.

The extensive circulation of these tokens rendered
some protection from counterfeits necessary. A bill
was, therefore, passed to this effect; and Lord Stanhope's
act of the previous year was continued until three
months after the opening of the next session. A
clause was proposed by Lord Archibald Hamilton for
confining the dividend of profits to proprietors of the
Bank to £10 per cent., in order to give them an
interest in the recommencement of specie payment.
This was negatived; and Mr. Spencer Percival carried
an amendment in its place, by which the landlord
was deprived of the right of ejectment after a tender
of Bank notes from the tenant; and, in 1814, the
bill of Lord Stanhope was protracted during the Bank
Restriction Act.

The frequent motions made by Mr. Pascoe Grenfell
relative to the Bank of England, some to limit the
profits, and others to procure accounts and documents
from the Corporation, must be familiar to the readers
of parliamentary history. Though the motions were
almost invariably negatived, and the good or evil
tendency of a regular publication of the affairs of the
establishment is a disputed question, there can be
little doubt, from the decided ability with which they
were conducted, that they tended greatly to prepare
the public mind for the system which prevails at

present. Among other things, he contended that the Bank did not pay sufficient stamp duty ; and, in 1815, the Chancellor of the Exchequer announced that he had negociated with the Bank on the subject of a composition for stamps on their notes, the result of which would be communicated. The arrangement formed was on the average of the circulation during the preceding year, the principle being, that the Bank should pay £3500 for every million sterling issued of their paper.

On the 21st of February, 1814, the Bank of England and its neighbourhood wore an appearance of great excitement. The military operations of Buonaparte, by which he checked the great allied powers, had depressed the funds. Deep anxiety for the result was felt throughout England. On that day, however, although what is termed " a private day," the clerks in all the stock offices of the establishment were busily employed in preparing transfers, which, contrary to the custom on such a day, poured in from the members of the Stock Exchange. Reports and rumours spread rapidly. Many of the transfers remained unfinished, as a plot, intended to deceive all London, was discovered in time to prevent their execution. The following is a brief narration of this important conspiracy.

On the 21st of February, 1814, about one o'clock in the morning, a violent knocking was heard at the door of the Ship Inn, at Dover. On being opened, the intruder annnounced himself as Lieutenant Colonel Du Bourg, aide-de-camp of Lard Cathcart. His dress supported the assertion. The richly-embroidered scarlet uniform, the star on the breast, the silver medal suspended from his neck, the dark fur cap, with its broad band of gold lace, gave the wearer a military appearance. His clothes appeared wet with the sea spray, and he stated that he had been brought over by a French vessel, the seamen of which were afraid of landing at Dover, and had placed him in a boat about two miles from the shore. His news was important. Buonaparte had been slain in battle. The allied armies were in Paris. A great victory had been gained; and peace was certain. He immediately ordered a post-chaise and four horses to be prepared; enquired the residence of Admiral Foley; and, with the appearance of great haste and excitement, wrote the following letter.

"To the Right Hon. T. Foley, Port Admiral, Deal.

"Sir,—I have the honour to acquaint you that L'Aigle, from Calais, Pierre Duquin, Master, has this moment landed me near Dover, to proceed to the capital with despatches of the happiest nature. I have pledged my honour that no harm shall come to the crew of L'Aigle. Even with a flag of truce, they immediately stood for sea. Should they be taken I entreat you immediately to liberate them. My anxiety will not allow me to say more for your gratification than that the allies obtained a final victory;

that Buonaparte was overtaken by a party of Sachen's Cossacks, who immediately slaid him and divided his body between them. General Platoff saved Paris from being reduced to ashes. The allied sovereigns are there; and the white cockade is universal. An immediate peace is certain. In the utmost haste I entreat your consideration, &c. Signed,

M. Du Bourg, Lieutenant-Colonel, and Aide-de-camp to Lord Cathcart."

A special messenger was dispatched to Deal; and the letter reached the admiral between three and four o'clock. The morning proved foggy; the telegraph could not work; and Admiral Foley was saved from an involuntary deception. Directly the letter was forwarded, Du Bourg entered the post-chaise, and, with every appearance of haste, departed for London. Wherever he changed horses the news was spread, and the post-boys rewarded with napoleons. On his arrival at Bexley-heath, the intelligence was acquired that the telegraph could not have acted; on which he told them not to drive so fast. He then added that the war was over; that Buonaparte was cut into a thousand pieces; and that the Cossacks fought for a share of his body. At the Marsh-gate, Lambeth, he entered a hackney-coach, after informing the post-boys that they might spread the news as they returned. In the mean time information reached the stock exchange; and by a little after ten it was filled with rumours of general officers, despatches for government, victories, and post-chaises and four. Expresses from the various places where Du Bourg had changed horses poured in to the principal speculators. The funds rose on the news. Application was made to the Lord Mayor, but, as his Lordship had received no intelligence, they declined.

On the morning of the same day, about an hour before daylight, two men in the habiliments of foreigners landed in a six-oared galley, called on a Mr. Sandon, at Northfleet, and handed him a letter purporting to be written by one whom he formerly knew, begging him to take the bearers to London, as they had great public news to communicate. The request was complied with. Between twelve and one o'clock in the afternoon of that day, three persons, two of whom were dressed as French officers, proceeded in a post-chaise and four, the horses of which were bedecked with laurel, over the then narrow and crowded thoroughfare of London Bridge. While the carriage proceeded with an almost ostentatious slowness, small billets were scattered among the anxious gazers, announcing that Buonaparte was dead, and the allies in Paris. Through busy Cheapside and crowded Fleet-street, the occupants of the carriage paraded their intelligence. They passed over the fine bridge of Blackfriars, drove rapidly to the Marsh Gate, got out, took off their military, put on round hats, and speedily disappeared. The news again spread far and wide. The neighbourhood of the Stock Exchange was once more full of exaggerated reports. The funds rose. What could resist such accumulated evidence ? The aide-de-camp of Lord Cathcart at Dover; two foreigners at North-fleet with dispatches; private expresses from various places; all tended to convince the members that there must be some foundation for the reports. Application was made to the ministry, but they knew nothing. Large bargains were made. The scene at the Stock Exchange is described by those who witnessed it as baffling all description. Yet still there was some doubt, so long as government remained ignorant of the important intelligence. And as hour after hour of anxious doubt passed by, it would be difficult to imagine the feelings of many who had suffered from the delusion. "To this scene of joy," says one, "and of greedy expectation of gain, succeeded, in a few hours, that of disappointment, shame at having been gulled, the clenching of fists, the grinding of teeth, the tearing of hair, all the outward and visible signs of those inward commotions, of disappointed avarice in some, consciousness of ruin in others, and, in all, boiling revenge." A committee was appointed by the Stock Exchange, and various circumstances tending to prove a conspiracy were discovered. On the Saturday preceding the Monday on which the deception was attempted, consols and omnium to the extent of £826,000 were purchased for various individuals, many of whom were seriously implicated.

A name known and loved in England was said to be included. Lord Cochrane, endeared to the English people by the most gallant naval successes ever achieved, was, on the 21st of June, 1814, tried with some others at the Court of Queen's Bench, and sentenced to twelve months imprisonment. His Lordship and another were fined £1000 each. They were also in addition to stand one hour in the pillory, but this was remitted. The decision with regard to Lord Cochrane (now Earl of Dundonald), excited great animadversion. A conviction was very generally expressed that there was some doubt, and the public feeling was disposed to accord him the benefit. This might perhaps have been a national sympathy towards one of the most gallant sailors in the royal navy. The actions of Lord Cochrane have been rarely surpassed; and if, as he always steadily affirmed, and as many circumstances tend to prove, he was more sinned against than sinning, it is one of the most melancholy instances in modern record of great achievements being followed by great misfortunes. The name of Cochrane, for the last thirty years, has been associated with fraud, because mankind are too prone to take on trust the traditions of their fathers. It is pleasant to be able to add that the present sovereign has rewarded his lordship for his past sufferings, and evinced her belief in his innocence by restoring to him those honours of which he should never have been deprived.

CHAPTER XIV.

PEACE OF 1815—CONTINUATION OF RESTRICTION—COMMERCIAL
DIFFICULTIES—BONUS ON THE CAPITAL—PARTIAL RESUMPTION
OF CASH PAYMENTS—LEGAL DECISIONS—MR. PEEL'S CURRENCY
BILL—RETURN TO CASH PAYMENTS—THE DEAD WEIGHT—PEN-
SION LIST—DIMINUTION OF DIVIDEND—FORGERY OF FAUNT-
LEROY.

IN 1815 a universal song of triumph arose, from the
prospect of that peace which had been denied to
Europe for nearly a quarter of a century. The terrible
excitement of "the hundred days" had passed. The
earth ceased to be nourished with human blood. The
field of Waterloo, that field which was described by
the great man there as a "battle of giants," had
darkened every gleam of hope for him who in
three years had destroyed the compact strength of
Austria, crushed the military power of Prussia, and,
by forcing the Czar to sign the treaty of Tilsit, had
placed the sceptre of the continent in his own hands.
Throughout the world there was a general yearning
after repose. The sight of an empty treasury was
attended to when the voice of humanity was scoffed at.

The tranquillity, which gave independence to Holland and freedom to the Swiss, which rewarded the guerilla of the Spanish hills and the patriot of Portugal for their unyielding defence of their country, was of no less importance to England. The relations of commerce, "the golden chain of nations," which tend to bind the whole earth in one tie of brotherhood, were once more resumed. Since then, civilization has asserted its proper influence. The developement of science, for social benefit, its true end and aim, has rapidly progressed. The poor man is no more regarded as a serf. The horrors of war, and the ancient antipathies of nations, are passing into traditions. " Poverty preserved the peace of Europe," says an eloquent writer. The gold which had kept the despot at bay, had been gained in greater proportions from the artizan and the sons of the soil, than from the master manufacturer or the country gentleman. The war, indeed, had affected all classes ; and the Bank of England, in its different departments, had experienced its effect. The funds, which had drooped or risen from hour to hour, as good or bad fortune prevailed, had created business to an extent varying with the excitement of the period. The large advances to the State, the cessation of cash payments, the general prosperity of trade, made a period of hostilities a period of profit. The prospect, therefore, of recommencing payments in specie, to accomplish which it would be necessary to collect a large amount of bullion, was an important consideration. On the restoration of peace, however, the restriction was continued by a new act, until the 5th July, 1816, and was again renewed until July, 1818.

In 1814 the State repaid the three millions advanced in 1800 without interest, and continued in 1806 at three per cent., until six months from the ratification of peace. The three millions also, lent without interest in 1808, became due in December, 1815. This money had been advanced principally in consideration of the large public balances in the Bank. In consequence of these deposits remaining undiminished, the Chancellor of the Exchequer addressed a letter to the Governor, claiming the continuance of the loan until April, 1816. This proposal was produced before a general Court of Proprietors, and agreed to.

A long list of declarations was entered on the books of the House of Commons, by Mr. Mellish, affirmatory of the services rendered by the Corporation to the State. It was chiefly enumerative of those which have been already alluded to, and were the result of some resolutions proposed by Mr. Grenfell. Among others was one which stated that, during the existence of the income tax, the Bank had made the calculations on the dividend warrants, deducted the money from the interest of the fund-holders, and paid it in, without charge, to the account of the Government, and that, in one year, the number of warrants from which this reduction had been made amounted to 565,600. The cost of this was very great; but it bore no comparison whatever to the enormous saving effected by the government, through the interference of the corporation.

The distress of 1811 had been relieved. The expulsion of the French from Portugal, and the noble achievements of our army in Spain, had once more unclosed the trade with the Peninsula. These, with other causes, again produced the temptation to over-trade. "The departure of the French from Portugal," says an authority of the day, " has once more opened commerce with that country; and vast quantities of goods of the manufacture of Great Britain are now shipping for Lisbon and Oporto." " Large orders for all kinds of woollen, linen, and cotton goods, have arrived here for Portugal and South America." The warehouses were soon filled, though not with so much rapidity as in the first trade to South America. " It was not yet marked," says Mr. Tooke, " by such eagerness of speculative shipment as had distinguished 1808 and 1809." A sufficient quantity was however exported to glut the markets; prices were ruinously low, and goods were sold on terms which scarcely paid the charges of insurance and shipment.

Circumstances connected with the South American speculations have, perhaps, been too lightly passed over. They form an episode in history, which approaches nearly to romance, and, therefore call for a brief record. Tempted by the reports, which were plentiful, of the wealth and weakness of the Spanish Colonies, Sir Home Popham set sail from the Cape of Good Hope, which he had just taken, for South America, and, on his arrival, attacked and carried Buenos Ayres. The adventure had been undertaken on the sole authority of Sir Home; and knowing that success is often the great justifier, he sent a circular manifesto to the merchants and manufacturers of Great Britain, which occasioned much excitement. A land, abounding with gold, had been conquered; a whole continent was open to British enterprize. A million of dollars was sent to London, and a sufficient amount was retained for contingent expences.

When information of the wild expedition first arrived in London, orders were sent to recal Sir Home; but when the news of the conquest arrived, when the dollars came home, and the commercial prospects were known, an order of Council was gazetted, stating that a lawful trade might be carried on in Buenos Ayres and its dependencies. The trading interest was filled with exultation, and Sir Home Popham's adventure was sanctified by success. "Ministers sanctioned the whole scheme," says an historian; "but before people at home had finished rejoicing for the conquest, the conquest was no more, and the capturers captive." A popular insurrection was organized; and Sir Home narrowly escaped being made prisoner in the place which he had carried with a mere handful of men; while those who had sent their merchandize keenly lamented their thoughtless confidence.

Mr. Tooke, says, in his "History of Prices," that from 1814 to 1817 there was a considerable depression in nearly all productions, and in the value of all fixed property." In Holland our goods were bought cheaper than in England, and many merchants purchased them for home consumption. In 1815 and 1816 there were 5014 bankruptcies, 63 of which were bankers ; the number of stoppages and compositions being probably in proportion.

The various periods of excitement and depression from 1797 to 1816, during the whole of which the company had been restrained from paying its notes in gold, appear to have worked altogether beneficially for the interests of the proprietors of Bank stock. The years 1799, 1801, 1802, 1804, and 1806, had each produced a money bonus. In the following year the regular dividend was raised from seven to ten per cent. These modes of enlarging the profits of the proprietary were legitimate and just. In 1816 a bonus of a more extraordinary kind took place. It can indeed be only accounted for by the constant success which had attended the company, by the large gains which accrued to them as the great circulating medium of the country, and above all by there being no necessity to keep a large amount of bullion to meet the payment of their notes. The interest saved by the latter circumstance alone must have amounted to an enormous sum, and these facts united must be accepted as some cause for the policy which dictated the announcement that an addition of twenty-five per cent. would be made upon the capital stock of each proprietor, in proportion to his share. An act of Parliament was necessary to carry this into effect ; and the Bank directors were authorised to increase the capital from £11,642,400 to £14,553,000, at which amount it now remains.

It was not possible for the ministry to witness such an evidence of wealth without endeavouring to partake of it. They compelled the Bank, therefore, in return for this permission to give a bonus to their proprietors, to lend three millions at three per cent. for two years, thus making them pay about eighty thousand pounds for the privilege of dividing their own capital, although the Chancellor acknowledged,—"This is in other words only granting permission to the proprietors to divide among themselves three millions of their own money, in consideration of their advancing a similar sum for the public service."

The policy of this bonus is not even questionable. It has entailed a heavy charge upon the management of the Bank since that period. The interest of three millions at ten, eight, and seven per cent. respectively, has necessarily pressed on its resources. The prosperity however which had marked the progress of the corporation from 1797, the continuance of the war, the demand for discounts, the large circulation of its issues, must be received as an apology. The time

named for the return of cash payments had two years
to run. The war which had tended to enrich the
company for so many years might again break out.
Their charter embraced a considerable period before
its expiration. All these circumstances, combined with
the great success that had hitherto distinguished the
career of the institution, tended doubtless to produce a mental intoxication, resulting in an act which,
though favourable to the proprietary in many respects,
caused a fall in the price of their stock. The period
was equally beneficial to other corporations. The
private bankers benefitted. The merchant made
larger gains. The employé was paid a higher salary.
The master made more profits. The servant received
increased pay. And amid all this scene of public
welfare the Bank alone was censured for advantaging
with the rest, and was accused in the House of
Commons of being favoured too much by government,
because prosperity followed in the wake of skill. A
reference to the dates when many of the existing
companies were founded, will show that they owe
their existence to this period. The principle of Life
Assurance, that principle which cannot be urged too
strongly, received a further impulse; and the origin
of many of those companies now holding a high
position, may be traced to the general enterprise
excited by war prices and war profits.

In 1817, the directors, desirous, perhaps, of testing
the feeling of the public with regard to metallic

payments, announced that, after the 2nd of May of that year, they would pay cash for all their notes of one and two pounds, dated prior to the 1st of January, 1816, or exchange them for new notes of the same value. The confidence, however, of the public was great; and scarcely any demand was made on their coffers. In October of the same year a further notice was issued, that on and after the 1st day of October, they would be ready to pay gold for all their notes dated prior to 1st of January, 1817. Every exertion, since the commencement of peace, had been made to resume specie payment with safety. The collection of bullion had been rapid, and to a large amount; and it was soon found that these precautionary measures had not been thrown away. The difference between a legitimate demand for gold by the public, and a demand for the same material by speculators, was rapidly witnessed.

When the one and two pound notes, that description of paper held principally by the poor man, were called in, the amount of cash claimed was not more than one million. When, however, it was announced that all notes prior to a particular date would be paid in specie, the bullion speculator stepped in, took advantage of the exchanges, and sent more than five millions to the continent. On the report of Mr. Peel, the house passed a bill in two nights, restraining the Bank from paying the notes alluded to.

That a great increase in bullion tended to justify this measure is indisputable. In 1816 and 1817, some of the country bankers found it difficult to dispose of their coin. Preference was shown to their notes; and it cost one firm £100 to transmit its surplus specie to London. At another period, in bringing one thousand guineas to a London banker, the latter begged as a favour that the gold might not be left, as he had sent so much to the Bank, and did not like to trouble the establishment with any more.

During the imperial career of Buonaparte, it had been his favourite idea that England would be eventually rendered powerless, by draining her of gold. In this he was strengthened by the language held by the opponents of government, and especially by the report of the Bullion Committee. In Knight's "History" we read: "The members of the Parliamentary opposition and the opposition newspapers had assured the world that Great Britain was altogether incapable of continuing a struggle which was draining up her resources, that she was exhausted and impoverished, and that every effort she made against the power and will of France, only hurried on her final ruin. But here was a voice of another kind; here a committee of the House of Commons, composed of men of name and reputation, some of whom had recently belonged to the ministry, declared in a report to the whole country that the paper currency was depreciated, was becoming every day more and more like the *assignats* of the French revolutionists, and that the only remedy that could be proposed was the impracticable and impossible resumption of cash payments; here a noble lord, who was lately prime minister, supports the principles laid down in the report; here another noble lord tells his tenantry he will not take depreciated bank notes for his rent, and finds other peers ready to back him, and support the argument that a national bankruptcy is imminent and inevitable. These men must know better than we the real state and prospects of the country. *Allons* then! let us persevere a little longer; let us burn all English merchandize, wherever found, let us punish all who attempt to bring British goods into the continent, and for the triumph of this great system let us brave and despise the remonstrances and the enmity of the Czar." "Yet, after all, the bullionists may be said, without perhaps intending it, to have done a fatal injury to the Emperor of the French, for through them he was encouraged to persevere, and even to attempt to coerce the Czar, and hence followed the Russian campaign, and the disastrous retreat from Moscow."

Another attempt was made, in 1818, to procure a dividend of the entire gains of the Corporation. Nathaniel Grundy, having been negatived in his endeavour in the Bank parlour, had recourse to the Queen's Bench, where he met with that success which the nature of his application merited. It is difficult seriously to entertain the idea of dividing all the profits of an establishment like the Bank, liable to pecuniary calls of great magnitude ; and the affair may be dismissed as an evidence of the short-sightedness of those who would act either without evidence by which to judge, or capacity to comprehend the consequences.

A curious scene took place in May at the Bank. On the 26th of that month, a notice had been posted, stating that books would be opened on the 31st of May, and two following days, for receiving subscriptions to the amount of seven millions, from persons desirous of funding Exchequer bills. It was generally thought that the whole of the sum would be immediately filled, and great anxiety was shown to obtain an early admission to the office of the chief cashier. Ten o'clock is the usual time for public business ; but at two in the morning many persons were assembled outside the building, where they remained for several hours, their numbers gradually augmenting. The opening of the outer door was the signal for a general rush, and the crowd, for it now deserved that name, next established themselves in the passage leading to the chief cashier's office, where they had to wait another hour or two to cool their collective impatience. When the time arrived a further contest arose, and they strove lustily for an entrance. The struggle for preference was tremendous ; and the door, separating them from the chief cashier's room, and which is of a most substantial size, was forced off its hinges. By far the greater part of those who made this effort failed, the whole £7,000,000 being subscribed by the first ten persons who gained admission.

In 1819, a trial, well worthy recording, took place. Mr. Ransom, an engraver, having paid a one pound note to a Mr. Mitchener, the latter found it was detained by the Bank, upon the ground of its being a forgery. Upon this Mr. Mitchener claimed a repayment of the amount from Ransom, which was refused until the return of the note. Mr. Mitchener immediately summoned him, and procured the attendance of Mr. Fish, an inspector of the Bank, with the note in question. Ransom requested to look at it, and permission having been granted, he deliberately placed it in his pocket, and avowed his intention of keeping it. An appeal to the magistrate was of no avail, as he declined to interfere ; on which Ransom went to Mitchener's house, and paid the twenty shillings.

This style of treatment was rather too decided for the Corporation quietly to permit ; and Fish, it is to be presumed, at the instigation of the directors, made a charge in writing against Ransom for knowingly having a forged note in his possession. On this the magistrate committed him to Cold Bath Fields, to remain there till duly discharged by law. After a

few day's incarceration, he was liberated on bail.
Mr. Ransom, however, was not to be so quietly dismissed. He brought an action for false and malicious
imprisonment against Fish ; and, after producing
several witnesses, the evidence of whom went to show
the note was genuine, and no person being present
from the Bank to prove the contrary, as the directors
were quite unprepared for this statement, the jury
brought in a verdict for the plaintiff of £100.
Previous to this period it had always been the practice
of the Bank to detain the forged notes which were
offered to them for payment, with the view of saving
the public from being again imposed upon. Since
the circumstances enumerated, however, the notes
have been returned to the parties presenting them ;
the same beneficial result being obtained by stamping
the word " forged " upon them in several places.

The value of the Bank paper, which, in 1815 and
1816, was about 16¾ per cent. below that of gold,
rose, in 1817 and 1818, to within 2½ per cent. of
bullion; and, in 1819, the depreciation amounted to
about 4½ per cent. On 20th January, 1819, the
directors submitted a resolution to government to the
effect, that there was little probability of a return to
cash payments by March, 1820, and that it would
be preferable to submit to a parliamentary enquiry
rather than to delude the public with an expectation
not likely to be realised. A committee of secrecy
was appointed ; and after an examination of mer-

chants, bankers, and Bank directors, from all of whom opposite opinions were elicited, the committee concluded by recommending a certain mode of action embodied in a report which Mr. Peel presented to the house. Lord Brougham says, the attention of Parliament, chiefly through the press, was awakened to the state of our affairs. The government saw that something must be done to stop the depreciation of bank paper, and to restore the standard. At length the government of Lord Liverpool, under the influence of Mr. Peel, who was one of its most powerful supporters, though not then in office, undertook the settlement of the question; and a committee was appointed, which, after a full investigation of the subject, reported in favour of an unqualified resumption of cash payments.

By this report the Bank were liable to pay on

30th of January, 1819	£33,894,550
While their assets were . . .	39,096,900
	5,202,320

exclusive of the permanent debt due from government to the Bank of £14,686,800, re-payable on the expiration of the charter.

The act, known so well as Mr. Peel's currency bill, passed in 1819, and was, perhaps, one of the most important of the kind which ever met the sanction of both houses of legislature.

A remarkable feature in its history is to be found in a petition from the merchants of the city of

London, presented by the late Sir Robert Peel, against
the measure proposed by his son. After stating that
his petitioners were the best calculated to judge on so
important a point, and that a meeting which he had
attended for this purpose was composed of the very
men who had so nobly supported the government in
1797, he proceeded to say, in language as feeling
as the subject was interesting, that " he well remembered, when that near and dear relation was only a
child, he observed to some friends who were standing
near him, that the man who discharged his duty to his
country in the manner which Mr. Pitt did, did most
to be admired, and was most to be imitated; and he
thought at that moment, if his own life and that of
his dear relation should be spared, he would one day
present him to his country to follow in the same path.
He was well satisfied that the head and heart of
that relation were in their right places ; and that
though he had deviated a little from the path of
propriety in this instance, he would soon be restored
to it."

When Mr. Peel introduced this currency act to the
house, it was with one of those elaborate speeches for
which his name is distinguished. After an elegant
and powerful tribute to Mr. Horner, he proceeded to
state that the house must now resolve whether the
old metallic standard should be restored or not, and
he thought it impossible that any considerate man
could hesitate on that question. One witness only

had been an advocate for the indefinite suspension of cash payments, and had stated that the pound should be the standard of value. When required to define what he meant by the pound, his answer was, " I find it difficult to explain it ; but every gentleman in England knows it ; it is something that has existed without variation in this country for eight hundred years." Mr. Locke could not define what he meant by an abstract pound. Sir Isaac Newton came to the doctrine that the true standard of value consisted in a certain quantity of gold bullion. Every sound writer arrived at the same conclusion. After an able historical exposition of the three distinct periods of difficulties which had stood in the way of the restora- tion of the standard of value, and a graceful allusion to the great public duty imposed upon him, from which he would not shrink whatever might be his private feelings, he proceeded to the resolutions, which, after various forms and modes of opposition, were passed.

This memorable bill provides that, from the 1st of February to the 1st of October, the Bank shall deliver on demand gold of standard fineness, not less than sixty ounces, in exchange for bank notes, at £4 1s. per oz. From 1st of October, 1820, to 1st of October, 1821, the same plan to be adopted ; but the gold to be at the rate of £3 19s. 6d. per ounce. From the 1st of May, 1821, to the 1st of May, 1823, the Mint price of gold of £3 17s. 10½ per oz., to be the rate, with the adoption of the same plan ; and from the 1st of May, 1823, the notes to be paid in the gold coin of the empire if required. Between the 1st of February and the 1st of October, 1820, the Bank were empowered to deliver gold at any rate between £4 1s. and £3 19s. 6d. per oz. ; and from the 1st of October, 1820, to May the 1st, 1821, they were also allowed to do the same at any rate between £3 19s. 6d. and £3 17s. 10½d, in ingots or bars of gold, weighing sixty ounces. They were permitted also the option of paying in specie on or after the 1st of May, 1822. By the same act the laws which restrained the exportation of gold and silver coin, or prohibited it from being melted, were repealed.

This bill was the first commencement of that great principle enunciated by Mr. Peel, that the national Bank should always be prepared to pay specie for its notes on demand, a principle he has since worked out in the last Bank charter. Mr. Peel's act, says one writer, was passed amid general acclamations. Mr. Canning pronounced the question to be settled for ever. Among the public, various opinions, comprised in pamphlets and octavo volumes, were disseminated. Mr. Tooke, however, has, perhaps, paid the highest compliment to the bill in the observation, that had it not been for the derangement of our currency, occasioned by the large financial operations of the continental states, in 1817 and 1818, in which loans were raised to the amount of

38,600,000, the renewal of cash payments in this
country would have taken place as a matter of course
in 1818. These words prove that Mr. Peel, with that
remarkable power which distinguishes him, of com-
prehending and replying to the demands of the time,
had chosen the proper period for the resumption;
while, by the gradual tone of the bill, he prevented any
sudden, and, perhaps, mischievous, return to specie
payments.

On the 22nd of January, 1819, a committee appointed to enquire into the mode of preventing the
forgery of bank notes made their report, in which
they stated that the directors had furnished them with
a detailed account of one hundred and eight projects,
regularly classed and arranged, together with the
correspondence concerning them, a statement of the
trials to which they had been subjected, and speci-
mens of the proposed originals, and of the imitations
executed by order of the Bank. They had also received and answered communications from seventy
individuals, and in some cases held a personal interview with them. They had examined forged notes
of various kinds, and the tools and instruments of one
forger which were taken upon him; and that from the
capital and skill employed in carrying out the crime
there must always be a liability of imitation. "One
plan," they concluded by saying, "has been, with the
liberal assistance of the Bank directors, for some time
past in a course of trial, for its greater perfection.

The result, if our expectations be not disappointed, will afford a specimen of great ingenuity in the fabric of the paper, of great excellence in the workmanship, and of a very peculiar invention and difficult machinery in the art of printing." The following is a description, from a contemporary authority, of the improved note. A number of squares will appear in chequer work upon the note, filled with hair lines in elliptic curves of various degrees of eccentricity, the squares to be alternately of red and black lines ; the perfect mathematical coincidence of the extremities of the lines of different colours on the sides of the squares will be effected by the arrangement of machinery of singular fidelity. But even with the use of this machinery a person who has not the key to the proper disposition would make millions of experiments to no purpose. Other obstacles to imitation will be also presented in the structure of the note ; but this is the one principally relied upon. It is plain that any failure in the imitation will be manifest to the observation of the most careless ; and the most skilful merchants who have seen the operation declare that the note cannot be imitated. The machine works with three cylinders, and the impression is made by small convex cylindrical plates.

In 1821, after a quarter of a century, the Bank re-commenced specie payments. The currency bill of Mr. Peel allowed them the option of paying in gold coin on and after the 1st of May, 1822.

Anxious, however, to meet the spirit of the act, which required a return to a metallic currency whenever it should be safe to all interests, the directors commenced paying on the 1st of May, 1821. Of the beautiful coin so well known as the sovereign, which was produced in 1817, 9,971,364, were issued during the ensuing year.

It is a curious fact that, a few weeks before, a writer who possessed considerable weight with the public, confidently affirmed, that the carrying out of the measure which prescribed the Bank to pay the bullion at mint prices, on the 1st of May, 1822, would be attended with most unfortunate circumstances to the country. His assertion, for the fulfilment of which he offered to stake his life, had not long been made known, when the Bank came forward, begging that they might be permitted to anticipate by a year the term fixed on for their payment in coin.

When this subject was mooted in the House, Mr. Baring proposed the establishment of a double standard, to consist of gold and silver. He also condemned the committee appointed to enquire into the question of forgery, who had failed because they had entertained an overweening solicitude to discover something absolutely perfect.

A singular and very intricate fraud was discovered this year. The perpetrator was William Swiney Barnard Turner, one of the clerks in the service of the corporation. It is painful to record internal

treachery; but it has, at least, been some gratification to the writer, that such instances have not
often presented themselves.   It was the duty of
Turner to post, on a certain day, £4,795. 15s. in
the navy 5 per cents., to the account of Sir
Robert Peel.   In place of this, he gave him credit to
the extent of £14,795. 15s., thus increasing the
amount due to Sir Robert by £10,000.   Having
secured the foundation of the object which he had in
view, the next movement was to dispose of the
amount which he had thus created by a single stroke
of his pen.   The second step was effected with almost
as much facility as the first, by opening an acccount
in the fictitious name of J. Penn, of Highgate, whom
he credited to the amount of £10,000.   A purchaser
was found, the stock appeared to the credit of the
seller, and the transfer was effected.

The fraud was found out by the accidental discovery
that a leaf had disappeared from the transfer book;
and that it was not accidental was proved from the
circumstance that the paging of the leaves was altered
in order that they might be consecutive.   Various circumstances pointed to the probability that Turner was
the culprit ; and he was taken before the directors, in
the Bank parlour, where he underwent an examination.   The result was a confirmation of the suspicion;
and Foy, the officer, was directed to detain him till the
next day.   From the respectability of Turner, and
from the confidence which had previously existed in

his integrity, Foy was permitted to take his prisoner
to any place which he thought might be most convenient, and where as little abridgment of his comforts
might take place as possible. With this permission,
he was taken to an inn in the neighbourhood, in a
bed-room of which he was secured. About one
o'clock in the morning, as the watchman proceeded
on his rounds he was suddenly startled by the sound
of breaking glass, and looking up saw a figure
suspended from the third floor window, which the
next moment fell heavily to the ground. The unfortunate adventurer proved to be Turner, who had thus
attempted to make his escape. In a most deplorable
condition he was removed to the hospital; and, on the
18th of September following, supported on crutches,
he appeared to take his trial.

Out of fifteen notes received for the forgery, twelve
had been traced to Turner. Great difficulty in bringing the crime home was occasioned by the fact that
he had destroyed many evidences of his guilt. On
the trial, as the only witness who was disposed to
swear decidedly to the writing of the prisoner was
answering the questions put to him, Turner whispered
to his counsel, who immediately said, "Do you believe
the New Testament to be a revelation from God?"
The witness hesitated, and the question was repeated.
"Yes, I do," was the reply, uttered in a faint tone.
He was, however, again pressed, and evidence being
produced to prove that he had frequently avowed his

disbelief, he was at last compelled to acknowledge it. The prisoner's fate was greatly decided by this, and the jury returned a verdict of "not guilty." With the money thus disgracefully obtained Turner went to Italy, and resided for some time on the banks of the beautiful lake of Como. He soon dissipated his property, and returned to England; nor was it long before he was found, early in the morning, behind the tables of the Bank of England, examining some books which were exposed. His object was never known; but it is presumed it was to assist him in some further fraud. A retributive justice overtook him, as it overtakes all who depart from the path of rectitude, and he died in an obscure street in London, in great distress.

"The Bank directors," says a periodical writer, "have adopted a resolution likely to be of essential service. They have fixed their interest at four per cent. The effect will be to produce an extensive alleviation upon all persons having charges upon their landed estates hitherto paying five per cent. Ten thousand pounds is the minimum of any application to be entertained, but the extent of accommodation is unlimited, provided the rental of the estate is double the amount of interest at four per cent." An extension of the time of such bills as were discounted was also allowed, from sixty-one to ninety-five days. The effect on public securities was very soon seen, as consols immediately rose.

The purchase of the dead-weight has been variously commented upon, Mr. Loyd believing that both for the Bank and the state it was an "injudicious arrangement," while Mr. Ward termed it "the best undertaking in which the Bank could have been engaged." With regard to the negociable character of the security, Mr. Norman considered it was equal to Exchequer bills, with the simple difference of the one being a debt to be repaid, and the other an annuity for a given term. The following is copied from Mr. Mc Culloch's "Dictionary of Commerce," to enable the reader to form a clear and comprehensive view of the transaction :

"At the end of the war the naval and military pensions, superannuated allowances, &c., all included under the term dead weight, amounted to about £500,000 a-year. They would of course have been gradually lessened, and ultimately extinguished, by the death of the parties. But it was resolved, in 1822, to attempt to spread the burden over the whole period of forty-five years, during which it was calculated the annuities would continue to decrease." "In 1823 the Bank agreed, on condition of receiving an annuity of £585,740 for forty-four years, commencing on the 5th April, 1823, to pay on account of the pensions, &c., at different specified periods, between the years 1823 and 1828, both inclusive, the sum of £13,089,419."

The discontinuance of notes under £5 lessened to

an important extent the internal business of the corporation. When the £1 notes were first introduced the number of clerks had been considerably increased, and on their abolition it was found necessary to part with a considerable number. In 1822, therefore, many of them left the establishment. The liberality of the directors on this occasion, who gave pensions to all, in proportion to the number of years they had served, "was highly liberal, and met with universal approbation." This liberality is yet remembered with respectful gratitude. Tending, as such conduct unquestionably does, to create a beneficial union of interests between the employer and the employed, it is pleasant to be able to record the consideration of the one, and the kindly remembrance of the other. The moral claim of a servant, worn out with years or work, is indisputable. In all government situations in Austria a plan is adopted by which the employé, when certain stipulations are performed, and after a certain period of service, is entitled to claim a pension. The plan adopted is simple, and might be advantageously introduced into England.

In 1822, the ministry proposed to the Bank directors that they should concede their exclusive partnership privileges immediately, in all parts of the kingdom, sixty-five miles distant from London. The Earl of Liverpool and Mr. Vansittart entered into correspondence with the governor; and the proposal was acceded to by the authorities of the Corporation, upon the condition that the integrity of the remainder of the charter should be continued for ten years longer. The treaty was, however, abandoned. The country bankers remonstrated strongly; and it was reprobated in the house, where Mr. Pascoe Grenfell presented a petition against it. To the extension of the monopoly beyond 1833, he stated that he had the greatest possible objection. To the proposal which tended to remove the restriction on the number of partners engaged in country banking, he entertained a yet greater ; and after the conduct of the Bank, after their immense profits, which amounted to twenty-five millions in twenty-five years after seven per cent. was divided, it was amazing that government should be so unwise as to propose a renewal of the Bank charter. Mr. Manning denied that the gains of the Bank were more than were made by others. The Royal Exchange Assurance had made immense additions to their capital in consequence of their profits. Mr. Ricardo announced that he would oppose it to the utmost of his power. If a paper currency were required ministers could do it better without, than with the Bank. Under these circumstances, the ministry deemed it advisable to withdraw the negociation, as there appeared but little probability of the legislature sanctioning the measure.

In the same year, during a period of considerable agricultural distress, the country bankers were permitted to continue the issue of their notes below the value of £5, up to the year 1833. Only six votes were recorded against the bill.

On the 11th of June, 1822, Mr. Western attempted to make an inroad on the provisions of Mr. Peel's currency bill. "He assumed," says the "Annual Register," "that the landholder had a right (we suppose a Divine right) to enjoy all the advantages, and be protected from all the inconveniencies, that might at any time flow from fluctuations in the currency, and took for granted that the change which had occurred in prices had been occasioned solely by the resumption of cash payments; with the help of these two postulates he easily arrived at whatever conclusion seemed good to him." Mr. Huskisson replied that, as the foundation of his plan, he asserted, "that the standard of value in every country should be that article which forms the constant and most general food of its population." It followed that wheat could not be the standard in Ireland. Potatoes must be the measure of value. We had heard of fanciful standards; the ideal unit; the abstract pound sterling; but we had never heard before of a potatoe standard. What a beautiful simplicity of system; a wheat standard for one part of the empire, a potatoe standard for the other. The proposition was for a depreciation of the standard of the currency. A measure reprobated by all statesmen, and all historians, the wretched but antiquated resource of barbarous ignorance and arbitrary power, the last mark of a civilized nation's weakness and degradation. If such a proposition should be entertained, all pecuniary dealings would be at an end ; all pending transactions would be thrown into disorder; all holders of paper would insist upon its being converted into coin. Neither the Bank, nor the London bankers, nor the country banks, could survive the shock.

Mr. Ricardo maintained that the inconveniences of the return to a metallic standard had been infinitely increased by the Bank directors, in making premature purchases of gold to a large extent. They ought not to have paid in specie until 1823. Mr. Peel's bill was in truth to try whether a bank could not be advantageously carried on upon the principle of paying the notes in bullion ; and if the Bank had gone on wisely in their preliminary arrangements the bullion part of the plan would have worked for a number of years beyond the time originally stipulated.

Mr. Peel trusted that the house would pause before they adopted a proposition which would reduce the value of one pound to fourteen shillings. The effect of the measure would be to disturb all mercantile transactions. If the house should proceed upon the principle of this bill, there would be an end for ever to the very idea of national faith ; that faith which had supported us under every difficulty, and which constituted the pride, the glory, and the support of the country. The measure of Mr. Western was lost by a large majority.

A sudden and unexpected fall in Bank stock of sixteen per cent., produced by an equally unexpected diminution of dividend, occurred in 1823. The customary meeting was held to hear the rate of interest announced, attended by the usual small proportion of proprietors. For many years they had heard gratifying statements, sometimes concluding with an increased dividend, and sometimes with a considerable bonus. With this result the holders of stock willingly concurred, applauded the wisdom of the direction, passed a vote of thanks to them for their united capacity, and went home happy and contented. A change, however, occurred this year. It is probable that the return to a metallic currency was one cause of the proposition that the half-yearly dividend should be reduced from five to four per cent. For this, however, the meeting were by no means prepared; and the prospect of the reduction produced some very energetic speeches. All were quite willing to allow great capacity to the directors while a high dividend was maintained; but no sooner was there a hint of lowering it, than they practically evinced their doubts of the wisdom of that body which year after year had received a vote of thanks. A counter proposition was made for retaining the old dividend; but it was lost by a large majority. The suggestion was offered to reduce it only half per cent., but in vain. A ballot was then demanded, and granted on the demand being signed by nine proprietors. The monetary portion of the stock-holders are generally aware of the importance of supporting the direction. At this period also, the affairs of the corporation were private, and it was far from judicious to oppose those who were well acquainted with the accounts, and who were naturally far more pleased to declare an enlarged rather than a decreased dividend. But while it must be acknowledged that many of the Bank stock proprietors represent the wealth, the rank, and the intelligence of the country, it must also be remembered that a diminution of interest of two per cent. per annum might cause some distress to the small holder, by its occasioning him to reduce his expenditure ; and he would, therefore, express warmly what he felt keenly. Of course the directors gained their point.

Although most of the following occurrences are familiar to all, there are some portions of the relation sufficiently novel to claim the perusal of the reader.

The father of Henry Fauntleroy was originally clerk in a city banking house, and obtained a partnership in the firm of Marsh, Sibbald and Co., in 1792, from his knowledge of banking. On his father's death, in 1807, Henry Fauntleroy, from his superiority over his co-partners in banking information, was chosen to occupy the same position. The business, from the first, was unfortunate. Two years after its establishment a loss was sustained of £20,000; and at the early age of twenty-two, the subject of this narrative found, to use his own words "that the whole weight of an extensive, but needy, banking establishment at once devolved upon him." He had not occupied his post above three years, when another sudden demand of £170,000 was made upon the house.

Mr. Fauntleroy has said that he was not a gambler; nor was he in the ordinary acceptation of the term. But, in the funds, his speculations were considerable ; and it is probable that his losses there made him first alter, as he was nightly in the habit of doing, the balances of the house after the total was made up. It is, indeed, hardly credible, that he should resort to forgery, until the exhaustion of all other means. Upwards of £100,000 were thus withdrawn ; and the fraud was so artfully concealed, that it required the utmost keenness of the accountant, aware as he was of some such fact, to detect the imposition.

About 1816 other losses occurred ; and the Bank of England, undoubtedly aware, from its extensive information, of the slight means of the house, refused to discount its bills. This was a further severe blow. In May, 1815, a power of attorney was presented at the Bank, purporting to bear the signature of Frances Young, of Chichester, for the sale of £5,000 three per cent. consols. That power was forged; but it passed the ordeal of the Bank examinations, and the money was procured. From this period many powers, bearing the names of Marsh and Co., as Attornies, were acted on by Mr. Fauntleroy. Most of these were attested by two of the clerks of the banking house. Some of them were to replace stock previously sold, while others provided funds for different purposes. No doubt appears to have been excited at the Bank, or it was at once allayed by the fact, that the power was given to a banker, and therefore genuine. From 1815 to 1823 large sums were thus obtained; but in the latter year the supply ceased. Mr. Fauntleroy was joint trustee in an acccount with some other gentlemen, in the imperial three per cents. In the management of the trust some difficulties arose; and the only plan which could save the executors from a heavy responsibility, was to throw the property into Chancery. Mr. Fauntleroy strenuously objected. In the course of the dispute, one of the co-trustees visited the Bank, and learned the fearful intelligence which first led to the discovery of a series of forgeries, so gigantic in their extent, and so unparalleled in their nature, as to border on the regions of fiction.

The information was communicated to the Bank authorities. Orders were issued for the examination of all powers granted to the house of Marsh, Stracey, and Co., and the result may be anticipated.

In September, 1824, Plank, the Bow Street officer, might be seen proceeding in the direction of the banking house of Marsh, Stracey, and Co. A person, who accompanied him, entered first, and requesting an interview with Mr. Fauntleroy, was ushered into his private counting house. Within a minute he was followed by Plank. The interior of a bank is nearly sacred ; but the officer pushed boldly by the clerk, who would have interrupted him, merely saying he wished to speak with Mr. Fauntleroy. On entering, he closed the door, announced his name, and produced a warrant for the apprehension of Henry Fauntleroy on a charge of forgery. A deadly pallor passed over the face of the latter ; he was fearfully agitated, and hurriedly exclaimed, " Good God ! cannot this business be settled ? " Plank begged him to make no noise, but to walk out quietly for a few minutes, and they could talk about it. Mr. Fauntleroy then signed a few blank cheques for the business of the house, with a hand so unsteady, that it was difficult to recognize his signature ; and said he should go out for a few minutes. He was then conducted to the private residence of Mr. Conant, the magistrate ; and after an interview of the prisoner with one of his clerks, Mr. Freshfield, Solicitor to the Bank, accompanied by Plank, proceeded to the banking house to search the papers.

The search was successful. Documents unparalelled in the history of crime were discovered. In a private room, a box, bearing no name, was found. What must the surprise of the Bank solicitor have been to find in it a list, in the prisoner's hand writing, of forgeries which he had committed, amounting to

£112,000, with the following extraordinary acknowledgment. " In order to keep up the credit of our house, I have forged powers of attorney, and have, thereupon, sold out all these sums, without the knowledge of any of my partners. I have given credit in the accounts for the interest when it became due. HENRY FAUNTLEROY." These words followed, " The Bank first began to refuse our acceptances, and thereby destroy the credit of our house. The Bank shall smart for it." At the period of his apprehension he had a power of attorney by which he would have replaced the stock that produced the discovery.

In a conference the forger had with a partner, he expressed great anxiety to obtain possession of a " blue book." Mr. Graham searched, and brought one with a blue sheet for a cover. " No, no," he said, " this is not the one I want. It is a bound book." Mr. Graham informed him that it had reached the hands of Mr. Freshfield, " Then," said Fauntleroy, " I'm a dead man. I could have set the Bank at defiance." This book was said to contain an account of the forgeries in which he had been engaged.

The crime of Mr. Fauntleroy excited great interest. " Hardly anything else," says one writer, " was talked about." The newspapers teemed with anecdotes. His past life was enquired into. His portrait was in the windows. His behaviour was analysed. His person was described. The very way in which he held his hat was repeated. The magistrate apologized for an intrusion ; and, when the forger heaved a sigh, the scribe was ready to draw the attention of the public to so memorable a fact. The whole affair from beginning to end was a bitter satire upon those English people who rest the importance of a criminal on the magnitude of his crime, and interest themselves in exact proportion to the respectability of the offender.

The human mind is always disposed to sympathize with great criminals ; and those who had heard week by week of executions of small people, for small sums, were filled with horror at the position in which a gentleman was involved, and evinced a most misplaced sympathy at the idea of hanging a banker. The loss which the Company sustained from this wholesale forger was stated by the governor to a committee of the House of Commons at £360,000 ; and the interest alone, which was regularly paid, must have been nine or ten thousand pounds a-year. The care required by these accounts, and the constant anxiety weighing on the mind of Fauntleroy, from the knowledge of his perilous position, were, in themselves, a punishment. His exertions at the banking house were extraordinary. So energetic was he that his services were noticed as being equal to those of three clerks ; but such care and such energy should have produced better fruit. The last time he received from the Bank the warrants due to the firm

was the day on which Thurtell and Hunt were tried.
During the payment, he entered into conversation on
the crime, with the clerk who paid him ; imagining
but little that within a year the same judge who had
tried them would try him; that the very list of
warrants he was receiving would be brought in
evidence ; and that the clerk with whom he was so
familiarly conversing would be a witness against him.
Before the debtors' door at Newgate, and amidst a
vast concourse of spectators, the unhappy man
expiated his crime.

CHAPTER XVII.

THE year 1823 witnessed the early dawning of a
prosperity, which, regarded as solid by many, ended
in an almost national ruin. In the previous year,
with a view of reviving speculation, then dormant,
the Bank, at the instance of the state, had issued
about four millions in advances to the government, and
in enlarged discounts ; but, in Mr. Horsley Palmer's
opinion, the first step towards the excitement was
lowering the interest on public securities, which was
effected in 1822, by reducing the navy five per cents.
to four per cent., and a smaller stock to three-and-
a-half per cent. This reduction in the interest of
upwards of two hundred millions caused some distress
and great dissatisfaction. To meet the dissentients
the Bank advanced five millions, to be repaid in

quarterly instalments. Many persons who had hitherto been contented with the dividend they had received, were compelled either to reduce their expenses to meet a diminished revenue, or endeavour to obtain a larger interest than was offered by government. A feverish feeling was thus excited, and as there are always plenty of schemes, which, if not safe, are specious, the discontented man embarked his capital in speculations, the great promises of which blinded him as to their insecurity. Unwilling to reduce his expenses, he thought he saw a safe mode of enlarging his income, and he " entertained any proposition for investment, however absurd, which was tendered." In the year 1822 another cause occurred, of which the entire responsibility must rest with the government. This was the act of Parliament extending the circulation of the small notes of country bankers till 1833, instead of ceasing at the period allotted to them by the bill of Mr. Peel. That act, said Mr. Canning, hedged the one pound note with a divinity which was never supposed to belong to it before. Only six opponents were seen arrayed against the bill. The Bank had made a provision of bullion for the country notes, with the full conviction that the law would remain unaltered. In the memorandum delivered to the House of Commons the directors state, " the consequence of that measure was to leave in the possession of the Bank an inordinate quantity of bullion ; £14,200,000 in January, 1824 ; and fur-

ther to afford the power of extension to the country
banker's issues, which it is believed were greatly
extended from 1823 to 1825." Mr. Richards, in his
evidence before the committee of the House of Commons in 1832, bore testimony to the efforts of the
Bank in preparing to meet its outstanding engagements. " When it was determined that the country
should return to cash payments, a vast deal of anxiety
was created in the minds of the public. As the
period approached that anxiety greatly increased, and
many who had previously issued freely, and given fair
and legitimate accommodation, were afraid to continue. The Bank had put itself in a position faithfully
and honestly to fulfil that law—that I assert most
fearlessly—and succeeded in procuring a large quantity
of bullion. They anticipated the period when, by law,
they were bound to return to cash payments, and
enabled themselves to assist the country bankers to
meet their engagements in gold."

In 1822 the aggregate currency was low; but no
sooner was the country banker allowed to issue more
small notes, than it began to increase, and with it
an apparent prosperity as dangerous as it was delusive. In 1825 the issues of the country bankers were
fifty per cent. more than in 1822. From the middle
of the latter year to the commencement of 1825,
prices of commodities improved, in some cases twenty-
five, and in others fifty per cent. At the end of 1824
the stock of manufactures was shorter than usual.

The whole country wore a promising appearance, and every one became ready to embark his capital in anything which promised great profit. The people congratulated themselves on being wiser than their forefathers ; and part of the press, at first, re-echoed their congratulations. Every one seemed smiling and satisfied. The shopkeeper sold his goods. The merchant made large profits. The manufacturer could not produce sufficiently fast. " Even country gentlemen, the most querulous of all classes," says a periodical, " the least accustomed to suffer, and the most incapable of struggling with difficulties, could no longer complain."

The South Sea bubble was a tradition about which many talked, who knew nothing but the name. Those who were familiar with the story, little expected to see a repetition of scenes which had shaken the foundations of commerce. " The schemes so lately afloat," says a writer at the time, " carried with them a much greater mass of fraud and deception, in the aggregate, than the South Sea bubble." It is instructive to read the comments of a portion of the press. The following extract from the " Annual Register," as a calm survey of the events of the year, aspiring to the dignity of history, may be regarded as most important, from the time allotted it, to form an opinion.

"There was in the present year no diminution of that prosperity which the country had enjoyed throughout the whole of 1823. All agricultural produce was slowly but steadily on the rise.   In the cotton trade there was a rapid increase ; and the manufacturers of wool, iron, and hardware, were equally prosperous. The abundance of capital led to the formation of numerous Joint-Stock Companies, directed, some of them, towards schemes of internal industry ; others of them towards speculations in distant countries. The " Mines of Mexico," was a phrase which suggested to the imagination of every one unbounded wealth; and three Companies, the Real del Monte Association, the United Mexican, and the Anglo-Mexican, were formed for the purpose of extracting wealth from their bowels, by English capital, machinery, and skill.   Similar companies were formed in the course of the year, for working the mines of Chili, of Brazil, and Peru, and of the province of Rio de la Plata.   In the month of March there were upwards of thirty bills before the House of Commons, for the purpose of giving legal existence to different companies.   In all these speculations, only a small instalment, seldom exceeding 5 per cent., was paid at first ; so that a very moderate rise in the price of shares produced a large profit on the sum actually invested. If, for instance, shares of £100, on which £5 had been paid, rose to a premium of £40, this yielded on every share a profit equal to eight times the amount of the money which had been paid.   This possibility of enormous profit, by risking a small sum, was a bait too tempting to be resisted.   All the gambling propensities of human nature were constantly solicited into action ; and crowds of individuals of every description, the credulous and the suspicious, the crafty and the bold, the raw and the inexperienced, the intelligent and the ignorant ; princes, nobles, politicians, placemen, patriots, lawyers, physicians, divines, philosophers, poets, intermingled with women of all ranks and degrees ;—spinsters, wives, and widows, hastened to venture some portion of their property in schemes, of which scarcely anything was known but the name."

The speech from the throne evidenced the general feeling of security and satisfaction.   It congratulated the Commons and Lords on the "prosperous condition of the country.   There never was a period in its history, when all the great interests of the nation were in so thriving a condition.   An increasing activity pervades almost every branch of manufactures."   But another source of high profit appeared to offer through the acknowledgment of the independence of · the South American States.

Any petty commonwealth putting forth pretences to a popular government, had only to publish magnificent assertions, and yet more magnificent promises, and loans were made as freely as required.   Upwards of thirty-two millions were thus subscribed by infatuated men, the principal of which will never be seen ; while a pretence of keeping up the interest is scarcely made.   The following will afford some idea as to the mode in which these loans were managed, and will yield an insight into the madness, to which a state of monetary excitement will sometimes lead soberminded men. This desire to invest capital in foreign loans amounted to a mania. The way in which the Peruvian loan was arranged, together with the circumstances which attended it, may serve as a specimen of others. No sooner was it understood that the State of Peru had consented to borrow, than the utmost anxiety prevailed to lend. The ostensible contractor was overwhelmed with applications. The reply was that he would dispose of the scrip in the open market. At the time appointed a crowd of speculators surrounded him, begging to know the terms, and pressing for an early delivery. All voices were lost in the confusion, and the agent calmly waited the bidding of the eager multitude. Various prices were vociferated; but the contractor maintained a reserved silence. By this it was understood that the point desired was not reached. After a pause, 88 was named by him. This was known to be a premium of 8 per cent. on the contracting price, and a storm of indignation arose at the idea of any one, but the assembly, making so large a profit. "Shame, shame!" "Gross extortion!" met the contractor's ears. Still there was an eager pressure to get near him, and those who could approach sufficiently close considered themselves fortunate in taking sums varying from £5000 to £10,000. The practical reception of his terms appeared so satisfactory that the contractor soon advanced the price to 89; on which he was once more met with the same expressive language. Again, however, his acuteness proved correct; and some of the scrip was taken at the increased rate. The noise became so great, and the confusion so excessive, that few could be supplied; and though many applications were made, there was no answer. The attention of the crowd was soon diverted by the offer of a broker to supply any person, who required the scrip, at 88. The speculator was taken at his word, and very large amounts were sold. By this time the news had reached the Stock exchange; and in a short period a considerable number of the members assembled, and pressing round the contractor, with great indignation, moved him and his agents from one part of the edifice to another. The crowd soon became so exasperated, that they forced them out of the building. A desperate struggle followed, and at last they were allowed to re-enter. Being tumultuously called upon to name a price, one of them mentioned 90 as the minimum; soon after this they left; with their departure, the mania appeared to subside; and many of the purchasers, fancying their bargains were imprudent, actually sold on the spot at a lower price than they had given. Such was the anxiety to obtain a portion of the loan to be granted to Peru, a loan which now bears no interest whatever.

The year 1825, like its predecessor, was ushered in

with a flourish of trumpets. The ancient golden age
had revived. Gladness and gaiety were in the land.
" The hum of successful industry was heard throughout the fields ; every man was contented and happy ;
joy beamed in every face," and, as Lord Leveson
Gower expressed himself, his poetic spirit waxing
•warm within him, " distress had vanished from the
face of the land." The delusion was general. The
song of triumph universal. The Earl of Liverpool
rejoiced in the success which had attended that great
measure, introduced with his sanction by Mr. Peel.
" The task had been accomplished ; we were enjoying
our reward." Lord Dudley said, the country " now
reaped in honour and in repose all that they had sown
in courage, in constancy, and in wisdom."   " Our
prosperity extended to all orders, all professions, all
districts, enhanced by those arts which ministered to
human comfort, and by those inventions by which
man seemed to have obtained a mastery over nature
by the application of her own powers."

The contagion spread to the Commons. No year
had ever exceeded that of 1824 in its exports ; and
the Chancellor of the Exchequer, in an exultant tone
of triumph, congratulated the house on the auspicious
circumstances of the period, adding, " we may safely
venture to contemplate with instructive admiration
the harmony of its proportions and *the solidity of its
basis.*" Joint Stock Companies of every conceivable
description were put prominently forward. In 1824

and 1825, six hundred and twenty-four new ones made their appearance. Royal and imperial mines ; a Mint Company, to coin the gold when it should be procured from Mexico ; associations to provide bread ; with others, which rivalled one another in outrageous assertions and extravagant protestations, possessed the public mind. The upper classes found their representatives in the direction of these companies. A violent love of lucre was as prevalent among the higher as the lower ranks. Mr. Grenfell asserted in the House of Commons, that he had seen the prospectus of a new speculation, to which the name of a prince of the blood was attached. Another bore the title of the Archbishop of Canterbury. The highest mercantile names in the land were in the direction of others. All were confident ; and all hoped to reap enormous profits. A Mr. Peter Moore boldly said in the House of Commons, " Upon his honour, he believed that not one of the companies with which he was connected had less probity or less stability than the Bank of England." Every description of property rose greatly. The artizan was in full employment. New buildings were in progress of erection. Men of enterprize, without capital, could command funds for any plausible undertaking.

When introducing his motion on the address to the King, Lord Leveson Gower said, " Such is the general state of prosperity at which the country has arrived, that I feel at a loss how to proceed, whether to give precedence to our agriculture, which is the main support of the country, to our manufactures, which have increased to a most unexampled extent, or to our commerce, which distributes them to the ends of the earth, which finds daily new outlets for their distribution, and new sources of national wealth and prosperity."

END OF THE FIRST VOLUME.

WILLOUGHBY AND CO., PRINTERS, 97, ST. JOHN STREET, SMITHFIELD.

604484